Also by the Author
Development without Aid
The New Protectionism
The Economics of Integration

HOW
NATO
WEAKENS
THE
WEST

MELVYN KRAUSS

SIMON AND SCHUSTER
New York

Designed by Carla Weise/Levavi & Levavi
Manufactured in the United States of America

10 9 8 7 6 5 4 3 2 1

Library of Congress Cataloging in Publication Data
Krauss, Melvyn B.
    How NATO weakens the West.

    Bibliography: p.
    Includes index.
    1. North Atlantic Treaty Organization.   I. Title.
UA646.3.K72 1986   355'.031'091821   86-14019
ISBN: 0-671-54455-1

The author gratefully acknowledges the following for permission to reprint the material indicated:

The poem "Dane-geld" by Rudyard Kipling, excerpted from *The Years Between and Poems from History.* Copyright © 1919; copyright renewed. Reprinted by permission of Charles Scribner's Sons.

The chart "The Economics of National Defense" by Daniel I. Okimoto, from *Japan's Economy: Coping with Change in the International Environment.* Copyright © 1982. Used by permission of Westview Press.

The chart "Protest Howls Belied by Opinion Polls," by Gerhard Herdegen and Elizabeth Noelle-Neumann, from *German Tribune-Political Affairs Review*, June 3, 1984. Reprinted by permission.

Acknowledgments

The major part of the book was written during the academic year 1984–85, while I was on sabbatical from New York University. I am grateful to NYU for its support. The book was actually written at the Hoover Institution at Stanford University. I owe a debt of gratitude to my colleagues at Hoover, and especially to Henry S. Rowen, without whose help this book could not have been completed. "Harry" Rowen is not responsible for my views, of course— I would not want to stick anyone, especially a friend, with that onus. But Harry's vast knowledge of economics and foreign policy helped make an amateur look, if not good, at least better than he would have looked without Harry's useful interventions. Thanks a lot, Harry; I really appreciate it.

W. Glenn Campbell, director of the Hoover Institution, claims any good idea I think up he already thought of at least twenty-five years before. Actually, I don't doubt him. Judging by the enormous success he has made of the Hoover Institution, I would believe anything he tells me. The truth is, Glenn Campbell richly deserves all the praise he gets from me, and all the Hoover scholars, for he has created an atmosphere of true intellectual freedom and excel-

5

lence. No wonder the Hoover Institution is the preeminent think tank in the country. Even Mikhail Gorbachev thinks so. My heartfelt thanks to W. Glenn Campbell for his support.

The first germ of the idea that perhaps it had become time to change the Atlantic Alliance came to me in a conversation with Tom Bray when he was associate editor of *The Wall Street Journal*. Bray was not convinced—he still may not be—but he published my work anyway. My thanks to him for his initial support, which gave me the confidence to go on with this project. Later on, Tamar Jacoby, at *The New York Times*, encouraged me by publishing my Op-Ed pieces in her favorite newspaper.

William Hammett, president of the Manhattan Institute, deserves credit for his support, as does Richard Turner, ex-dean of New York University. I have greatly benefited from my many conversations with Roman Frydman of New York University and Gregory Fossedal of the Hoover Institution. Steve Stedman was a first-class research assistant, and Betty Oates did a fine job of typing the manuscript.

Most of all, I am indebted to my wife, Irène Krauss, for her tolerance and understanding. It is never easy living with an author, and it's next to impossible living with this one. As a small token of my appreciation, I am dedicating this book, which means so much to me, to her.

MELVYN KRAUSS
New York
January 10, 1986

To Irène

Contents

PART II

PART III

Illustrations

The "Dane-geld"

It is always a temptation to an armed and agile nation,
   To call upon a neighbour and to say:
"We invaded you last night—we are quite prepared to fight,"
   Unless you pay us cash to go away."
      And that is called asking for Dane-geld,
      And the people who ask it explain
      That you've only to pay 'em the Dane-geld
      And then you'll get rid of the Dane!

It is always a temptation to a rich and lazy nation,
   To puff and look important and to say:
"Though we know we should defeat you, we have not the time
   to meet you,
We will therefore pay you cash to go away."
      And that is called paying the Dane-geld;
      But we've proved it again and again,
      That if once you have paid him the Dane-geld
      You never get rid of the Dane.

It is wrong to put temptation in the path of any nation,
   For fear they should succumb and go astray,
So when you are requested to pay up or be molested,
   You will find it better policy to say:
      "We never pay anyone Dane-geld,
      No matter how trifling the cost,
      For the end of that game is oppression and shame,
      And the nation that plays it is lost!"

RUDYARD KIPLING

PART 1

PART 1

1

The Trouble with NATO

That mutual confidence is a necessary ingredient of a successful partnership is self-evident. There are, however, some partnerships whose structure is such that it exaggerates the normal requirements of confidence. These are lopsided partnerships, in which there is a single dominant partner. The weaker partners must have extraordinary confidence in the stronger one, since their interests are profoundly affected by the stronger partner's policies and actions. To protect themselves, they are likely to strive for control over the dominant partner and are apt to be more suspicious about its motives than would be the case in a more balanced arrangement. The North Atlantic Treaty Organization (NATO) is a lopsided partnership because the United States has an exaggerated influence over the fortunes of other members.

The key element of U.S. dominance in NATO relates to nuclear weapons. The United States has given its European allies a nuclear guarantee: Should any of these nations be attacked, the United States is pledged to come to its aid with nuclear weapons if necessary. The United States also maintains troops in Europe. These troops are linked with America's nuclear guarantee through what is known as the "trip-wire" strategy. The physical presence of U.S. troops in Western Europe is intended to reassure the Europeans that America will make good on its nuclear guarantee should the occasion arise. The idea is that no American president would be able to ignore a Soviet invasion of Western Europe that would decimate American as well as European soldiers. The United States would be forced to act even if it preferred otherwise.

EUROPEAN DEFENSE FREE-RIDING

European defense dependence on the United States is a legacy of the early post–World War II period, when defending U.S. allies against Soviet expansionism was necessary because of their ravaged economies. Today, however, economics no longer justifies this dependence. In 1984, for example, the U.S. GDP (gross domestic product) share of total NATO GDP was 44.50 percent while Europe's GDP share, at 34.18 percent, was not that much less. Yet, the U.S. defense spending share of total NATO defense spending was 64.73 percent in that same year, while Europe's defense spending share was only 29.45 percent.

Table 1.1 lists defense expenditure as a proportion of GDP for the several NATO countries. In 1983 the United States spent 6.6 percent of its GDP on defense while Japan spent 1.0 percent, Luxembourg 1.2 percent, Canada 2.0 percent, the Netherlands 3.2 percent, Belgium 3.3 percent, West Germany 3.4 percent, France 4.2 percent, Britain 5.3 percent, non–U.S. NATO 3.6 percent, and non–U.S. NATO plus Japan 2.8 percent. In contrast, the Soviet Union is estimated to spend *at least* 15 percent of GDP. Fig. 1.1 shows that the U.S. defense effort, as measured by the ratio of defense spending to gross domestic product, has been consistently and substantially higher than both non–U.S. NATO and Japan since 1961.

The reason we allocate a greater portion of our economic product to defense than the Europeans is not that we are more warlike than our allies, but that we subsidize Europe's defense needs. The nature of defense as an economic good explains the mechanics of the subsidization process. Defense is a good which, once provided, benefits

TABLE 1.1 *Total Defense Spending as a Percentage of GDP*

	1971			1983			TOTAL % CHANGE
	%	% OF HIGHEST NATION	RANK	%	% OF HIGHEST NATION	RANK	71 vs 83
Belgium	2.9	39.2%	10	3.3	50.6%	8	+15.3
Canada	2.2	30.2%	13	2.0	30.6%	13	−9.7
Denmark	2.4	32.8%	12	2.4	36.7%	12	−0.2
France	4.0	54.1%	6	4.2	63.2%	5	+4.2
Germany	3.4	45.5%	9	3.4	51.3%	6	+0.6
Greece	4.7	63.3%	4	6.4	96.5%	2	+35.9
Italy	2.7	36.5%	11	2.7	40.7%	11	−0.6
Luxembourg	0.8	10.8%	15	1.2	18.9%	14	+56.3
Netherlands	3.4	46.5%	7	3.2	48.8%	9	−6.4
Norway	3.4	45.8%	8	3.1	46.8%	10	−8.9
Portugal	7.4	100.0%	1	3.4	50.8%	7	−54.7
Turkey	4.5	61.3%	5	5.0	75.7%	4	+10.2
United Kingdom	4.9	66.6%	3	5.3	80.5%	3	+7.8
United States	7.1	95.3%	2	6.6	100.0%	1	−6.4
Japan	0.8	11.4%	14	1.0	15.1%	15	+18.1
Non–U.S. NATO	3.6	48.1%		3.6	55.0%		+2.0
Non–U.S. NATO and Japan	3.0	40.4%		2.8	42.8%		−5.4
Total NATO	5.5	74.4%		5.3	79.6%		−4.6
Total NATO and Japan	5.0	67.7%		4.5	68.8%		−9.3

everyone within the defended area regardless of their contribution to its costs. Economists call this type of good a "public good." When the United States makes a defense expenditure, for example, it renders a benefit to all members of the Atlantic Alliance even though it is only Americans who pay the cost.

Because of the benefits that accrue to other countries from a nation's defense spending, there is an obvious economic incentive in an alliance to get the other partners to spend more on defense than you do. In that way, the partner countries subsidize your own defense needs. In the Western Alliance, the Europeans have been

FIG. 1.1 *Total Defense Expenditures as a Percentage of GDP*

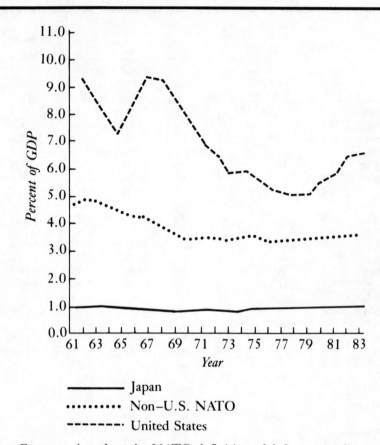

———— Japan
•••••••• Non–U.S. NATO
-------· United States

Footnotes based on the NATO definition of defense spending

Source: "Report on Allied Contributions to the Common Defense," a report to the U.S. Congress, Caspar W. Weinberger, Secretary of Defense, U.S. Department of Defense (March 1985), p. 31.

able to get the Americans to bear the lion's share of Western defense expenditure by following a classic free-rider strategy. By pooh-poohing the Soviet military threat and generally taking a more neutralist line than they would if Uncle Sam was not there to pay the bills for them, the Europeans have created a mentality in the United States that if we don't make the defense expenditures, no one else in the Western world will.

The basic source of European defense free riding is the U.S. nuclear umbrella. Not only do U.S. taxpayers pay the entire cost of the umbrella, but, more important, the nuclear umbrella encouraged Europe to economize on its conventional forces at a time when the Soviet Union spared little effort in building up theirs. The funds the Europeans saved on defense were used instead to build up their welfare states. In OECD Europe, for example, welfare state expenditures increased by an enormous 12.7 percentage points of gross domestic product from 1955–57 to 1974–76, while defense expenditures actually fell by .8 percentage points. This could not have happened without the American defense guarantee.

THE HOLE IN THE UMBRELLA

From the European point of view, underinvestment in defense could be defended so long as the United States had nuclear supremacy over the Soviet Union. The inability of the Soviet Union to respond in kind to an American nuclear attack gave the U.S. nuclear guarantee an unquestioned credibility. "Today, however, the American nuclear umbrella is 99 percent bluff," writes Irving Kristol.[1] Nuclear disparity between the Soviet Union and the United States no longer exists. Under these circumstances, it is inconceivable that the United States would risk a nuclear exchange with the Soviet Union over Western Europe—no matter what our leaders might say or how many guarantees they might make. The stakes simply are too high.

"When NATO was founded in 1949," writes Jay Winik in *The Wall Street Journal*, "it was basically a unilateral American nuclear guarantee of European security in the guise of an alliance. This situation has remained largely unchanged. But with the advent of at least strategic parity, the U.S. nuclear commitment to defend Europe has been reduced to a pact of mutual suicide. It has lost much of its credibility, if not sense."[2]

The hole in the American nuclear umbrella began to appear in 1963 or 1964, according to the noted French general Pierre Gallois. He argues:

> Ever since 1956, when we saw how easily the Russians put down the Hungarian revolt and, after it, the resistance there, a number of political and military spokesmen in France have begun to wake up to the fact that once the Russians achieved the capability of striking

American territory—which happened in 1963 or 1964—the U.S. guarantee would fall apart. And that is just what has happened.[3]

Former U.S. Secretary of State Henry Kissinger is another distinguished voice among the growing chorus of informed opinion questioning the credibility of America's nuclear guarantee. At a private gathering of American and European strategists in Brussels in September 1979 he said:

> Perhaps even today, but surely in the 1980s, the United States will no longer be in a strategic position to reduce a Soviet counter-blow against the United States to tolerable levels. . . . If my analysis is correct, we must face the fact that it is absurd to base the strategy of the West on the credibility of the threat of mutual suicide . . . and therefore I would say—what I might not say in office—that our European allies should not keep asking us to multiply strategic assurances that we cannot possibly mean or if we do mean, we should not want to execute because if we execute, we risk the destruction of civilization.[4]

DÉTENTE AS DEFENSE

The theory behind détente is that by intelligent use of its economic lever, the West could tame the Soviet beast. Moscow would be both less apt to misbehave for fear of the stick of economic sanctions and more apt to cooperate in the hope of the carrot of increased Western trade and economic subsidies. The stark reality behind détente for the Europeans, however, is that it is a policy to bribe the Soviets not to invade Western Europe. The Europeans reason that if the Soviets could be given a greater vested interest in the status quo in Western Europe through economic subsidies and increased East-West trade, they would have less reason to attack. European reliance on a "détente as defense" strategy has increased in tandem with diminished credibility in the American nuclear guarantee.

If the "public good" interpretation of Western defense is correct, European and American defense efforts should be inversely related—the greater U.S. efforts, the less European efforts and vice versa. This see-saw relation, however, does not show up in the statistics. As Chart I shows, European defense expenditure as a percentage of gross domestic product has been fixed more or less at the 3.5–4.0 percent level during the 1970s, while the U.S. defense-spending ratio declined rather sharply, from 8 to 5 percent of gross domestic product. The reason the statistics fail to show the see-saw relation is that Europeans came to view détente as a *substitute* for explicit defense expenditure during the 1970s. Instead of increasing their defense expenditures as American defense efforts declined and confidence in the U.S. nuclear guarantee waned, Europeans increased their practice of détente.

The fact that détente has become Europe's second "line of defense" against the Soviet Union—behind the U.S. guarantee—is a very dangerous development for the United States. Resources are fungible, and a good deal of détente-inspired economic transfers to the Soviets and increased East-West trade wind up as part of the Kremlin's military machine. The danger of sending Moscow high-technology goods, of course, is self-evident. But even when the United States and Western Europe export such "humanitarian" goods as butter and wheat to the Soviet Union, domestic resources within that nation are freed that can be used to build tanks, missiles, and ammunition. One result of Europe's détente-as-defense strategy, then, is that the United States must spend more on its own defense because the Europeans are adding resources to the Soviet war-machine. This can be called the "defense-feedback effect" of détente.

Unfortunately, the amounts involved in European economic transfers to the Soviets are far from trivial. In recent years, for example, Great Britain, France, and West Germany subsidized exports of pipeline equipment to help the Soviets build the Siberian natural-gas pipeline. The Dutch economics ministry has estimated these subsidies at $1.2–$1.6 billion.[5] The Organization for Economic Cooperation and Development (OECD) gives export credit subsidies to the Soviets and Eastern Europe. The Rand Corporation estimates all OECD export credit subsidies to all Communist countries at $3.0 billion in 1981.[6] These are but two examples of the many subsidies the Europeans give the Soviets. The European Common Market sells surplus agricultural goods to the Soviets at below-cost prices—a subsidy worth billions of dollars to the Kremlin. West German banks have made subsidized loans available to East Germany and Poland. How ironic that East German goods enter the European Common Market duty-free while American goods have to pay a tariff.

American charges that the Europeans subsidize the Soviets often are countered by resentful Europeans who point out that the United States does it too. While two wrongs do not make a right, it is true that, like the Europeans, the United States does subsidize its agricultural exports to the Soviets, that as a member of the OECD we share to some extent in its export credit subsidies, and that American banks also made subsidized loans to Poland with U.S. government guarantees. One dollar of subsidy given by the United States helps the Soviet war-machine as much as one dollar given by the Europeans.

There are, however, critical differences between the subsidy practices of Western Europe and those of the United States. Most experts are agreed that, quantitatively, Europe gives far more subsidies to the Eastern bloc than we do. Europe's subsidies and desire for increased East-West trade are systematic, part of their détente-as-defense strategy. U.S. subsidies are haphazard and ad hoc, part of periodic efforts on the part of Washington to bolster American exports to the Soviet bloc. From the standpoint of equity, the United States bears the "defense feedback" costs of its own subsidies to, and trade with, the Soviets. When we foolishly enrich the enemy, at least we pay the corresponding increase in defense costs such enrichment implies. When West Europeans enrich the enemy, they pass the defense-feedback cost along to Americans.

A second danger to the United States from Europe's détente-as-defense strategy relates to the nuclear threshold. The nuclear threshold is that critical point in an armed conflict when one of the combatants is faced with the choice of either surrendering or going nuclear. At present, the nuclear threshold is dangerously low. If Moscow were to attack Western Europe by conventional means, according to the present NATO commanding general, Bernard Rogers, NATO could fight for "days, not weeks" before facing the doomsday decision.

How ironic that the low nuclear threshold is itself caused by the American nuclear guarantee. Shielded by the nuclear umbrella at a time when the United States held a clear nuclear advantage over the Soviets, the Europeans built up their welfare states rather than their conventional defense. Now, despite the danger posed to mankind by the low nuclear threshold, the Europeans resist adding to their conventional forces because additional defense spending would reduce their welfare states from current levels. This explains the enormous appeal détente has for the Europeans. Détente allows Europe to keep its conventional defense spending low and its welfare spending high, and still feel safe vis-à-vis the Soviets despite the onset of U.S.–Soviet nuclear parity.

While the Europeans find it cheaper to subsidize the Soviets than add to their conventional defense, Uncle Sam continues to spend an enormous amount of money on NATO. In an article in *Foreign Affairs*, Earl Ravenal estimates that our financial commitment to NATO will cost American taxpayers $134 billion in 1986 alone and $2.2 trillion over the next ten years.[7] An analysis by the General Accounting Office put the U.S. cost of NATO at $122 billion for fiscal 1982, or 56 percent of total U.S. defense outlays for that year. A Defense Department report estimates the 1985 figure at $177 billion.[8] Senator Sam Nunn (D-Georgia), who in 1984 proposed that 90,000 of the 360,000 American troops in Europe be withdrawn within five years unless the European allies increase their military spending—the so-called "Nunn Amendment"—argues that "the citizens of . . . this nation . . . will, and should, question why their hundreds of billions in defense investment buys such a limited conventional defense that NATO must rely on the untenable military strategy of early resort to nuclear weapons."[9] Détente and the welfare state may be a satisfactory equilibrium for Europe, but it is a dangerous, and costly, one for the United States.

Not only has Europe's high-welfare, low conventional defense-spending equilibrium given the world a low nuclear threshold, but it also has given Europeans a strong vested economic interest in maintaining the present system of nuclear deterrence known as Mutual Assured Destruction, or MAD. "Many European officials say they believe that fear of nuclear retaliation has kept the peace in Europe for decades," according to a Congressional study on European reaction to President Ronald Reagan's Strategic Defense Initiative (SDI; also known as "Star Wars"). "Should a reliable shield be developed against nuclear weapons, these officials fear, a conventional war might become more likely, setting off a conventional arms race and subjecting Europe to the risk of devastation by conventional arms."[10] Surely, though, the dangers to mankind from a conventional arms race are less than those of the present nuclear arms race. The Europeans appear to oppose changing the present system of nuclear terror to one of strategic defense and conventional deterrence because, given present Soviet conventional superiority, the changeover to the safer alternative would compel the Europeans to cut into their welfare states to finance the necessary conventional arms buildup. European addiction to the welfare state has kept the world on the nuclear precipice.

The Soviets are well aware of European reluctance to scale down their welfare state to build up their conventional forces and are using this fact to help undermine the Strategic Defense Initiative. At present, the Soviets are refusing to negotiate missile cuts in Europe unless the United States puts the SDI on the bargaining table in arms control talks. This tactic is intended to put the Reagan administration in a bind: If it agrees to bargain away the SDI, the Soviets, who for years have been building up their own SDI system, score a big strategic victory; if it disagrees, the Europeans, who want arms control to keep their military spending low, will be angry with the United States for undermining the arms control talks. So far, the Soviet strategy seems to be working. The Europeans have let it be known that "no one envisions an agreement at Geneva so long as the Reagan administration refuses to treat SDI as a bargaining chip and trade it for Soviet missile cuts."[11]

European attempts to undermine American interests in order to pacify the Soviets have not been limited to strategic defense. According to Henry S. Rowen of the Hoover Institution:

> The last occasion in which a European consensus existed for acting to combat the extension of Soviet power was in supporting democratic forces in Portugal in the 1970s. The now-normal stance of the Europeans towards the extensions of Soviet influence in the Third World is (1) to regard such extensions as deplorable but not warranting action by them (Afghanistan), (2) to regard them as provoked by actions by a U.S. ally (the Soviet presence in Syria as a response to Israeli action in Lebanon), (3) the natural response of shaky democratic—or potentially democratic—governments which are being subjected to U.S. hostile pressures (the Sandinistas), (4) over-reaction by the U.S. to local difficulties of no wide importance (Grenada), or (5) understandable self-defense actions which result in calls on Soviet support taken by governments subject to systematic hostile

actions (Angola and Mozambique in response to South African pressure).[12]

Perhaps the arena in which European obstructionism has been most apparent is the United Nations. Western Europe often votes against the United States on key strategic issues in the United Nations—Nicaragua, El Salvador, Grenada, and so forth. Here are two examples from 1983:

—Resolution 38/101 of the 1983 U.N. General Assembly Meeting reads as if it had been written in the Kremlin. It expresses "deepest concern that the gravest violations of human rights are persisting in El Salvador, recommends reform, calls for comprehensive negotiated political solutions, and urges all states to abstain from intervening and to suspend any type of military assistance." Seven of our NATO allies supported this resolution and five abstained. None supported the United States.

—When the United States liberated Grenada from a Marxist-terrorist regime, the "Iron Lady" of Great Britain, Margaret Thatcher, denounced the move even though the U.S., at some cost to its regional interests in Latin America, supported Mrs. Thatcher in the Falklands War. U.N. Resolution 38/7 of the 1983 General Assembly Meeting "deplores U.S. armed intervention in Grenada and calls for immediate withdrawal of foreign troops from Grenada." Nine of our NATO allies supported this resolution and three abstained in the voting. None supported the United States.[13]

Europeans rationalize their indifference to the extension of Soviet power in the Third World by arguing that the United States overestimates the Soviet threat in these and other areas. Peregrine Worsthorne, a prestigious British Conservative, admits:

[there is] . . . a difference in perception between the two sides of the Atlantic about the magnitude and urgency of the Soviet menace; a difference which prompts the European allies to be less easily convinced than are the American neoconservatives of the necessity to stamp out every Communist growth anywhere in the world, even if this means, say, using right-wing dictatorships to do the job.

As we understand it, their view is that Communist totalitarianism, rather like AIDS, constitutes a uniquely dangerous threat, since any country once infected by the dread virus can never hope to recover.

> ... Without wanting in any way to play down the Orwellian 1984-
> ish side of Communism, cannot we Europeans legitimately point
> out that this apocalyptic view of the effect of Communism does not
> seem to be borne out much by what has been happening recently
> in Eastern and Central Europe. . . . Communism, except in Russia—
> not even in China—does not seem to us quite that uniquely dreadful
> that it once appeared to be, and I suspect that the more the virus is
> exposed to different climes, the weaker it will become, to the point
> where its capacity to spread to, and dominate, all parts of the body
> politic will be less than once feared.[14]

If a leading European conservative has come to view communism
with such rose-colored glasses, can there really be any doubt as to
the long-range debilitating effect wrought by the American security
blanket on European perceptions of external danger?

In conclusion, the biggest threat to the West today is not that
the Soviets will invade Western Europe, but that Western Europe
will "Finlandize" itself to the point where a Soviet military invasion
is redundant. The message the Europeans appear to be sending the
Kremlin is this: "We will close our eyes to the horror you do in
Afghanistan and Poland. We will enrich you by increased trade and
subsidies. We will conspire with you to obstruct the Americans in
Central America and frustrate their efforts to build a strategic defense. We will do all this, and all we ask in return is for you not
to invade us."

A convincing case thus can be made that, under American protection and posing as friends, the Europeans have made a Faustian
deal with the devil that severely undermines U.S. national security
interests.

2

Europe on $134 Billion
a Year

An elephant in the dining room is unlikely to escape notice. Yet NATO is eating up an elephantine portion of the U.S. defense budget and few Americans appear to be aware of it. An unscientific sampling of friends recently yielded estimates of 10–20 percent to the question of the size of NATO's share of U.S. defense expenditures. When told that the debate today is whether the figure for fiscal year 1985 lies closer to the 42-percent estimate of a leading private analyst or to the 58-percent estimate of the U.S. Defense Department, they simply refused to believe it.[1] One reason the public tends to underestimate the economic costs of NATO is that a good part of the costs are hidden.

MEASURING THE ELEPHANT

Even the military's highest-ranking field officers have an incomplete picture of the costs of their commands, according to defense analyst Earl C. Ravenal of the Cato Institute. "The commander-in-chief of a given unified or allied command does not see all the costs," writes Ravenal. "The American forces that he commands are just the tip of the iceberg; *most of the costs involve support units and Pentagon overhead.* The money is spent in the United States, but it is attributed to our commitment to defend each specified region." According to Ravenal, "the forces the United States keeps in Europe are only about one-third of the forces it maintains for the support of NATO.[2]

Ravenal attempts to measure the budgetary costs of U.S. regional commitments by using a simple and indirect methodology. First, the defense budget is divided into two components: "Strategic" and "General Purpose." Then Ravenal attributes "general purpose" costs—estimated to be $241 billion in 1986—to each specific command on the basis of the share of total active ground divisions allocated to each region. "Land divisions are the most practical and the most accessible measure," according to Ravenal, "and they quite well represent the allocation of tactical air wings, whether Air Force, Navy, or Marine." NATO/Europe and its southern flank (the Eastern Mediterranean) gets 11⅔ of the 21 active ground divisions deployed by the United States. The costs of NATO/Europe are thus computed at .56 times $241, or $134 billion. East Asia and the Western Pacific get 3⅔ of the 21 divisions; its cost is computed at .17 times $241, or $42 billion. Other regions and the Strategic Reserve, which includes what is now called the "Rapid Deployment Forces," absorb $65 billion, which is .27 of $341 billion. Almost $50 billion of this is for the Persian Gulf.[3]

What, precisely, does Ravenal's $134 billion cost estimate for NATO actually mean? To an economist, the relevant definition of cost is "opportunity cost"—the alternative use of resources. When the United States uses some portion of its national resources—land, labor, capital—in defense of Europe, it cannot use these resources for other purposes—military or social, public or private. The true costs of NATO thus are the variety of military, social, and private goods Americans could have, but do not—because the resources needed to produce them are spent on the defense of Europe.

How can Ravenal's figure of $134 billion be reconciled with the concept of opportunity costs? If the United States were to totally negate its commitment to Europe by (1) withdrawing the troops from Europe, (2) freeing its support troops stationed in the United States for other duties or demobilization, and (3) shrinking the Pentagon bureaucracy proportionately or using the Pentagon overhead for other military functions, Ravenal claims that $134 billion worth of resources would be made available for the production of other goods and services. Note that it is not necessary to precisely specify what these other goods and services might consist of in order to ascertain the economic costs of NATO. Whatever permutation and combination of goods and services $134 billion can buy in world markets at the present time, that is the total cost of NATO.

One can, of course, imagine a multitude of alternative uses of $134 billion worth of resources that would be more profitable for this country than the defense of Europe. For example, in a recent *New York Times Magazine* article, Zbigniew Brzezinski, Robert Jastrow, and Max Kampelman claim that a strategic defense capable of reducing the prospect of a Soviet first strike to almost nil could be available for deployment by the early 1990s at an estimated cost of $60 billion.[4] Sixty billion dollars is less than half of what the United States currently spends on NATO *in one year*. In fact, it is quite possible that the Strategic Defense Initiative favored by President Reagan will not be adequately funded because of the U.S. deficit problem. Yet, if the United States were to pull out of NATO, the country could fully fund strategic defense at the same time that it reduced its deficit by $74 billion.

Skeptics may point out that while it is possible to cashier troops, shrinking the Pentagon is another matter. Its size may be immutable for political reasons. If, then, one makes the assumption that the Pentagon overhead costs are roughly half of the total costs (more in the air force, less in the army), instead of $134 billion as maximum potential savings from negating the U.S. commitment to NATO, the savings figure becomes $67 billion. In this case, the gain from decommitment would finance the Strategic Defense Initiative but would not allow for a substantial reduction in the U.S. budget deficit. Europe would be on its own, and the United States would be able to negate the Soviet ability to use a first strike against it.

It is important to note that while the debate about Europe often is carried out in terms of whether the United States should—or should not—pull its troops out of the old continent, withdrawing the troops from Europe will not, in and of itself, save this country any of its resources. From the point of view of determining NATO's costs, the important thing is not where the troops are deployed, but where they are committed. Thus, it makes little difference whether or not the troops committed to the defense of Europe are actually deployed in Europe or stationed in the United States. To save resources, the United States must decommit them from Europe's defense wherever they are located. Only then can the nation use the released resources for purposes other than European defense.

Though Ravenal's figure of $134 billion as the cost of NATO is a surprisingly large number, it may actually underestimate the true burden of NATO to the United States. The reason is that Ravenal's definition of NATO's cost is incomplete; it leaves out some very important indirect costs that bias his estimate downward. One such omission, for example, is the "defense feedback" cost of European free riding.

When U.S. allies trade with, overtrade with, and subsidize the Soviets, our enemy gains economic resources which they can—and do—use to augment their military machine. The United States in turn must counter the Soviet military buildup with one of its own to maintain the military balance. The increase in the U.S. defense budget by comparison with what it otherwise would have been—made necessary by the enrichment of the Soviet Union by its allies—can be called the "defense-feedback" costs of the détente policies of America's allies.

If all U.S. allies engaged in détente to essentially the same extent, Ravenal's methodology—attributing general purpose costs to each specific command on the basis of the share of total active ground divisions allocated to each region—would yield an unbiased estimate. But this is not the case: Only Western Europe has a détente-as-defense strategy that puts disproportionate upward pressure on the U.S. defense budget via the defense-feedback effect. Thus, when Ravenal makes his NATO calculation by multiplying the general purpose budget by the NATO fraction of .56, he does not capture the NATO–induced increase in the general purpose budget. NATO is imposing more costs on the United States than Ravenal's $134 billion figure indicates.

Ravenal's estimate also leaves out the strategic costs of NATO.

While it is true that specifying NATO's share of U.S. strategic expense may be extremely difficult, this does not make the costs nonexistent. The United States gives the Europeans a nuclear guarantee. The marginal resource costs of extending the American nuclear umbrella to cover Western Europe may be minimal, but the United States has developed certain nuclear weapons (like the Pershing missile) for use primarily in the European theater. This weapon helps neutralize the Soviet SS-20s which are targeted on European, not U.S., cities. The costs of the Pershings are purely NATO costs, which must be added to the $134 billion figure if an accurate cost estimate of NATO is to be obtained.

ADJUSTING TO A NATO-LESS WORLD

A reallocation of domestic resources of the magnitude implied by the negation of our commitment to defend Europe will involve nontrivial adjustment problems for the United States. Not everyone would gain from the change. Even in the case where the total U.S. military budget remains constant, the transfer of resources from NATO to other defense programs could cause sufficient short-run dislocation. Consider, for example, the possibility that the savings from pulling out of Europe would be used to finance a full-blown strategic defense system. When the United States withdraws, it is likely that many of the demobilized American soldiers, both in Europe and in the United States, will be unable to find employment in the expanding research-intensive strategic defense program. This would be particularly true of the unskilled soldiers. The result will be unemployment of unskilled labor unless wages in the private sector fell sufficiently to absorb those who either cannot find, or do not want to accept, jobs in the expanding military programs. Increased unemployment of unskilled labor is not likely to be a long-run consequence of the reallocation of the military budget, but lower wages for low-skilled workers than otherwise would have been the case can be expected. Of course, if a portion of the saved NATO money is used for social programs to benefit the income groups that are hurt by the otherwise beneficial change, the negative consequences of the transfer of resources could be moderated.

On the other hand, allocating resources to the strategic defense program will increase the demand for—and wages of—skilled workers, particularly in the high-tech field. It also will increase the demand for capital made necessary by the need to invest in strategic defense hardware. Under *ceteris paribus* assumptions, this could lead to an increase in interest rates as the "crowding out" pressure of the Strategic Defense Initiative made its impact felt. The increase in interest rates, in turn, would lead to a general slowdown of economic activity unless it led to an inflow of foreign capital to meet the increased demand. Whether the latter occurred or not would depend to a large extent on the general economic climate in the United States at the time in comparison with that abroad. The more favorable the relative economic climate in the United States, the more likely that foreign savings would help finance a significant portion of the Strategic Defense Initiative. The point of this analysis, it should be noted, is not to make precise predictions about what will happen to each and every economic variable, but to give a general schema for the kinds of distributional changes that could result from the envisaged transfer of domestic revenues should the United States decommit.

Very different distributional results obtain, for example, if instead of using the freed resources for strategic defense, the United States used them to reduce the budget deficit. In this case, instead of interest rates rising because of an increased demand for funds for capital investment, they could decline because government borrowing declines. The decrease in interest rates, in turn, would increase the demand for both skilled and unskilled labor in the private sector of the economy, because there would be an increase in general economic activity induced by the fall in interest rates. This chain of reasoning leads to the conclusion that the cashiered American soldiers would be absorbed in the burgeoning private sector. Thus, the unemployment presumed in the first case would not be a problem in the second one. Indeed, if private economic activity responds strongly to the fall in interest rates, not only would there be jobs for the cashiered American soldiers, but total employment in the economy would increase as well.

A third possibility occurs if the resources freed by U.S. withdrawal from NATO are transferred to the private economy *via* a general tax cut. The transfer of resources from the public to the private sector implied by a dollar-for-dollar cut in government expenditure and taxes would affect economic change through its effect on the composition of total demand for goods and services in the economy. As the public sector shrinks and the private economy expands, there will be an increase in the demand for goods for which the private sector has a marginal preference by comparison with the public sector. For example, the demand for military goods such as tanks, ammunition, and electronic military devices would fall, while the demand for television sets, automobiles, and other consumer goods increases. Moreover, because of these changes, the income of the factors of production used intensively in the military sector would fall relative to those used intensively in the production of civilian goods. The fortunes of some companies and citizens would rise and those of others would decline, depending on the industry one happens to work and invest in. Those lucky or skillful enough to be in the expanding civilian-goods sector gain while those in the military-industrial complex lose from the resource reallocation due to demilitarization.

In addition to changing the composition of overall demand in the economy, the dollar-for-dollar reduction of tax rates and military expenditures increase can be expected to increase economic growth. The tax cuts will stimulate greater work effort and savings in the economy. This means that the expanding investment and employment opportunities from the growing sectors of the economy should more than offset those in the declining military sector. The number of winners will be greater than the number of losers, though losers there will be. As far as the budget deficit is concerned, the immediate impact of the dollar-for-dollar reduction in government expenditure and taxes would be to leave the deficit unchanged. But because increased economic growth increases tax revenue, the budget deficit should—over time—be reduced. This serves to reinforce the positive growth implications of the tax and government expenditure reduction.

Whatever economic adjustments take place as a result of a U.S. negation of its defense commitment to Europe, the adjustment process will go smoother the more flexible the domestic economy. The more flexibility there is, for example, the less the likelihood that the transfer of labor from one sector to another will create unemployment or labor shortages. Gluts and shortages of commodities are less likely when commodity prices are more flexible. In the modern economy, however, prices tend to be flexible upward but not downward. Workers and capitalists in threatened industries make common cause, using the political process to resist the adjustments that change requires (see chapter 7). Government policy should be geared to increasing flexibility of the economy precisely to minimize the dislocations caused by beneficial transfers of resources of the type that would occur should the United States decommit from Europe.

THE EUROPEAN RESPONSE

When I argued, in *The Wall Street Journal*,[5] that the United States should adopt a "Fortress America" strategy to counter Finlandization arguments and to end European defense free-riding, Richard R. Burt, the then assistant secretary of state for European affairs and present ambassador to West Germany, responded:

> The Soviet Union remains the preponderant military power in Europe. The Soviet Union also continues to employ its military power to achieve political objectives, including the intimidation of Western Europe. In such circumstances, the withdrawal of American troops and of the American security guarantee would have the reverse effect from that Professor Krauss suggests. American withdrawal would leave European leaders with no realistic means to provide for their national security except through accommodation with the dominant regional power, the USSR. American withdrawal would, as a result, depress, not stimulate, European defense efforts, while driving the U.S. into increasing international isolation.[6]

When Ambassador Burt argues that a U.S. withdrawal from Europe would depress European defense efforts from present levels, he assumes to know what European defense efforts would be in the absence of U.S. subsidization. How does he know this? Economists postulate that in market economies the demand for private goods can be judged only by market behavior. But defense is a public good, not a private one. What the Europeans demand in the way of defense when the United States pays the bills in no way indicates what they would demand in the absence of U.S. contributions. Indeed, public goods theory predicts that Europe presently understates its demand for defense precisely to get the United States to pay more. This is the essence of the defense free-riding argument.

Despite the fact that Europe no longer would have an economic motive to deliberately understate its demand for defense should the United States withdraw, a purely economic analysis does not give an unambiguous answer to the questions posed by Ambassador Burt. The increase in the demand for defense that results from the elimination of deliberate demand understatement means that, at any given price (or cost) of defense, quantity demanded increases. At the same time, however, the elimination of U.S. subsidization of European defense means that the price of defense to the Europeans would increase. Quantity demand decreases as the price goes up. Thus, American withdrawal should give rise to two contradictory effects: one that increases the quantity demanded of defense by the Europeans and one that decreases it. Which effect will dominate depends on the relative strength of the two opposing forces. If the defense free-riding effect dominates, then American withdrawal will increase European defense efforts. The opposite occurs if the price effect dominates.

While a purely theoretical analysis cannot, by itself, give an unambiguous answer to the question of how termination of U.S. subsidies to European defense can be expected to affect European defense efforts, imposition of a quite reasonable empirical assumption as to the nature of defense demand can settle the issue. Defense is not one of those goods where demand is particularly sensitive to price. When choosing which missile system to deploy, cost often plays a secondary role, if only because the government officials who make the decisions do not bear the financial implications of their choice; the taxpayers do. Thus, an increase in price is likely to have a small quantitative effect on defense demand. The presumption of a small price effect means that the defense free-riding effect is likely to dominate the price effect; hence, the removal of U.S. subsidies can be expected to increase, not decrease, European defense efforts on its own behalf.

3

Restraint and Containment

Worle World War II marked an important cross-over point in the evolution of American foreign policy. Despite U.S. entry into World War I, isolation remained the cornerstone of American foreign policy during the interwar period with such formidable spokesmen as President Herbert Hoover, Senator Robert A. Taft, and Senator Arthur H. Vandenberg. The Second World War, however, changed the political landscape of the United States in quite remarkable ways. American isolationists had counseled against U.S. entry into World War II on the grounds that it would irreparably and irreversibly damage the country. War, said Senator Vandenberg in 1939, would result in the complete regimentation of American life, the imposition of a dictatorship, ruinous deficit spending, and radical domestic change. Whatever the apparent benefits from U.S. intervention abroad, isolationists argued they would be far outweighed by domestic costs.

Where the isolationists went wrong is that they did not foresee Pearl Harbor. The Japanese sneak attack convinced the vast majority of Americans that the isolationists not only had it wrong but that they had it backward. Preserving the American way of life required that the United States get militarily involved, not turn the other cheek. Isolationist credibility was further undermined when their predictions of dire domestic consequences from U.S. entry into the war failed to materialize. Not only did the United States not get the totalitarianism that isolationists had promised, but it helped rid the world of Japanese, German, and Italian dictators in the process.

A TIME FOR CONTAINMENT

If ever there was a perfect time for U.S. interventionist policy, it was the post–World War II period. The United States emerged from the war with two important gaps in its favor—the "economic gap" and the "nuclear gap." No other country, or group of countries, had as productive an economy as the United States had after the war. No other country, or group of countries, had its nuclear punch. Moreover, the war brought to the fore a new and dangerous enemy—the Soviet Union—whose imperialistic ambitions made it a worthy candidate for containment. The United States thus had both a purpose and an unparalleled ability to effectively pursue intervention after the war.

The prime architect of America's containment policy was the diplomat and historian George Kennan. In *American Diplomacy*, Kennan wrote:

> . . . the main element of any United States policy toward the Soviet Union must be that of a long term, patient but firm and vigilant containment of Russian expansive tendencies. . . . It would be an exaggeration to say that American behavior unassisted and alone could exercise a power of life and death over the Communist movement and bring about the early fall of Soviet power in Russia. But the United States has it in its power to increase enormously the strains under which Soviet policy must operate, to force upon the Kremlin a far greater degree of moderation and circumspection than it has had to observe in recent years, and in this way to promote tendencies which must eventually find their outlet in either the break-up or the gradual mellowing of Soviet power.[1]

In the public's eye, containment is most commonly identified with military intervention. But to its architects, the economic component of containment is at least as important as the military. Kennan himself, in a 1975 interview, stresses the economic and downplays the military aspect of containment.

> When I talked about containment, what I had in mind was an effort on our part to stiffen the hope, the confidence of European nations in themselves, and to persuade them that they didn't need to yield to one great power or another.... In 1948, when the talk of the formation of the NATO pact began (it was actually the Europeans—the French and the British and the Benelux people—who came to us and wanted it), I was quite surprised. I said, "Why are you giving your attention to this? We're just getting the Marshall Plan through. For goodness sake, concentrate on your economic recovery. Nobody's going to attack you." But I found that all of Western Europe had what the French call *la manie d'invasion*—the mania of invasion.[2]

According to Kennan's analysis, the Soviet threat was not so much military invasion but subversion from abroad.

> What I thought was essential in 1945, in 1946, and in 1947 was to prevent the political influence and predominant authority of the Soviet government from spreading any farther in the world, because we had had it demonstrated in the period of World War II that you didn't always have to occupy another country in order to dominate its life. You could threaten it or you could subvert its government by various ways, including the time-honored phenomenon of puppet government.[3]

True as this may be, there is nothing particularly inconsistent between Kennan's dictum that "you don't have to occupy a country to dominate its life" and excessive fear of military invasion. Indeed, as we have learned in the postwar period, the two go together hand in glove. Increasingly, the Soviets are dominating life in Western Europe, and they certainly have not militarily occupied the old continent. The threat of military invasion has been sufficient to turn Western Europe to policies that give the Soviets much of what they want without the need to bloody their hands. Today, as much as forty years ago, a strong military deterrent is required if subversion is to be avoided.

The North Atlantic Treaty Organization was organized in 1949 to give Europe that military deterrent. Owing to the influence of George Kennan, however, it also was recognized that military support alone could not do the job. "Western Europe, as the war ended, was in a sorry state," according to Kennan. "People were disoriented, discouraged, apprehensive, frightened by the experiences of war, and it would not have been too difficult for Italy or for France, if they had lost their confidence in us then, to turn to the Soviet Union and let their communist parties take over."[4] Under these circumstances, it was imperative that the United States help Europe get back on its feet again. If economic recovery from the war did not take hold, there was a real danger Europe would be lost.

To prevent this, a powerful idea took shape in Washington: An economically strong Europe was essential for American security. Whatever economic sacrifices the strengthening of the European economies might imply for the United States, they were deemed smaller than the cost of American isolation should Europe fall under Communist control. The most important initiative taken to effectuate this idea was the Marshall Plan, to give economic aid to Western Europe, including West Germany, on an unprecedented scale. The estimated four-year total of Marshall aid was $17 billion. Most of this aid went to finance U.S. exports to Europe—food, feed, and fertilizer accounted for the largest percentage of aid; then raw materials and semifinished goods; then fuel; and finally machinery and vehicles. This part of Marshall Plan aid provided important relief to the Europeans and helped lay the basis for a sustained economic recovery. A smaller amount of Marshall Plan aid went to finance the European Payments Union, whose purpose it was to restore currency convertibility in Europe. The European Payments Union proved extremely important for economic recovery because, unless the European currencies were freely exchangeable one into the other, the growth in intra-European trade necessary for European recovery could not take place. The true sign Marshall Plan aid was doing its job is that between 1947 and 1951, intra-European trade grew at a much faster rate than European imports from the United States.

A second and related initiative undertaken by the United States to rebuild Europe during this period was its sponsorship of regional economic integration in Europe. Aware of the advantages that the United States has enjoyed through the existence of a large domestic market with no internal trade barriers, and believing that similar advantages could accrue to the countries of Europe, the U.S. Congress wanted to encourage these countries, through a joint organization, to exert substantial common efforts as set forth in the Report of the Committee of European Economic Cooperation signed in Paris on September 22, 1947.

What Congress did not mention in the European Cooperation Act, however, is that in addition to the absence of *internal* trade barriers, the United States always has had trade barriers against foreign countries. The same would be true of a "United States of Europe," except the party discriminated against in this instance would be the United States. Thus, in actively promoting regional integration in Western Europe to the extent that Marshall Plan aid actually was made conditional upon progress toward this objective, the United States actively promoted organized institutional discrimination against itself. This type of economic interventionism, which promotes discrimination against one's own exports rather than the opposite, is truly rare.

There were several reasons why the Truman administration favored regionalism as a containment policy in Western Europe after World War II. Regionalism was perceived to be a self-help measure to make the European economies less dependent on the United States. The United States wanted Europe back on its feet, not tied to its apron strings. Second, European integration was viewed as a way to contain the nationalisms that many considered to be the chief cause of European wars. In particular, regionalism was viewed as a mechanism for controlling West Germany as it recovered from the war and rehabilitated itself. Finally, many Americans simply had faith that economic integration works. Look what it had done for the United States, after all.

There can be no doubt that the vision of a united, integrated, and prosperous Europe was an inspired one. As we have learned from Adam Ulam, director of the Russian Research Center at Harvard University, the Soviet nightmare is to be confronted not by one superpower in the West but by two—the United States of America on one side of the Atlantic, and an independent and powerful United States of Europe on the other. American political leaders in the early postwar period understood this and pushed for the regional option in Europe even though it meant organized trade discrimination against their own country. The United States has received more than its fair share of credit for its generous Marshall Plan aid to Europe. American support for a United States of Europe, however, represented an act of far greater vision and statesmanship.

Unfortunately, though U.S. statesmen had inspired vision for postwar Europe, either they did not have—or did not use—the ability they possessed to impose that vision on the Europeans. True, American enthusiasm for a United States of Europe was in tune with European federalists like Jean Monnet of France. But the voices of Monnet and his European supporters were not strong enough. Almost from the beginning, U.S. efforts on behalf of a united Europe were met with caution, reserve, and resistance by Europeans of real influence who seemed more interested in what regionalism could do for their nation-states than what their nation-states could do for regionalism. The truth appears to be: that so long as the United States has stood ready to defend Europe against communism, European anti-communism has taken a backseat to European nationalism. By neutralizing the Communist threat, defense of Europe undercut the very regionalism the United States had hoped to achieve. The failure of regionalism in Western Europe raises, or at least should raise, questions about the efficacy of American interventionism.

THE LIMITS OF INTERVENTIONISM

Nowhere have the limits of interventionism been more apparent than in U.S. relations with Western Europe. American economic and military support clearly was required to discourage Soviet Adventurism in Western Europe in the immediate post–World War II years. The idea was that the United States would help out during the critical period of readjustment to normalcy, but that support would be cut back as soon as Europe got back on its feet.

Things did not work out that way, however. American leaders, corrupted by the apparent control military support of Europe gave them over European defense and foreign policies, have worked to keep Europe dependent, while European leaders, corrupted by the enormous defense subsidies the United States provided them, learned that by skillful diplomatic maneuvering they often could eat their cake and have it too—the tail-wagging-the-dog syndrome. Thus, as the old continent recovered from World War II, elitist groups on both sides of the Atlantic conspired to maintain the status quo of American subsidization and European dependence—despite the fact that increasing Soviet influence over Western Europe had made it clear that the old formula no longer worked. How ironic that opposing the Soviets by excessive and uncritical internationalism produced the very result—growth of Soviet influence over Western Europe—that such action is supposed to prevent. Instead of building up Western Europe, the U.S. open-ended commitment to Europe built Europe down.

"Internationalism reached its rhetorical high-water mark with John Kennedy's 'bear any burden' inaugural pledge," writes Charles Krauthammer in *The New Republic*.[5] But in openly declaring that this country would "bear any burden and pay any price" for defense of the free world, Kennedy made our allies an offer they couldn't refuse. The unintended result of Kennedy's carte blanche approach to containment has been that, too often, the marginal or incremental contribution of U.S. military aid to Western defense and containment has been disappointing simply because this intervention has induced offsetting substitutions of defense efforts by our allies. U.S. military assistance in these cases does not increase Western deterrence. It merely redistributes the cost of financing a given amount of defense from our allies to ourselves.

The recognition that American assistance, by inducing weakness and dependence in its allies, can benefit our enemies raises an important distinction between opposing Soviet influence and power on the one hand, and American internationalism on the other. The conventional wisdom is that support of U.S. allies, whether economic or military, is necessary to stymie the imperialistic Soviets. But the debate in the United States over Europe's persistent weakness in the face of the Soviet threat is splitting the internationalists from strong anti-Communists for the first time in the postwar period. Many respected foreign policy experts, such as Irving Kristol, William Safire, and Henry Kissinger, have publicly expressed doubts about the wisdom of open-ended commitments to U.S. allies and friends. There can be too much of anything in this world, and there is a growing recognition that there can be too much support for friends as well as too little of it.

Does recognition of the fact that there can be too much support for an ally make one an isolationist? Charles Krauthammer, an expert on isolationism, thinks that it does. He writes:

> Right isolationism has yet to capture a party, but its proponents, still in opposition, are growing in strength and confidence. Kristol, for example, in his essay "Does NATO exist?" (his answer is no), makes the most radical case for the United States to get out of Europe. Henry Kissinger probes the idea more tentatively with a proposal for cutting U.S. forces in Europe by "perhaps up to half." Owen Harries follows with a proposal to turn from an Atlantic to a "Pacific Community."... In Congress, the leader of the effort to cut U.S. troops in Europe is a conservative Democrat, Sam Nunn.[6]

What Krauthammer fails to appreciate is that true isolationists in this country do not believe in actively opposing Soviet foreign adventures. Their motto is: "If the Soviets want it, let them have it." Neither Kristol, Kissinger, Harries, nor Nunn take this position or anything close to it. All four are concerned about Europe's persistent reluctance to defend itself, and wonder whether it may be due to American overprotection. Why label as isolationists those who want to see Europe strong?

Perhaps the answer to this question is that Krauthammer views the proposal that the United States get out of Europe as an American "beggar-my-neighbor" policy—with America gaining at the expense of its European allies. "Although rightist isolationists draw different lines," he writes, "the sentiment animating their efforts is the same: *a sense that America has let itself be drawn into commitments that serve not its interests but that of others* [emphasis mine]. From Washington's farewell address on, that sentiment has always animated classical isolationism, particularly pre-war right isolationism."[7]

But what should America's policies be when the "other interests" served by NATO include those of our principal enemy—the Soviet Union? The United States may not like it, but the Soviets have their "silent allies" in Western Europe who (1) enrich them with loans, subsidies, and international trade which, because it is so one-sided, might better be called "unrequited transfer"; (2) attempt to restrain American power in the Third World, and particularly in Central America, when it seeks to oppose communism or forces sympathetic to communism; and (3) do their best to sabotage American defense initiatives like Star Wars, which the Soviet Union has deemed threatening to its interests. It is isolationist to argue that the multilateralist net in which the Europeans hope to entangle the United States in the fight against communism should be cast off; that unless an assertive unilateralism can be restored to American foreign policy, not only Nicaragua but Costa Rica, Honduras, and Guatemala may be lost to the United States as well? The military weakness NATO has imposed on the Europeans, which leads them to flack for the Soviets, is in neither Europe's long-term interests nor that of the United States. Withdrawal of the U.S. defense commitment to Europe is not "beggar-my-neighbor" because, in the long run, it is likely to benefit Europe as well as the United States.

THE NEW INTERNATIONALISM

Traditionally, American isolationists and internationalists could be defined in terms of how far each would go in opposing the Soviet menace—the internationalists going the full distance, the isolationists barely a step. Since Vietnam, however, internationalism has taken on a new meaning that not only is different from, but whose implications are opposed to, the old one. Internationalism, in the post–Vietnam War era, has come to mean "multilateralism"—that in the fight against the spread of communism, the United States should never act by itself, but always in concert with other nations. The Communists must be delighted with "revisionist internationalism," since multilateralism has become little more than a euphemism for inaction by the United States in the face of the Soviet advances.

Even critics of American unilateralism admit this. Peregrine Worsthorne writes:

> Whereas alliances once upon a time facilitated what was, to all
> intents and purposes, American unilateralism, today they tend some-

times to be more a hindrance than a help. This is why, of course, Democratic Party opponents of the energetic use of American power are nowadays all for alliances, precisely because concerted action in present circumstances is often the equivalent of no action, or at any rate, delayed and possibly half-hearted action.[8]

"Multilateralism," according to Charles Krauthammer, "now a true hindrance to American action, is a synonym—an excuse—for paralysis. It has become what [Walter] Lippmann once called 'the internationalism of the isolationists.'"[9] But if multilateralism indeed has become the "internationalism of the isolationists," has not unilateralism then become "the isolationism of the internationalists"?

Irving Kristol writes: "So long as the Soviets enjoy success in foreign policy, an internal crisis can be indefinitely postponed. U.S. policy, therefore, should try to inflict a series of defeats, however minor, on the Soviets. That is the significance of our support, or lack thereof, of 'liberation' movements in Angola, Nicaragua, Afghanistan, and wherever else they emerge."[10] It is more than unfair, it is ridiculous, to call the man who wrote these words a "right-wing isolationist" just because he wants to escape the paralysis multilateralists seek to impose upon this country. An important step the United States can take toward a new policy of unilateralism—what Irving Kristol calls "global unilateralism"—is to pull out of NATO.

Europe's détente-as-defense strategy has made U.S. membership in NATO inconsistent with its containment objectives. NATO has been transformed from an old-style "internationalist" institution into a lever European multilateralists can, and do, use to hamstring American efforts to counter the extension of Soviet influence in the Third World. Its very existence helps perpetuate the dangerous notion that the United States should consult with, and where possible, act in concert with, its allies in trouble spots like Nicaragua, El Salvador, and the Middle East. "An important element in gaining public support for a foreign action," writes Harry Rowen, "is the perception that it is not just the United States helping some beleaguered party abroad, but that other nations are willing to pitch in also."[11] When the legitimacy of U.S. foreign activities comes to depend upon what the consensus in Europe believes to be prudent, however, not only are the Europeans given veto power over U.S.

foreign policies, but because of Europe's détente-as-defense strategy, the United States virtually gives the Soviet Union a veto as well. Containment of Soviet influence under such conditions is obviously impossible.

AMERICA'S MORAL ISOLATIONISTS

To argue that unilateralists are not right-wing isolationists is not to argue that American right-wing isolationists do not exist. In fact, they do. Although the Libertarians are not a very influential political force in the United States, they are interesting for two reasons: First, they represent a type of "moral isolationism" that is important; and second, their foreign policy views are virtually congruent with left-wing isolationists. Right-wing and left-wing isolationists are cut from the same cloth in the post-Vietnam era.

Many Libertarians believe that the pursuit of a containment policy by the United States has reduced the country to a position analogous to that of the Soviet Union. "The world," according to Robert W. Poole, Jr., of the Reason Foundation, "has grown accustomed to the United States and the Soviet Union opposing each other as equivalent superpowers, intervening in other countries, threatening each other's populations with mass destruction, and leading a pack of allies and client states around behind them."[12]

Poole thinks this has blurred the moral difference between the United States and the Soviet Union. "U.S. statesmen," Poole claims, "embark on grandiose plans 'to make the world safe for democracy' or 'bear any burden, pay any price'... While such open-ended claims on the lives and fortunes of the citizenry might be consistent with a collectivist society... they are hardly consistent with the limited government of a society of free and independent individuals." Moreover, both superpowers are dedicated to MAD, "the fundamentally immoral doctrine by which the United States' and the Soviet Union's principal means of defense is the threat of destroying each other's society." Poole believes the United States could "reclaim the moral high ground" by removing the threat of man's destruction and shifting to a defensive strategic posture.[13]

It is indeed ironic that Poole's "moral isolationism" on the right is mirrored by the left in the United States by the foreign policy views of most of the aristocrats of the Democratic Party—O'Neill, Hart, Kennedy, Mondale, Dodd, and Cuomo. Despite the fact that they operate from radically different assumptions concerning the proper role of government in society—the Libertarians believing in limited government, the Democrats in big government—there are striking similarities in these groups' views on American foreign policy. Both place considerable emphasis on the moral factor in world politics. Both agree that the United States has lost the moral high ground to the Soviets in the Cold War. And both argue that in trying to rebuff the Soviets at every turn, the United States has become as evil as the Soviets themselves.

Like the Libertarians, the left-wing isolationists are against the use of military assistance to contain the spread of communism. Charles Krauthammer writes:

> In the 1984 Democratic campaign, the principal disagreement over Central America was whether the United States should station 20 advisors in Honduras (Walter Mondale's position) or zero (Gary Hart's). On Angola, El Salvador, Grenada, Lebanon, and Nicaragua, the Democratic position has involved some variety of disengagement: talks, aid, sanctions, diplomacy—first. In practice this invariably means—only. Force is ruled out, effectively if not explicitly.[14]

Why? The reason is morality.

In the view of left-wing isolationists, containment has been an immoral policy because it has led the United States to support certain regimes in the Third World alleged to be responsible for the economic poverty and social injustice that exists in those countries. We have trouble in Nicaragua today—because the United States backed Somoza. We have trouble in El Salvador—because the United States backed the oligarchies. We have trouble in Iran—because the United States backed the Shah. And we have trouble in Cuba—because the United States backed Batista. The reason the United States backed these "evil" regimes, the argument goes, is that they were anti-Communist. American pursuit of anticommunism abroad, therefore, has been morally wrong because it has led to social injustice and poverty. Indeed, the suspicion exists that many left-wing isolationists would welcome additional Communist regimes in Central America if only to punish the United States for the moral sins they claim Americans have committed there.

This clearly is an absurd and self-defeating foreign policy. While it is certainly true that the United States did support the Shah, Somoza, Batista, and many other authoritarian regimes because they were anti-Communist, and that U.S. support made a difference to the longevity of these regimes (the reason Somoza fell, in fact, was because the Carter administration refused to continue U.S. support of them in the face of opposition), history shows that the "cure" for communism or Islamic fundamentalism always has proven worse than the "disease" of authoritarianism.

Castro, for example, has damaged the lives of Cuban people by reducing their freedoms and ruining what had been a thriving economy in Cuba. Can there be any doubt that the Cuban people today are both less free and less wealthy than they were under Batista? President Carter was concerned with the "human rights" record of Somoza in Nicaragua. Did his subsequent failure to support Somoza lead to increased human rights for the Nicaraguan people, or did not the well-meaning President from Georgia increase their suffering even further? Ayatollah Khomeini has been a major source of international terrorism and has sent hundreds of thousands of Iranians to premature deaths in his war with Iraq. Even from a human rights point of view, was the Shah not infinitely superior to the Ayatollah?

The next time an American President decides to pull the rug out from under one of the country's anti-Communist allies for reasons of morality, there should be someone in the White House to remind him of Maurice Chevalier's celebrated response to a reporter's question on how he felt when he reached the age of eighty: "It feels fine," Chevalier said, "when you consider the alternative."

George Kennan makes a similar point in a recent issue of *Foreign Affairs*. Commenting on the irresponsibility of the moral isolationists, Kennan writes:

> While we are quick to allege that this or that practice in a foreign country is bad [for moral reasons] and deserves correction, seldom if ever do we seem to occupy ourselves seriously or realistically with the conceivable alternatives. It seems seldom to occur to us that even if a given situation is bad, the alternatives to it might be worse— even though history provides plenty of examples of just this phe-

nomenon. In the eyes of many Americans it is enough for us to indicate the changes that ought, as we see it, to be made. We assume, of course, that the consequences will be benign and happy ones. But this is not always assured.... We are demanding, in effect, a species of veto power over those of their practices that we dislike, while denying responsibility for whatever may flow from the acceptance of our demands.[15]

A FOREIGN POLICY TRAP?

Is U.S. foreign policy, then, in a trap? If the United States pulls the rug out from under right-wing military regimes, it will wind up with anti-American dictators whose human rights record is even worse than their predecessors. If the United States supports them, it still is stuck with an SOB, though, at least, the SOB is the United States' SOB (as President Franklin Roosevelt once delicately put it). The peaceful revolution in the Philippines—when Corazon Aquino replaced Ferdinand Marcos in a bloodless transition of power—demonstrates that the answer to this question is no!

America's moral isolationists, who claim that events in the Philippines vindicate their view that the United States should not support right-wing dictatorships, are on their usual path down the slippery slope. For the return to democracy in the Philippines demonstrates nothing if not the validity of Jeane Kirkpatrick's view that between totalitarian dictatorships, such as found in Communist nations, and authoritarian dictatorships, as in right-wing military regimes, it is the latter alone that offers the possibility of democratic change. U.S. support for right-wing dictators does not inevitably lead to disaster for itself or the peoples of the nations involved. The United States supported Marcos for more than twenty years. And the result is what it sees today: a leader who represents the will of the Filipino people.

A question now presents itself to the "human rights first" crowd who are so enamored of the policies of Mr. Reagan's predecessor, Jimmy Carter: Why did Ronald Reagan succeed in the Philippines when Jimmy Carter failed so miserably in Iran and Nicaragua? For one thing, Reagan did not attempt a moral crusade that sought to impose democracy on Third World countries not yet ready for it. He waited until the time was right to distance himself from Marcos.

For another, Carter, the moralist, tragically discounted the strategic implications of his policies. Ronald Reagan did anything but—as his administration refrained from pulling the rug out from under Marcos until it was clear an acceptable alternative was available.

Some conservatives are attacking Reagan because he did not support a friend. But the usefulness of Marcos' friendship to the United States had diminished to the point where his continuation in power would have been a boon to the Filipino Communists. In short, Reagan broke with Marcos because the U.S. alliance with him had become too costly.

The result has been a turn of events that proves the bankruptcy of left-Liberal claims that U.S. support for right-wing dictatorships inevitably leads to bloodshed and anti-American regimes. On the contrary, the peaceful revolution in the Philippines amply justifies the principle that the United States must continue to back right-wing allies such as South Korea, Chile, Taiwan, and so forth.

But it also serves to remind those allies that U.S. support is not unconditional. They, too, could share Marcos' fate if they become more a liability than an asset to the United States: which could occur if, as in the Philippines, their abuse of human rights, corruption, and general incompetence brings acceptable opposition forces to the fore—forces which have now learned that they can count on U.S. backing if they are untainted by Communist influence and generally reflect the popular will.

It is no small irony that by following a strategy policy, Ronald Reagan has achieved more human rights progress for a country hitherto under the thumb of dictatorship than anything his predecessor, Jimmy Carter, was able to do.

It should be obvious that the call for moral isolationism in the United States, whether from the right or the left, reflects a desire by the isolationists to introduce "moral restraint" as the critical component of the country's foreign policy. Moral restraint argues that the United States restrain itself in the struggle with the Soviet Union for moral reasons. The United States should, for example, refrain from intervening in foreign countries because intervention is immoral; it should drop out of the nuclear race because MAD is immoral; it should eschew covert aid because covert aid is not fair; and so on. To the "moral isolationists," the strategic implications of moral restraint are more than beside the point; they are themselves an evil. Indeed, according to isolationist logic, strategic concerns are what got the United States into a moral quagmire in the first place.

The basis for the United States' moral isolationism appears to be the existence of a peculiar need in U.S. culture that makes many Americans unable to face an enemy unless they feel morally superior to him. The fact that an enemy tries to undermine U.S. institutions, wealth, influence and freedoms in the world, does not seem to be enough for a significant segment of the American population. The Soviets appear to understand America's puritanical need to feel morally superior to them and use it against the United States by arguing, through surrogates of course, that the United States and the U.S.S.R. are moral equivalents because both are nuclear powers ("two scorpions in a bottle") who threaten nuclear peace.

Not only does this particular propaganda line give a certain moral credibility to the Soviet-appeasers in Western Europe, but it spurs the holier-than-thou gang in the United States to nonsensical acts of greater and greater moral purity to prove the moral equivalency thesis false. "We're not as bad as the Soviets," they argue, "and we're going to prove it by refusing covert aid to countries under Communist attack." Moreover, when sensible people protest the moral equivalency thesis by noting, for example, that the U.S. intervention in Grenada to serve the people's choice is the opposite of the Soviet intervention in Afghanistan to impose a pro-Moscow regime, the moral isolationists respond with the dubious argument that "the assault on moral equivalency leaves too little room for *fair* and necessary criticism of one's own government and society."[16] Surely, though, there already is enough room for "fair and necessary criticism" in the United States without subjecting the American people to the enormous slander that their society is the moral equivalent of the Soviets'.

STRATEGIC VERSUS MORAL RESTRAINT

It is critical that the citizens of the United States not equate the call to withdraw U.S. troops from Western Europe and pull out of NATO with moral isolationism. Strategic restraint begins from a different set of premises and makes a different argument than moral restraint. Actively opposing the foreign adventures of the Soviet Union is morally correct precisely because combating an evil—the Soviet Union—is a moral good. In the fight with the "Evil Empire," morality dictates that there be no hesitation, no equivocation. The pursuit of containment by economic and military assistance to countries threatened by communism must be restrained, however, for strategic reasons. When U.S. support weakens the resolve of its allies to combat evil or, worse, encourages them to give comfort to the enemy, the enemy is strengthened, not weakened. This is most likely to occur when the United States commits its ground troops abroad. The single most important operational component of strategic restraint is that U.S. ground troops not be committed to actual or potential foreign conflicts.

To illustrate the differences between strategic and moral restraint, the proposed withdrawal of American troops from Western Europe can be contrasted with the withdrawal of American ground troops from South Korea ordered by President Jimmy Carter in 1977. Carter's Korean pullout is a prime example of American foreign policy based on isolationists' moral restraint. The reason President Carter ordered the withdrawal of 27,000 combat soldiers from South Korea was because he was concerned with the "human rights" policies of the then-President of South Korea, Park Chung Hee. The American President wanted to put greater distance between the United States and a regime he considered immoral.

No one is arguing, of course, that the United States negate its defense commitment to Western Europe because European governments are undemocratic or totalitarian. The thesis for withdrawal from Europe is based exclusively on strategic grounds. Perhaps the best way to characterize the difference between the two proposed withdrawals is that Carter's withdrawal from Korea reflected a reduced commitment to oppose communism, while the proposed withdrawal from Europe reflects a new and greater anti-Soviet commitment. Whether or not one agrees with the argument that America's open-ended defense commitment to Europe has weakened Europe to the point where it has in effect become a proxy of the Soviet Union, the desire to turn the strategic situation around in Western Europe and resurrect Europe's containment objective is what motivates the withdrawal proposal—not a misplaced moralism that attempts to impose American moral standards on others.

4

The Tail that Wags the Dog

When the Soviets deployed and targeted their new and sophisticated SS-20 missiles on West European cities in 1977, they already had a plethora of deadly missiles pointed at Europe. Strategic analysts agree that what made the SS-20 deployment different was not that it fundamentally turned the strategic balance against the West, but that Helmut Schmidt, then West German chancellor, demanded that NATO do something about it. West European confidence in the leadership of the United States had fallen to a new low under President Jimmy Carter, and Schmidt wanted to make the SS-20s a test of America's commitment to defend Western Europe. Would the United States respond to the new Soviet missiles, Europe wondered, and if so, what would be the manner of the response?

The fact that the NATO decision to counter the SS-20s with missiles of its own was initiated by the Europeans should not be taken to mean that there existed a true European consensus to support it. The December 12, 1979, NATO agreement to deploy 572 new nuclear warheads in Europe—108 Pershing II extended-range ballistic missiles and 464 ground-launched cruise missiles—

sparked violent protests in all but one of the allied countries. Outside of France, where the protests largely were organized by —and confined to—the French Communist Party, European opponents of deployment were able to forge a formidable "coalition for peace" around a hard core of youths, intellectuals, the media, clergymen, and women. How ironic that in West Germany, Helmut Schmidt's own Social Democratic Party made opposition to the Pershing and cruise missiles a part of the party's official political platform.

What started as a test of American resolve—a test the United States passed with flying colors—ended as a demonstration of European disarray and confusion about its link to NATO and the United States. Chancellor Schmidt obviously had misjudged badly the climate of public opinion in Europe when he asked for nuclear balance in the face of the Soviet SS-20s.

Perhaps the most startling aspect of the so-called Euromissile crisis for many Americans was the realization that a substantial body of European public opinion frankly doubted U.S. motives for wanting to put the missiles in Europe. "Peace protesters" throughout Europe argued that the United States was using Western Europe for its own private war against the Soviet Union, a war they wanted no part of. According to one German expert, Konrad Keller, "Many Germans reason that the Pershings make it possible to have a nuclear war between the Soviet Union and Western Europe without any United States involvement."[1] Michael Howard, of Oxford University, noted that "so far from Americans being in Europe to help the West Europeans defend themselves, they are seen in some quarters as being here to prosecute 'their' war—a war in which the Europeans have no interest and for which they are the first to suffer."[2] And Countess Marion Donhoff, publisher of the liberal weekly *Die Zeit* of Hamburg, went even further: "Europe," said the countess, "is frightened more by the United States than by the Russians."[3]

The deep-seated anti-Americanism that lies behind European doubts about U.S. motives was particularly severe in West Germany. John Vinocur wrote in *The International Herald Tribune*:

> Intellectuals such as Günter Grass, in the heat of the debate on new NATO missiles, said they felt shame for America, which they

pictured as an oafish, discredited bully....[This] view trickled through the layers of the mass media. A typical book of pop politics, written by Peter Merseburger, presented the United States as a reeling, incalculable force from which the Germans must keep their distance. It is not just that 'America has a permanent taste for violence'; that it has a 'lower horizon of political expectations' than Europe; that it admires Walt Whitman, 'the bard of American imperialism'; that it is a 'disturbed, rudderless' place; but that—by the television reporter's definition—it is deeply, organically flawed and dangerous.[4]

The main cause of West German anti-Americanism, however, goes deeper than, and antedates by many years, the controversy over the Pershing and cruise missiles. The location of 340,000 American troops on West German soil serves to remind-and humiliate-the Germans on a daily basis that they must now depend for their freedom on the very same country that conquered them only forty years before. "The Federal Republic is only on paper a sovereign state," claims West German author Günter Grass. And *New York Times* critic Walter Goodman underscores this point when, in countering Grass's anti-American outbursts, argues that West German authors "can write whatever they please because they live in a country backed by American power."[5] Thus, whatever the rational justification for the presence of American troops, on a emotional level, the Germans see the troops as a continuing army of occupation that keeps Germany impotent, dependent, and divided.

The response of the Reagan administration to European anti-American outbursts, and the real possibility that some European governments might backtrack on their decision to deploy the missiles, was measured. To convince the Europeans that the United States was not the warmonger the peace protesters were making it out to be, the Reagan administration adopted a less confrontational posture toward the Soviet Union. When, for example, the Soviets shot down Korean Air Lines flight 007, brutally murdering hundreds of innocent passengers, President Reagan limited his response to mere rhetoric. When the Europeans issued subsidized credit to the Soviets to finance the Siberian natural-gas pipeline, President Reagan backed off from the sanctions he had imposed against the West Europeans (indeed, Secretary of State George P. Shultz's first official act was to rescind the sanctions). President Reagan also could have had the U.S. loans to Poland called in default, thus disciplining West German banks for their excessively generous loans to the East European satellite, but he did not. In effect, the Europeans had threatened the United States with a "you-adopt-détente-or-else-we-won't-let-you-defend-us" proposition, and as outrageous as this might have been, the Reagan administration chose Atlantic unity on European terms rather than risk European rejection of the missiles—and hand the Soviets an even bigger victory than they already had won. The result was that all of the affected NATO countries voted to accept the missiles, although the Netherlands and Belgium delayed their final acceptance for two years.

To many Americans, the fact that Europe finally agreed to take the missiles represented a significant victory for the West despite the mutual accusations, recriminations, and anti-American demonstrations that took place during the Euromissile crisis. But President Reagan appears to have paid a heavy price for the European deployments. The administration apparently has given up on its efforts to bring the Europeans to adopt a tough anti-Soviet line. Instead, it has adopted the European policies of détente, summitry, subsidies, and arms control.

How ironic that while U.S. conservatives were hailing the 1985 Geneva summit as a Reagan victory, because the Soviets came back to the bargaining table after they said they would boycott arms-control talks so long as the Pershing and cruise missiles remained in Europe, the Soviets were getting precisely what they wanted— the "Europeanization" of Ronald Reagan's East-West policies. In December 1984, for example, the Reagan administration announced it no longer would block Poland's entry into the International Monetary Fund (IMF). "An appalling betrayal of Polish labor" is how *The Wall Street Journal* characterized the Reagan capitulation.[6] Not only did Poland's entry into the IMF render General Wojciech Jaruzelski badly needed subsidized credit—the epitome of détente—but because it gave the puppet regime undeserved international respectability, it undermined Poland's isolation among civilized nations. It came as no surprise, then, that some months after Poland's entry into the IMF, French President François Mitterrand formally received General Jaruzelski at the Élysée Palace.

Bailing out Poland with Western taxpayers' money was only part of the price the United States paid to get the Soviets back to the bargaining table. During the same week the arms control talks were initiated in Geneva (January 7–8, 1985), U.S.–U.S.S.R. trade negotiations were taking place in Moscow. These negotiations were the first formal trade talks between the two superpowers since the Soviet invasion of Afghanistan. "After a six-year hiatus, the United States is again prepared to engage in old-fashioned business diplomacy with the Soviet Union," writes John M. Starrels in *The New York Times*. "This is the clear message that Lionel H. Olmer, the Commerce Department's Under Secretary for International Trade, conveyed to his Soviet counterpart, Vladimir N. Shushkov, when they met in Moscow." Though the Reagan administration refused to concede linkage, "it is hardly coincidental," writes Starrels, "that Mr. Olmer's journey to the Soviet Union took place at the same time Secretary of State George P. Shultz and Soviet Foreign Minister Andrei A. Gromyko were meeting in Geneva to discuss future arms-control bargaining.[7]

The change of course in the Reagan administration, from a confrontational posture toward the Soviet Union to a more accommodating one, has both baffled the President's friends and cheered his enemies. During the first two years of the Reagan administration, relations between Europe and the United States became extremely strained because of Washington's tougher line toward the Soviets. The Europeans were concerned, first, that the Soviets might be provoked into some type of military action against Western Europe and, second, that the new administration would pressure them to discontinue or at least modify, their détente policies. For its part, the Reagan team was chagrined that the West European governments were subsidizing the Siberian natural-gas pipeline. This not only helped the Soviet economy, but gave the Kremlin an additional lever—a gas lever—that could be used against Western economies. Moreover, there was concern in Washington that the generous loans West European banks had made to Poland at below-market rates of interest were propping up the puppet regime Moscow had emplaced there. Solidarity, in particular, wanted the loans discontinued.

The Reagan administration had the leverage to get the Europeans to back out of the Siberian natural-gas pipeline deal and discontinue the subsidized loans, but refused to use it. It could have threatened withdrawal of U.S. troops from Europe—and thus, implicitly, withdrawal of the American nuclear guarantee—unless the Europeans gave up their détente-as-defense strategy. This would have been a perfectly reasonable response to Europe's détente policies. It makes absolutely no sense for the United States to spend billions of dollars to defend Western Europe from the Soviets if the Europeans turn around and use some of that money to subsidize the very enemy from whom they require protection.

But, alas, Europe also has a certain amount of leverage over the United States. So long as the United States insists on defending Europe, our allies can use the "you-do-as-we-say-or-else-we-won't-let-you-defend-us" threat against us. But why, Americans may ask, do we insist on defending the Europeans and thus give them the leverage they use so well in manipulating U.S. policies? Wouldn't it be better if we simply dealt with the Europeans on a take-it-or-leave-it basis? If the Europeans really do not want to be protected by us, why humiliate ourselves by foisting U.S. protection on them? Moreover, forcing "free goods" like nuclear protection down the throats of our allies can only strengthen anti-American, neutralist, and pacifist elements in allied countries.

The United States would be better off if it adopted a policy of "nuclear reciprocity" toward its allies: Nuclear weapons on American soil cannot be pledged to the defense of any country that refuses to allow American nuclear weapons to be deployed on its territory. Thus, if a European country refused to accept the Pershing and cruise missiles, by that act alone it would be forced to step out from under the American nuclear umbrella. Why, after all, should the United States accept the risks of having nuclear weapons on its soil to protect other countries if these very countries are not willing to accept the same risks, and for the same purpose, by allowing American missiles on their soil?

As reasonable as the doctrine of nuclear reciprocity may be, the idea of using U.S. troops in Europe—and thus the American nuclear guarantee—as leverage against the Europeans apparently never came up in discussions inside the Reagan administration over how to get Europeans to accept U.S. ideas on the proper limits of East-West trade. The reason undoubtedly is that the conventional wisdom considers a troop withdrawal from Europe to be counterproductive to U.S. national security interests because it would split Europe from America—which is precisely the result the Soviets are said to hope to achieve.

The theory—and it is little more than that—that the ultimate objective of the Soviet Union is to split the United States from the rest of the Atlantic Alliance is the most important lever the Europeans currently have over U.S. foreign policy. To deny the Soviets their victory, Atlantic unity has been made the sine qua non of U.S. foreign policy. An unintended, and unfortunate, consequence of American attachment to Atlantic unity is to give the Europeans license to disregard U.S. interests. If the United States protests Europe's policies, the doctrine of Atlantic unity is waved in American faces by a coalition of European and U.S. "Atlanticists" who claim the United States needs Europe at least as much as Europe needs the United States. This is why the European tail can wag the American dog.

A great irony of the European stratagem of using Atlantic unity to control the dominant partner in the Atlantic Alliance is that its underlying assumption—that the ultimate objective of the Soviet Union is to split Europe from America—may be false. "The Soviets are not so simpleminded as to believe that the Alliance must necessarily be a bad thing for them," say U.S. Senator Malcolm Wallop of Wyoming.

> Indeed, for two decades their instructions to communist parties in Europe have been not to demand a divorce from between the U.S. and Europe, but to work within the Alliance to *"empty it of its aggressive content."* One can hardly imagine a better situation for the Soviets, and a worse situation for us, than an increasingly rancorous marriage between the transatlantic partners in which the Europeans pay tribute, restrain the U.S., and keep 350,000 American hostages for them.[8]

Consider for a moment the dispute between the United States and Europe over the question of economic sanctions against Libya. The Europeans refused to follow the American lead and impose sanctions because they felt sanctions would not be in their best national interests. Many Americans deeply resented this precisely because the Europeans are our allies. Ben Wattenberg, the political commentator, is quoted in *The New York Times*: "Europeans have demonstrated again and again that they put money over principle."

He urged vacationing Americans to stay away from Europe "until our sometimes spineless *allies* show more spine."[9] One wonders, however, how vehement anti-European reaction in the United States would have been had NATO not existed. Our pique at the allies is magnified precisely because we expect more of them.

By no means is Senator Wallop alone in challenging the conventional wisdom that Moscow wants to split America from Europe. He has very good company in Adam B. Ulam, a leading Soviet specialist, who argues that "the ideal arrangement from the Soviet point of view is for the United States and Western Europe to be bound together in a less than happy marriage in which both partners continuously squabble rather than deciding on a trial separation, which might eventually result in a reinvigorated, politically united, more powerful Western Europe."[10] What the Soviets fear most is that someday Europe will emerge as a Third World superpower— more solid, more strong, more united, and better armed. What they fear least (and exploit most) is a supplicant Europe, ready to please them and anxious to do their bidding.

How interesting that the Soviets not only understand the U.S. obsession with Atlantic unity, but actively work to exploit it. When Gorbachev wanted to dispatch Reagan's Strategic Defense Initiative, for example, he went to Paris before going to Geneva. "Six weeks before he is to meet with President Reagan in Geneva," wrote James M. Markham in *The New York Times*, "Mr. Gorbachev appears o have developed a diplomatic strategy that aims at putting pressure on the United States through its allies in the North Atlantic Treaty Organization."[11] Mr. Gorbachev also understands how to use NATO to divide Europe from America. Thus, when the allies objected to Mr. Reagan's bombing of Libya, in May 1986, Mr. Gorbachev threatened to cancel the scheduled 1986 summer summit. "The Russians already smell opportunity in the NATO dissension," writes *The New York Times*. "This is why they want Europe to think the Reagan-Gorbachev summit meeting has now been jeopardized. *They'll do anything to make Europeans resent NATO and to make Americans resent standing guard over ingrates.*" [emphasis mine].[12]

If President Reagan's tilt toward détente was the price he had to pay to get the Europeans to accept the Pershing and cruise missiles, why, one might ask, hasn't the President reverted to more hard-line policies now that the missiles are in place? Apparently, the lessons of accommodating the Europeans have been learned all too well.

The battle over Star Wars is a case in point. The Reagan brain trust seems to believe that European participation in Star Wars research would make it easier to convince the American public—and American liberals, in particular—to accept a strategic defense program. That belief was a large part of the rationale behind the trips to Geneva and Eastern Europe. The President proved to the Europeans that he is no warmonger—and Britain and West Germany quickly reciprocated by signing on to do space defense research.

Because the President has been able to get the Europeans to go along with Star Wars research, he is being hailed as a great politician. But at what price? Not only has the U.S. paid Europe for its support of Star Wars by "Europeanizing" its policy toward the Soviet bloc, but there have been expensive economic strings attached to Europe's support as well.

The most obvious is the pledge that Europe will get a large share of the contracts for Star Wars research. According to private estimates, perhaps $300 million to $400 million in research will be farmed out to European companies in fiscal 1987. Officials at the SDI office say that no ally has been promised a specific dollar figure. They note that when British Prime Minister Margaret Thatcher asked Mr. Weinberger to guarantee Britain $1.5 billion over five years, she was turned down. Yet this well-publicized refusal, other officials say, was simply designed to cover SDI's lobbying tracks.

"We'll hear from the Europeans if they aren't getting enough," says one offical at the SDI office. Leaders of the other industrialized democracies, selling the program at home, have been quite explicit about their hopes—mentioning figures over the next five years as high as $1.5 billion for Britain, $1 billion for West Germany, $300 million for Israel, and perhaps 15 percent of the total SDI research budget for enterpreneur-rich Japan.

Still not satisfied, Europeans have now asked for, and apparently been granted, administration support for a specialized program designed to shield Europe from Soviet tactical missiles. Indiana Sen. Dan Quayle, a Republican, will propose a first-year subsidy of $50 million from the U.S. If it follows the trend of other Star Wars research, this figure will grow quickly.

These and other bribes, however, have not won European back-ing for strategic defenses. Most ally governments say they will oppose any steps toward defense deployment. Hence, the bidding for Eurosupport of Star Wars has just begun.

Ironically, by throwing money at the Europeans, the U.S. risks inflaming what may be Europe's central worry about Star Wars: the 1972 ABM Treaty banning such defenses. The treaty strictly prohibits America or the Soviet Union from constructing or fi-nancing a strategic defense located on the soil of an ally, as a way of circumventing its limits. It does not prohibit, nor can it, countries that didn't sign the treaty from building defenses on their own.

This is an important argument for the Europeans building their own SDI. But, of course, they may not wish to do so—and this is precisely what Pentagon officials, concerned that a shield is needed to protect U.S. troops in Europe, fear. Thus, because we subsidize European defense by maintaining U.S. troops there, we are told we must further subsidize the Europeans by helping finance a Eu-ropean SDI without even a commitment that the shield will be deployed.

One doesn't have to be a proponent of a U.S. troop withdrawal from Europe to see the folly of this argument. Even those who favor the troops in Europe understand that the troops will be de-fended only by deployed SDI, not research-and-development ex-penditures. And, given ABM Treaty limitations, deployment would be possible if, and only if, the Europeans built their own SDI. Thus, U.S. funding of R&D for a European SDI can only frustrate the shield deployment desired by the Pentagon.

Then, too, the attempt to link Europeans to all aspects of the Star Wars program elicits support in the least efficient way. It's like hiring five kids, each to mow one-fifth of your lawn, wash one-fifth of your car, paint one-fifth of your house, and so on. The best way for Europeans to aid the Star Wars effort would be for them to direct and finance their own specific project to build a tactical defense, a uniquely European concern.

But what if Europeans really did not feel the need for a defense against Soviet tactical missiles? In that case, America's Star Wars research would either have to ignore the problem or be stretched more thinly. And we might lose the unified support of our allies for Star Wars—at least in the short run.

Ultimately, however, Europeans are the best judge of what defensive systems they need. If they are not willing to pay for a shield against Soviet missiles, we should not bribe them into researching one.

Neither, however, should we worry about Europe's opinion of our own Star Wars effort. The correct answer to the argument that some American action might "divide the alliance" is, as George Will writes with concision, "So what?"

Managing an alliance is not chiefly a matter of choosing between unity and division. Rather, the question is how to promote a certain type of unity. The desirable unity is one in which weaker members align their policies with the strong. The unity the U.S. has practiced, out of an inordinate fear of dividing the alliance, is one in which the weakest member of NATO act as a check on the U.S., producing only a "consensus of the fearful," as Jean-François Revel puts it.

MULTILATERALISM AND INTERNATIONAL TERRORISM

The recent misguided multilateralism of the Reagan administration not only is being applied to this country's struggle with the Soviet Union, but to its battle against international terrorism as well. Robert B. Oakley, the head of the U.S. State Department's counterterrorism office, appeared on the NBC news program "Meet the Press" after the December 1985 attacks on the Rome and Vienna airports, and said the United States wanted the surge of terrorism to be dealt with by the wider international community, not just by individual nations. "We believe terrorism must be combatted," Mr. Oakley said. "It must be combatted by many different governments, not by one alone."[13]

But if U.S. action against Arab terrorism is made contingent on European participation, does not the United States condemn itself to a self-defeating paralysis that primarily benefits Qaddafi, Arafat, and Abu Nidal? How, one wonders, can a senior official in the Reagan administration lecture the American people about the need for a multilateral approach to terrorism when, only a few months before, in the *Achille Lauro* affair, Italy commandeered the Palestinian mastermind of the terrorist plot captured by the Americans and blatantly set him free? Indeed, as atrocious as was the murder of the American tourist, Leon Klinghoffer, the real story of the *Achille Lauro* affair turned out to be the conflict between Italy and the United States over the disposition of the captured terrorists. Above all else, this conflict demonstrated that a multilateral approach to international terrorism is a formula—and perhaps an excuse—for doing nothing in the face of increasing terrorism.

When U.S. jet fighters forced the Egyptian airliner carrying the terrorists to freedom to land at Sigonella, a NATO base in Sicily, U.S. troops surrounded the plane to transfer the terrorists to a waiting C-141 for transport to the United States. But the Italian troops at the base prevented the transfer by threatening the use of force against the American troops. President Reagan was reported to have personally intervened by ordering the ranking U.S. officer at Sigonella to hand the terrorists over to the Italians rather than risk a shoot-out with allies.

The spectacle of U.S. and Italian troops squaring off at Sigonella should prove sobering for even the most enthusiastic NATO supporters. Why, bewildered Americans may wonder, are we spending $134 billion on NATO in 1985 alone if, in carrying out a legitimate antiterrorist act, U.S. troops are opposed by Italian troops—at a NATO base, no less?

In any event, the decision to hand the Palestinian terrorists over to the Italian authorities proved a costly mistake. Within hours of the transfer, Rome released the mastermind of the seajacking, Muhammad Abbas, on grounds of insufficient evidence. At first, White House reaction to the release of Abbas was one of outrage. But when the White House issued a statement labeling Abbas' release "incomprehensible," it chose the wrong word to describe Italian behavior. Italian Prime Minister Bettino Craxi's reasons for failing to hold onto Abbas are no great mystery—Craxi feared the Palestine Liberation Organization (PLO) more than he feared the United States. And judging by the behavior of the Reagan administration in the immediate aftermath of the *Achille Lauro* affair, can it be seriously argued that Mr. Craxi's assessment of the relative risks of offending the PLO, by comparison with offending the Americans, was incorrect.

Mr. Craxi must have been comforted that at virtually the same time the White House issued its tough statement on the release of Abbas, a much more accommodating message emanated from the State Department. Bernard Gwertzman, of *The New York Times*, quoted Richard W. Murphy, assistant secretary of state for Near Eastern and South Asian affairs, to the effect that "while the United States was 'angry' with Egypt and Italy, it believed that 'they are too important to us' to permit 'any lasting damage to the two relationships.'" An anonymous State Department official concurs: "Look, we can't let things get to a point where we allow the *Achille Lauro* to put us at war with our friends over this thing."[14] The President obviously agreed. A few days after Abbas' release, President Reagan sent his deputy secretary of state, John C. Whitehead, to Italy with a conciliatory note for Craxi.

Acceptance of Atlantic unity as an overriding U.S. foreign policy objective in the *Achille Lauro* affair meant that the United States allowed European justice for the terrorists to substitute for American justice. As Italian treatment of Abbas demonstrates, the battle against terrorism was not furthered by this move. Clearly, there is a need for reciprocity in transatlantic relations—Atlantic unity is not, and must not be, a one-way street. In releasing Abbas, Italy showed no great respect for Atlantic unity; under these circumstances, why should the United States?

The United States should not "make war on its friends." But it needs to remind them that it expects a certain *quid pro quo* for the billions of dollars it spends annually for European defense. Instead of sending his deputy secretary of state with a conciliatory note, President Reagan might have informed Prime Minister Craxi that to avoid further confrontations with Italian soldiers, the U.S. troops at Sigonella were to be withdrawn. Mr. Craxi was reported to have told the Italian Parliament that "what happened at Sigonella air base in Sicily must, in the interests of both countries and NATO, never be repeated."[15] One way to ensure Mr. Craxi gets his wish is for the United States to pull its troops out of Italy.

THE CALCULUS OF ACCOMMODATION

America's refusal to discipline Italy for its treachery in the *Achille Lauro* affair had predictable consequences: It helped nurture our allies' belief that they might, at no great price, behave precisely the way the French behaved when they refused to permit American planes to fly over French territory on the way to bomb Qaddafi. Nor is there any reason for this pattern of obstruction to change. For when France and Italy calculate the potential costs of support for the United States—terrorist retaliation and Arab economic sanctions—and compare these costs with the negligible costs of not supporting us, they can only conclude that it is cheeper to accommodate the terrorists.

This calculus of accommodation is shortsighted, however. The Europeans fail to take account of the increasing number of Americans who wonder if Europe is worthy of their support. The United States spends some $135 billion a year on NATO, and, for good reason, many Americans are wondering why—particulary when, on several occasions, the NATO bases we pay for are not put at our disposal when we need them.

What is our alternative? The United States can, and should, impose costs on its European allies when they fail to support us. The point is not to punish them, although that would be a perfectly acceptable motive, but to provide incentives for more acceptable behavior in the future.

No one is more worried than France about the possibility that the United States might withdraw its troops from West Germany. Yet the French don't seem to understand that alliance means responsibilities for both sides. Imagine their reaction if the United States announced—in response to France's behavior—a symbolic withdrawal of a small number of the American troops defending France and the rest of Western Europe.

Why does the United States refuse to impose such costs on its uncooperative allies? The answer is the doctrine of Atlantic unity, which holds that no matter how outrageously our allies behave, we must not risk a dispute with them. It is no small irony that this doctrine, which minimizes the costs to Europe of opposing American interests, has worked toward our mutual estrangement.

5

The Soviets' Nightmare

There are two ways in which the Europeans attempt to control the foreign policy of the United States. The first, discussed in chapter 4, is the doctrine of Atlantic unity; the second is to take away the only real leverage the United States has over the Europeans—the withdrawal of its troops. American defense leverage over the Europeans has been neutralized by the threat that it has to keep U.S. troops in Europe or else Europe will become even more Finlandized than it is today. A distinguished French journalist, Michel Tatu, argues that "the Finlandization argument resembles more a stratagem—remain in Europe, otherwise you will lose it—than a reality."[1] It is the glue that cements the *status quo* in the Atlantic Alliance. No one dares breach it; otherwise, it is said, the Soviets will have all of Western Europe without firing a shot.

THE "SUPPLY SIDE" OF FOREIGN POLICY

In October 1949, six months after the North Atlantic Treaty was signed, Charles de Gaulle said: "France must first count upon itself, independent of foreign aid" and NATO "takes away the initiative to build our national defense."[2] Based on this succinct statement of the incentives case for present European military weakness, former French President de Gaulle may have staked a claim to being the first foreign policy "supply-sider."

The central tenet of supply-side reasoning is that incentives play a critical role in human behavior. When income taxes are too high, for example, individuals lose the incentive to work. High taxes on savings reduce the incentive to save. When residential rents are kept artificially low by government policy, landlords lose the incentive to rent for residential purposes. And when wages are made artificially high by laws such as minimum wage, business firms have an incentive to cut back on employment.

Properly interpreted, supply-side reasoning is as valid for foreign policy as it is for economics. Nations, like individuals, respond to incentives. When the United States gave Europe a defense guarantee, it also gave the Europeans an incentive to minimize their own defense efforts. When the credibility of the American defense guarantee diminished with the closing of the U.S.–U.S.S.R. nuclear gap, the Europeans were given a further incentive to follow a détente-as-defense strategy. The United States should not blame the Europeans for their minimalist defense posture, just as it cannot blame someone who, when faced with higher income taxes, works less hard or less often. To change European behavior, Washington must change the incentive structure faced by our allies.

Those who do not appreciate the role that incentives play in human affairs, or downplay their empirical significance, are at a loss to explain Europe's current military weakness and accommodation of the Soviet Union. As a result, they are forced to seek refuge in such explanations as a loss of political will or nerve in Western Europe, explanations which ultimately point to a decline in European attachment to Western values. Perhaps the leading spokesman for this point of view is the eloquent editor of *Commentary* magazine, Norman Podhoretz. He writes:

> If Europe is unable to defend itself ideologically, if it is unable to explain to itself why the life it now leads is worth making sacrifices for; if it cannot make itself understand why the willingness to risk war is the only way to avert war and surrender alike; if it cannot

remember the lessons of the 1930s and teach these lessons to its children—then we in the United States will be unable to go on with our commitment to the defense of Europe.[3]

Because defenders of the status quo lack a convincing explanation of European behavior, they have few cures to offer. What Podhoretz suggests is to exhort the "silent majority" in Western Europe to find its voice and to warn that if it does not, the United States will eventually have to pull out. Even this particular cure is advocated more in anguish than conviction. "I am poignantly aware of how wan, how lacking in vitality, the case has become," Podhoretz is quoted. "But what else can we do?"[4]

The problem with the analysis of those who fear a pullout of U.S. troops from Western Europe is that, because it leaves out the possibility of incentive effects, it puts its entire emphasis on a perceived decline in European attachment to Western values. This explains why defenders of the status quo in Europe are demoralized. Given Europe's alleged loss of political nerve, Podhoretz is convinced that the shock treatment of U.S. troop withdrawal would, in his words, "lead to the triumph of what might be called Red Vichyism everywhere in Western Europe."[5] At the same time, he believes that unless Europe's silent majority comes to its senses (an outcome he doesn't really expect), the United States will be unable to go on with its commitment to defend Europe. Thus a Finlandized Europe appears to be inevitable. To complete this tortured vision, Podhoretz believes that "in a Finlandized world, the United States would ultimately be Finlandized as well."[6] The Soviets thus are destined to win the Cold War—a result that we all can sympathize with Podhoretz in finding infinitely distasteful.

If Podhoretz and the many thoughtful people who agree with him could provide independent corroboration of the decline in European attachment to Western values assumed by his argument, his case would be more convincing. But the plain, and happy, truth is that there exists a substantial amount of evidence to indicate the contrary—that instead of a decline in European attachment to Western values, Europe actually has demonstrated a greater commitment to the values that distinguish us from the Communists in recent years.

The recent severe decline of the influence and popularity of the Communist Party in several West European countries is evidence that Western values have strengthened, not declined, in Europe. "There have been ups and downs of Communism," said Jean Ellenstein, a former French Communist Party intellectual, commenting on the state of an organization that has dramatically lost support in recent years. "But this is not that... it is an irreversible regression. There can be remission, but this is a fatal cancer."[7]

In France itself, the Communists have suffered a setback of monumental proportions, not solely in elections but also in the public's attitude toward them. "The French Communist Party has fallen into unprecedented decay and disarray," according to Flora Lewis in *The New York Times*. "The Communists have lost more than half their traditional vote of 22 to 25 percent in the last few years and, according to insiders, about half their formal membership."[8]

"The basic and universal reason for this decline is the realization that the Soviet Union is not a democratic system," said Henri Fiszbin, a former Communist who ran on a Socialist ticket in the March 1986 French parliamentary elections. Adds Annie Kriegel, a former French party member who now writes a column in *Le Figaro*: "Public opinion in Western Europe is extremely anti-Communist. Gorbachev comes to Paris and he is greeted by dissidents. Compare this to the tumultuous reception that the French Communists organized for Khrushchev."[9]

In fact, leading figures throughout France now look with active contempt on any person, or policy, that might seem to work in favor of the Soviet Union. Perhaps the most interesting of the new French anti-communists are those former members of the radical left who have had their eyes opened to the menace of Soviet Russia by Alexander Solzhenitsyn's *Gulag Archipelago*.

André Glucksmann is by background, training, and experience a man of the Left. Born to French Communist parents, Glucksmann was a member of the Communist Party from sixteen years of age to nineteen. He was an angry critic of the United States during Vietnam as well as a leader of the New Left during the 1968 student riots. But, today, the New Left is vilifying Glucksmann because the popular French philosopher has turned against the Communists with a vengeance.

"How a Leading Light of the French New Left Learned to Love the Bomb" is the put-down of Glucksmann used by American New Left journalist Paul Berman, obviously disturbed by the notoriety and influence enjoyed by Glucksmann and his thesis that survival is not enough.[10] Glucksmann disagrees with the "peace protesters" who have made nuclear war the single absolute evil of modern times. There are two evils, according to Glucksmann: Nuclear holocaust is one, the gulag is the other. It is true that a nuclear Armageddon would destroy life altogether. "But to the people who dwell on this fact and who, therefore, fear bombs more than camps, Glucksmann responds by asking: What does it mean for life to survive? Doesn't human life require some modicum of political liberty to be worth talking about? Human beings have a soul, not just a body, and the soul too, must have a life."[11] Thus, rather than accept the gulag out of fear of the bomb, Glucksmann accepts the bomb out of fear of the gulag.

In Italy, Prime Minister Bettino Craxi and his Socialist Party have taken a strong anti-Soviet, pro-Western line. In the May 1985 regional provincial and local elections, Italy's Communist Party was extremely critical of the popular Socialists. The result was a stunning defeat for the Communists at the ballot box. By comparison with the 1984 elections to Parliament, Italy's Communist Party (PCI) dropped from 33.3 percent of the popular vote to 28.5 percent in May 1985. The 1985 performance was its poorest since the early 1970s. Indeed, with the exception of the 1984 elections, when the Italian Communists made a strong showing, the trend since 1976 has been unambiguously negative. In 1976 the PCI won 34.4 percent of the popular vote; in 1979, 30.4 percent; in 1983, 29.9 percent; and in 1985, 28.5 percent. E. J. Dionne, Jr., writes in *The New York Times*:

> A quiet revolution is taking place in cities and towns throughout Italy. The Communist Party, which prides itself on the way it runs local administrations, is being thrown out of city halls by new coalitions of Christian Democrats and Socialists. . . . Particularly daunting for the Communists are losses of power in big cities like Rome, Venice, Milan, Turin, and possibly Genoa. Even Parma, in the northern Red belt around Bologna, was lost after decades under Communist leadership.[12]

The Italian people, most clearly, are sending Moscow a message: Soviet attempts to intimidate Italy through sponsorship of domestic terrorism and nuclear blackmail are not working.

The defeat of the domestic terrorists in Italy and West Germany through legal means is further evidence that Western values of due process and democracy are alive and well in those countries. Financed by the Soviet Union and trained by the Palestine Liberation Organization, terrorist organizations like the Italian Red Brigades and German Baader-Meinhoff group hope to subvert Western institutions and values by publicly demonstrating their inability to maintain their integrity when faced with extreme terrorist provocations. The courageous behavior of magistrates, lawyers, journalists, police officers, and ordinary citizens under death threats and worse have demonstrated that the terrorists bet on the wrong horse. It was the Soviet-sponsored Western destabilization program that was subverted, not Western society. Moreover, not only did the Italians eliminate the Red Brigades, they defiantly pointed an accusatory finger at the Soviet Union as the ultimate conspirator in the plot to kill Pope John Paul II. This, it must be noted, was considerably more than the normal Soviet-bashing the Reagan administration dared do at the time of the attempted papal assassination. These facts make the incentives case for Europe's accommodationist drift more persuasive by making the values case less so.

The rise of the neutralist Green Party in West Germany has been a source of concern for those who value the contribution of West Germany to Western security. The tendency has been to view the party's popularity as a barometer of neutralist sentiment in the Federal Republic—the greater the popularity of the Greens, the greater neutralist sentiment. If this indeed is the case, the recent defeats suffered by the Greens in German state elections—first in Saarland in March 1985 and then in North Rhine–Westphalia in May 1985—can be taken as an encouraging sign. "Green Party Is Fading into the Blues" is the way *The New York Times* put it in July 1985. "After two demoralizing drubbings in state elections," writes James Markham, "the anti-establishment, anti-nuclear, anti–NATO party is now at the very bottom of the roller-coaster run, fearful of going altogether off the rails."[13]

One reason for the decline of the Green Party is the defection of many of its youthful supporters. "Middle-class West Germans in their teens and early twenties are repudiating many of the rebellious anti-establishment values that gave birth to the leftist Green

Party and fed the campaign against the stationing of American missiles here three years ago," writes James Markham.[14] Interestingly enough, an important reason for this trend is precisely the failure of the campaign against the missiles. "The seminal political event for many young West Germans was the failure of the campaign to stop the deployment of American medium-range nuclear weapons in West Germany and other countries of the North Atlantic Treaty Organization. For most, the campaign was their first political experience, and a highly discouraging one. 'We did something,' said Stefi Battelini, a twenty-year-old Bonn University student, recalling the large demonstrations here against the missile deployment. 'We were 300,000. And then came the news on the radio that the missiles were coming. One didn't become more radical; one became totally resigned.'"

The British proved their values meant more to them than many had expected when, in 1982, they fought a war with Argentina to recover the Falkland Islands. "Four in every five adults, 81 percent, believe that the conflict has made people prouder to be British," reported *The Sunday Times* of London at the time. "Only two percent say that it has made them less proud. Despite the cost in lives and money, it was right to send the task force, say 81 percent of the sample. Only 14 percent disagree."[15] The British showed by their actions that they were willing to fight, and die, to keep the Falkland Islands British. Would they dare do less for Britain itself?

Michel Tatu has written in *Foreign Affairs* of the explicit effect European attachment to Western values can be expected to have should America indeed decide to withdraw its troops from Europe:

> Every government and every society seeks security not in order to become part of one or another system and thus as an end in itself, but because security will permit the government of the society to maintain its identity and its values. Just as a shipwrecked person who has lost one plank will not let himself drown but will look for another plank, so there is no reason to suppose that the European governments, not abandoned by America but simply invited to take charge progressively of their own defense, will immediately give up the values in whose name they so long attached themselves to America.
>
> Must one believe that the European attachment to liberalism and democracy is valid only so long as the United States is willing to

guarantee these values? Or is it rather the contrary, that the alliance with America springs from the Europeans' own attachment to these values. The argument that Europe would turn herself into another Finland lacks dignity as well as cogency.[16]

THE THEORY THAT DOESN'T WORK

Most observers believe that the Soviet Union would be delighted if the United States were to pull its troops out of Western Europe. The truth, however, may be the opposite. "The Soviet dream," according to Adam B. Ulam, "is that Western Europe will arm itself less and trade with the Soviets more, in the process becoming increasingly estranged from the United States. The Soviet nightmare is that Western Europe will unite politically and rearm itself vigorously, thereby leaving the Soviet Union facing two superpowers instead of one."[17] The U.S. troops in Europe have turned what the United States hoped would be a Soviet nightmare into their dream.

Advocates of containing Soviet power and influence have become so wedded to the theory that U.S. troops in Europe are an effective mechanism of containment that it appears they have stopped testing this theory against empirical reality and taken it as a matter of fact. The facts, however, have an important point to make: U.S. troops have been in Europe for the past forty years and, during the last twenty at least, Western Europe has become increasingly contentious with the United States at the same time that it has become increasingly accommodating to the Soviet Union. This is evidence that the U.S. troops in Europe have hurt, not helped, containment.

Soviet reaction to American troops in Europe provides further evidence that the troops may be more to the Soviets' advantage than ours. Consider, for a moment, Soviet reaction to the recent emplacement of the Pershing and cruise missiles in Western Europe. The Kremlin blustered, threatened, cajoled, and seduced the Europeans not to accept the missiles and, instead, make Western Europe into a nuclear-free zone. Why did it make such a fuss? Long ago the Soviets learned to live, and even prosper, with American nuclear weapons targeted on them from the continental United States. Was it only that the Pershing and cruise missiles have the decapitation potential that the intercontinental ballistic missiles

(ICBMs) lack, or was the basis of the Soviet objection more that the new missiles were to be physically located in Western Europe? It should be noted that the U.S. submarine-based ballistic missiles long have had the short flight time and short warning capacity that the Soviets complain about with regard to the Pershing IIs on West German territory.

The motives of the Kremlin are difficult to fathom at any time, but one thing can be said with certainty: Moscow fears the rearmament of Europe more than most Americans realize. It is particularly concerned that West Germany will obtain nuclear weapons. The emplacement of the Pershing and cruise missiles means that West Germany now has sophisticated nuclear weapons on its soil capable of reaching major Soviet population centers within a few minutes' time. And though control of the missiles presently resides with the United States, the transfer of control at some future date to a receptive West German government could be a relatively simple matter now that the trauma of the initial placement of missiles in the Federal Republic has been successfully overcome. The Soviet Union apparently is deeply concerned that it may be only a matter of time before the Federal Republic joins the nuclear club.

In contrast to Soviet reaction to the missiles, ask yourself when was the last time anyone can remember the Kremlin blustering, threatening, cajoling, and seducing the Europeans to send away the 360,000 American troops stationed in Europe? The answer is that they haven't. Ulam writes:

> Although the Soviets want to encourage tensions between Western Europe and the United States, they may not want to see the United States withdraw or greatly reduce its land forces in Europe. Such a shock might make West European leaders decide they have no choice but to unite politically. Or it might cause West Germany to reconsider its decision not to acquire nuclear weapons. Moreover, the present uneasy state of U.S.–Western European relations provides certain benefits to the U.S.S.R. America's European allies usually act as a moderating influence on Washington's anti-Soviet attitudes and initiatives.[18]

The Soviets have another and perhaps more important reason for wanting the American troops to remain in Western Europe: Our troops give the Soviets the excuse they need for stationing their

own troops in Eastern Europe. If the United States were to withdraw, the Soviets would be under substantial pressure to reciprocate
in the Eastern bloc countries. And even though they would not
follow the U.S. example, America's withdrawal would show the
Soviets to be the colonialists they, in fact, are. No longer could
they argue that their troops are in Eastern Europe because our
troops are in Western Europe. The Soviets make good propaganda
out of the American troops in Europe. Withdrawal would deprive
them of this leverage.

THE PROBABILITY OF WITHDRAWAL

No administration in Washington, whether Demoratic or Republican, is likely to withdraw American troops from Europe unless
there is a popular outcry of unprecedented proportions against
American defense support of the Europeans. The vested interests
in preserving the status quo are too strong on both sides of the
Atlantic. U.S. leaders have been corrupted by the illusion that
NATO has given them extraordinary influence over European defense and foreign policies; European leaders have been corrupted
by the American defense subsidies. Only a dramatic outburst of
anti-European sentiment in this country is likely to be able to get
the troops home. And this would occur only if the American public
comes to view the Europeans as working against American interests
in some fundamental sense.

Miscalculation of, and insensitivity to, American interests by the
Europeans is one reason a populist revolt against NATO may be
possible. A new spirit of nationalism is rampant in America. At
the core of the "new nationalism" is the idea that the United States
remain a great power capable of shaping the international order.
At the same time, the nationalist movement contains a strong isolationist element. Vietnam (and to a lesser extent, the hostage crisis
in Iran) taught the American people the dangers of getting involved
in disputes too far away from our continent. Despite these two
apparently contradictory elements, the new nationalist philosophy
demonstrates an underlying coherence.

A convincing case can be made that, a decade after Vietnam,
the American people have emerged from the trauma of that ordeal

dedicated to the proposition that what happened in that faraway country could not be allowed to happen again closer to home. And "home" to Americans very much includes Central and Latin America. "Military intervention in the Western Hemisphere, however controversial in specific instances, has never been regarded as a 'foreign' entanglement," writes Irving Kristol. "The Monroe Doctrine may be regarded as a dead letter in our State Department or at the United Nations, but it is still a valid doctrine so far as the majority of the American people are concerned."[19]

To resurrect the Monroe Doctrine, Kristol argues that U.S. foreign policy has to be made more assertive. And this necessarily means a more unilateralist approach, that is, a foreign policy less encumbered by entangling alliances and constraining treaties with foreign countries. Kristol calls the new nationalism a "return to an older, pre-Wilsonian conception of foreign policy, a Theodore Rooseveltian conception of foreign policy." No event better illustrates the new nationalist foreign policy than the American invasion of Grenada.

President Reagan did not inform the European allies about Grenada until after the American troops had landed on the tiny island in the Caribbean. The way it was done—as much as what was done—appears to have frustrated the Europeans, who have grown so accustomed to the tail wagging the dog that they became perplexed when the dog wagged back. It may be argued that the enormous popularity of Grenada with the American people was not only a consequence of its success—the conventional interpretation—but because it was a manifestation of a new, independent foreign policy with which they thoroughly approved. Surely, had Grenada failed, it still would have been far more popular than Reagan's 1984 fiasco in Lebanon.

When West Europeans severely criticized the American action in Grenada, they showed an insensitivity to American concerns that raises questions as to the compatibility of NATO and the new nationalism. The logic of the new nationalism is that the farther one proceeds from the continental United States, the less assertive and more isolationist U.S. foreign policy becomes. Though this implies the defense of Western Europe will cease to hold the priority it traditionally has held, in no way does it indicate a fundamental incompatibility between NATO and the new nationalism. How-

ever, should the Europeans try to frustrate U.S. nationalist ambitions where they are important, for example in Central and Latin
America, the U.S. commitment to NATO, not nationalism, would
likely go by the board. "The United States is not going to remain
committed to the defense of Western Europe, at the risk of nuclear
annihilation, if Western Europe is not equally committed to the
defense of Ameirca's interests," claims Kristol. "If our allies do not
support us when we are in trouble, it is highly improbable that the
American people will see much point in supporting them when
they are in trouble."[20]

Europe's "détente as defense" strategy, however, may have put
NATO and the new American nationalism on a collision course.
To ensure themselves against a Soviet invasion, the Europeans not
only have shown themselves indifferent to the extension of Soviet
power in the Third World, but actually may have aided the Soviets
by attempting to undermine a strong American response to the
subversion of poor countries by the Soviets and their client states,
Cuba and East Germany. Central America, in particular, has become an important focus of Soviet destabilizing activities. It is no
coincidence, then, that after decades of neglect, there is a renewed
European interest in that part of the world.

To justify this interest, the Europeans currently are arguing that
the admission of Spain and Portugal to the European Economic
Community (EEC) has made Central and South America an area
of European, as well as American, concern. "The European Community," reports *The Wall Street Journal*, "plans to strengthen its ties
with Latin America in the wake of the agreement to bring Spain
and Portugal into the EEC. . . . Jacques Delors, president of the
Commission, said in an interview that he sees a greater role for
Europe in what traditionally has been a U.S. sphere of influence.
'We, and especially Spain and Portugal, have a strong historical
affinity with these countries. We don't want to replace the U.S.
We know Latin America has a special link with the U.S. But we
also have a role to play.'"[21] Undoubtedly that role will be to soft-
pedal Soviet subversion in Central America while questioning
America's judgment as to the seriousness of the Soviet threat.

Jacques Delors is a Socialist, but it would be a mistake to think
that minimalization of the Soviet threat in Central America is a
monopoly of the left in Western Europe. "One does not need to be

a Communist sympathizer," writes Peregrine Worsthorne in *The American Spectator*, "to see that these neoconservative justifications for the exercise of American power outside U.S. borders really are a bit unsatisfactory since they seem, in effect, to argue that everyone interested in freedom should put America's security interests first, and if they don't, then they can't be interested in freedom."[22] But Americans neither ask nor demand that Europeans put U.S. security interests first. What Americans do ask—and must receive from their allies—is quid pro quo. If the United States helps Europe, it has the right to expect Europe to reciprocate. To argue, as the European Right does, that U.S. demands for quid pro quo in our relationship with Europe in effect is a demand that "the rest of the world slavishly follow America's lead,"[23] represents the ultimate in free-riding excuses for indifference in the face of Soviet expansion. Mr. Worsthorne certainly makes it clear what the United States can expect in the way of help from its European allies in Central America. "If the United States were to get involved militarily in Central America today," writes Worsthorne, "there would be no allied troops fighting alongside; and probably no diplomatic backing either."[24] With friends like these, Americans may wonder, who needs enemies?

CONCLUSION

Though Michel Tatu undoubtedly is correct that the Finlandization argument is more stratagem than reality, the issue nonetheless is not a phony one. Pulling U.S. troops out of Western Europe is a big step involving real risks. Two different types of risks can be identified. The first is that an American troop withdrawal might so demoralize the Europeans that they would turn to the Soviet Union for protection and a "peace treaty." But if European attachment to Western values has declined to the point where the Europeans would not sacrifice part of their welfare state to defend them, does the United States really want or need Europe as an ally? It is crucial that we find out the answer to this all-important question—and the sooner the better. Far better that U.S. national security policy be based on reality—no matter how unpleasant that may be—than on an assumption that the Western European allies would support the United States in a crisis if they really would not. Moreover, it is far better that the United States stop spending billions of dollars per year for the defense of a region whose allegiance to Western values is shown to be paper thin. Thus, the case is made. If Europe really would be Finlandized by a U.S. troop withdrawal, good riddance to a false ally. If not, then excessive U.S. defense support has been both unnecessary and unwise.

Assuming the more likely happenstance that Western Europe would respond to an American troop withdrawal by rearming and casting détente aside, there is a second risk attendant upon U.S. troop withdrawal. This concerns the transitional process in Europe from defense dependence to defense independence. The Soviet Union, unlike Hitler's Germany, is a state that is not risk-prone, but being risk-averse it works to manipulate circumstances so that it can get its way without war (e.g., suppressing revolts in Hungary, Czechoslovakia, and Poland) or, failing that, with a conflict that has a very low risk of escalation (as in Afghanistan). The relevant consideration here is whether the withdrawal of U.S. troops from Europe might create circumstances that the Soviets could exploit militarily.

Certain possibilities bring themselves to mind. For instance, the chance that the Soviets would move to reabsorb Yugoslavia into the Soviet empire might be higher if the United States were clearly out of Europe. Or that Finland would be reabsorbed and Norway made to move into the condition of Finland today? There is also the possibility of direct Soviet support for the Greek Communists, as in 1945–46. Probably such actions would so alarm the Europeans that it would accelerate European cohesion and rearmament, but there could be some important losses to the Soviets en route. Moreover, if instead of nibbling at the edges, the Soviets struck directly at the heart of NATO during the transitional period—by making a direct move against the Federal Republic of Germany with no use of Soviet nuclear weapons—just a rapid fait accompli that would put the Soviets on the Rhine in five to ten days—the results could be devastating.

These are not arguments to do nothing about the troops in Europe, but of ensuring that withdrawal is done over a period of time so that the Europeans, if they so desire, can phase in their forces as the United States phased out theirs. In order to make this phase-in go faster, the United States could sell its allies (even at cut-rate prices) a substantial amount of its weapons in Europe. The Soviets, on the other hand, can be expected to try to slow the phase-in of European troops and weapons. For that reason, Moscow is likely to be on its best behavior during the transitional period so as not to scare the Europeans into making the military buildup they seek to avoid. The transitional risks, in other words, may not be as great as some argue.

In the final analysis, pulling the troops out of Europe may be a little like having surgery to excise a cancerous growth. Clearly there are risks that the patient might expire during the operation, or that it will be discovered that the cancer has spread too far. But given the strong likelihood that the patient will die if nothing is done, there remains little choice but to operate. Those who do not want to take America out of Europe focus too much on the risks of the operation and not enough on what is presently happening to Europe—and what in all likelihood will continue to happen to it if the problem is ignored. The signs of cancer already are showing in Western Europe. Why wait until it is too late?

6

Will the Real Germany Please Stand Up?

The division of Germany is not limited to the purely physical—East Germany from West Germany or East Berlin from West Berlin. Today, neutralism is dividing West Germany from the Western alliance; pacifism is dividing it from its militaristic traditions; Europeanism is dividing it from its tradition of nationalism; and the West German economy is divided over whether it should take a more socialist or more capitalist path. Why, when asked, doesn't the "real" Germany stand up? Probably because it doesn't know who it is anymore.

GERMANY AND THE UNITED STATES

Despite the anti-American rhetoric of many of its intellectuals, the appearance of the Green Party that wants to pull Germany out of NATO, and the severe shift to the left by the German Social Democrats, many influential West Germans insist that relations between their country and the United States have not deteriorated. Fritz Ullrich Fack, publisher of the West German newspaper *Frankfurter*

Allgemeine Zeitung, maintains that public opinion polls show that the one constant factor in West German attitudes is the desire for cooperation with the United States. "In opinion polls this view has predominated for over thirty years and involves four-fifths of all those questioned," writes German media experts Gerhard Herdegen and Elizabeth Noelle-Neumann. "No other country has so many people in favour of friendship with America." In 1983, for example, results of the prestigious Allensbach poll showed that in response to the question, "Do you like Americans or don't you like them?", 53 percent of West Germans answered, "I like Americans," while only 19 percent answered, "I don't like them." In January 1957, the answers had been 37 percent to 24 percent, respectively.

Similarly, in the hot deployment-of-missiles summer of 1983, the Allensbach survey showed that 79 percent of West Germans favored close cooperation with the United States (see fig. 6.1). This was not much less than the figure in the calmer atmosphere of 1979 and 1980, when 80 percent of West Germans put the United States first, some distance ahead of France and Britain. And the United States was named by 48 percent of West Germans when asked who they thought their "best friend" was; France followed with 15 percent, Austria with 6 percent, and Switzerland with 3 percent. The German media experts conclude: "These results from the West German survey give the lie to reports, that are widespread, of tension in the U.S.–West German relationship and that there is mistrust on both sides."[1]

If only this were true! Focusing exclusively on West German attitudes toward the United States tells us very little about whether West Germany has indeed moved to the left, right, or center. For example, in answer to the question, "With which country would you like to cooperate most closely?", let us assume that a constant 80 percent of West Germans respond "the United States" over a period of several years. During the same period, let us also assume that an increasing percentage of West Germans answer "the Soviet Union" to the identical question. This indicates a deterioration of the U.S. position *relative* to the Soviet Union, even though the *absolute* level of support for the United States has remained fixed. Because the United States competes with the Soviet Union, it is the relative, not absolute, levels of support that count.

FIG. 6.1 *U.S.–West German Cooperation*

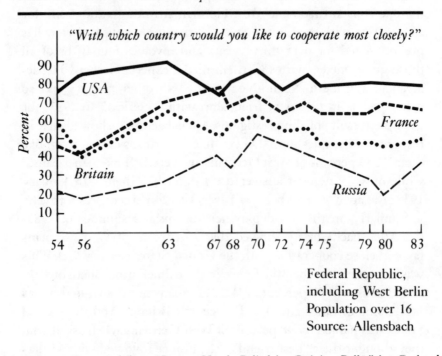

"With which country would you like to cooperate most closely?"

Federal Republic,
including West Berlin
Population over 16
Source: Allensbach

Source: Excerpted from "Protest Howls Belied by Opinion Polls," by Gerhard Herdegen and Elizabeth Noelle-Neumann, *German Tribune-Political Affairs Review* (June 3, 1984), p. 11.

Unfortunately, the deterioration of the U.S. position relative to the Soviet Union is precisely what occurred from 1980 to 1983 in West German opinion polls. In the Allensbach poll, a constant 80 percent of West Germans said they wanted to cooperate most closely with the United States. But during that same period, the percentage of West Germans who wanted to cooperate most closely with the Soviet Union increased from 22 percent to 36 percent. This represents over a 50-percent deterioration in the U.S. position relative to the Soviet Union during the three-year period, a statistic that can be taken as indicating a leftward drift in West Germany. Only during the Vietnam period (1963–67) does one find a similar deterioration of relative support for the United States in West Germany.

Other public opinion polls give a similar picture. When asked which of the listed facts or circumstances are the biggest contributory factors to international tensions, 50 percent of the Germans polled by the German weekly *Die Zeit* singled out Soviet rearmament. But 40 percent blamed America's rearmament. Next, 32 percent of the Germans polled said they were most concerned about the activities of both superpowers, and the same percentage expressed concern about the lack of European unity.[2] According to a Rand Corporation study by Peter Schmidt, "the most critical development (in West Germany) is an increasing belief that the Soviet Union is looking for reconciliation with the West and a decreasing belief that the United States is acting much more responsibly than the Soviet Union."[3] The fact that so many West Germans see so little difference between the United States and the Soviet Union is indeed disquieting.

DEPENDENCE AND NEUTRALISM

The changeover from an unambiguously pro-American stance to a more neutralist position in West Germany can be traced to the Federal Republic's extreme defense dependence on the United States. It probably is more than coincidence that Soviet appeasement is weakest in France—the European country least dependent on the United States for its defense and strongest in West Germany—the European country most defense-dependent on America. "No foreign weapons are allowed in France," writes Flora Lewis in *The New York Times*. "The pacifist movement in France, though it is growing, remains marginal because the French government retains full and exclusive control of its defense."[4]

The French can thank Charles de Gaulle for this. Former President de Gaulle's two critical foreign policy decisions of the 1960s—the withdrawal of France from NATO's military structure and its counterpart, the creation of an independent nuclear force—have insulated France from the neutralist disease. Michel Tatu writes in *The London Times*:

The first decision is now seen more as an anticipation of the present illness of NATO structures than what it was at the time: an affirmation of French independence and a rebellion against the "Anglo-

Saxons." If the Germans, the Dutch, and in some degree the British people today have second thoughts about American protection, so goes the reasoning in Paris, it is because the present NATO structure, with heavy American power and strategy, has deprived them of the necessary feeling of responsibility for their own defense.[5]

Irresponsibility, resentment, and self-hatred are the inevitable consequences of excessive dependence on others. "Western Europe is a frying pan on a stove whose controls are in the hands of others," writes Stanley Hoffman, professor of French civilization at Harvard University. "Nations which must rely on others for their defense, and consequently for much of their foreign policy, often tend to turn inward, leaving to those others the responsibility—and the blame—for difficult decisions."[6]

Hoffman's thesis is supported by the empirical fact that France today has the least amount of anti-Americanism while Germany has the most. "Leading French intellectuals, separating themselves from the influence of the Communist Party only in the 1960s and 1970s, now look with active contempt at any political position that might seem to work in favor of the Soviet Union," writes John Vinocur in *The New York Times*. "In West Germany, for a comparable group of intellectuals, the Soviet Union seems to be a subordinate problem to that of the United States—the factor they claim has smothered their identity, and in the process, made their country's democracy one they seem barely to respect."[7] While general public opinion remains favorable to the United States in the Federal Republic, German intellectuals, more than others, have sensed humiliation that their country must depend for its protection on the very same country that conquered it forty years ago.

The "incentives argument," that European attachment to détente is related to its defense dependence on the United States, predicts the greater a nation's defense dependence, the greater its attachment to détente. Evidence from Germany and France confirms this relationship. National security elites in West Germany and France were polled by the Science Center in Berlin in 1983 on how to deal with a number of East-West problems. The results show West German attachment to détente to be considerably stronger than French attachment:

—66 percent of the West Germans and only 30 percent of the French agree, or agree somewhat, that détente should be pursued independently of the military balance.

—96 percent of the West Germans and 73 percent of the French hold the opinion that the United States and the U.S.S.R. should reach an agreement on strategic arms reductions based on the concept of parity.

—19 percent of the West Germans and 62 percent of the French agree, or somewhat agree, on the question as to whether the West should agree on a list of economic sanctions to be used against the U.S.S.R. in case of such future actions as Afghanistan or Poland.

—86 percent of the West Germans and 38 percent of the French believe that the West should seek to increase trade with the East to establish a cooperative relationship and thus support the progress of détente in a mutual interest.[8]

There are, of course, other systematic differences between France and West Germany than differences in defense dependence on the United States. Because of this, it is useful to try to establish whether there exists a close statistical relationship between defense dependence and détente based on a more generalized sample than just two countries. If such a relationship can be established, there would be a greater level of confidence that differences in defense dependence, rather than some other difference, is the key explanatory variable behind French and German attitudes to détente.

To demonstrate that defense dependence on the United States and European attachment to détente are positively correlated in a statistically significant sense, a simple test can be performed. Table 6.1 ranks European NATO members according to their ratio of defense-spending share to economic product share in column 1. This ratio can be taken for "defense effort," and is used as a proxy for defense dependence. The greater the dependence on the United States, the less the defense effort.

An index of European attachment to détente appears as column 2 of Table 6.1. The détente index indicates how the European NATO countries voted in the United Nations on ten Third World issues that were judged by the United States to be of extreme importance to the United States in 1983—e.g., accepting Israel's credentials, aid to El Salvador, the invasion of Grenada, U.S. policy toward South Africa, etc. Low support for the United States in the UN votes are taken as indicating strong attachment to détente and vice versa. Greece and Turkey are excluded from the experiment because their substantial defense efforts are judged to be related more to their hostilities vis-à-vis one another than to the East-West conflict.

TABLE 6.1 *Rankings of Defense Effort and Soviet Appeasement by European NATO Members, 1983*

	RANKINGS OF DEFENSE EFFORT (FROM LOWEST EFFORT TO HIGHEST)[a]	RANKINGS OF APPEASEMENT (FROM BIGGEST APPEASER TO SMALLEST)[b]
Luxembourg	1	5
Denmark	2	1
Italy	3	7
Norway	4	3
Netherlands	5	2
Germany	6	9
Portugal	7	8
Belgium	8	4
France	9	6
United Kingdom	10	10

Source: [a]"Report on Allied Contributions to the Common Defense," A Report to the United States Congress, Caspar W. Weinberger, Secretary of Defense, U.S. Department of Defense (March 1984), p. 21; [b]"How NATO Countries Voted in the United Nations," Compiled by the U.S. Mission to the United Nations (Washington, D.C.: U.S. Government Printing Office, 1984).

In the experiment, positive correlation means that strong attachment to détente is correlated with low defense effort and weak attachment to détente is correlated with high defense effort. Using the well-known Spearman's rank correlation coefficient test, it is demonstrated that statistically significant positive correlation exists at the 10-percent significance level. That is, based on the data, the assertion of positive correlation would be correct nine out of every ten times. The correlation coefficient is .55, which is significantly different from zero. To demonstrate that the détente-defense dependency relation is essentially a European phenomenon, the same experiment can be performed with Japan and Canada included. If the addition of these two non-European NATO members undermines the positive correlation, then the thesis that greater defense effort reduces détente would be true for NATO Europe only. As it turns out, the correlation coefficient in this case is .35, which is not statistically different from zero at the 10-percent-significance level.

REUNIFICATION AND DÉTENTE

A second systematic difference between France and West Germany that explains their different détente preferences is reunification. The French have no reunification motive—the Germans do.

After the provision of national security, the most important foreign policy objective of West Germany is reunification of the two Germanies. The conventional wisdom in the Federal Republic is that reunification can be accomplished only by West German accommodation of the East, rather than the other way around. National security expert Richard Pipes, of Harvard University, writes:

> Since the 1960s, German policies toward the USSR have been strongly affected by the hope that *Ostpolitik*, the German variant of detente, will increase contacts between the two Germanies to the point where somehow, in the end, reunification will occur. The expectation is almost certainly misplaced: there is not the remotest chance that the Soviet Union will ever allow East Germany—its military and political springboard against Western Europe—to join with West Germany except on terms that would amount to the Federal Republic being detached from its allies and transformed into a Soviet client state. Nevertheless, the hope persists and affects policy in many ways.[9]

When Moscow forced East German Communist head, Erich Honecker, to cancel his planned visit to West Germany in September 1984, it confirmed Professor Pipes' point that German reunification on any basis other than the Soviet one simply is not possible.

Here's how the East Germans, and their Soviet backers, exploit the West German passion for reunification to their advantage. First, they put a wall between East and West Berlin to make certain East Germans do not leave the "worker's paradise" without official permission; then, their officials limit emigration to a trickle. They permit West Germans to visit East Germany, but they do it for a price: The fee at the time of writing was 25 deutsche marks, or about $9 per crossing, with old East Germans being allowed to visit West Germany under slightly less expensive terms. If the old refuse to come back, East Germany loses only a burden on its treasury, not a producer.

With immigration and visiting restrictions in place, the East Germans manipulate these restrictions for their own purposes. If the West Germans behave badly, the East Germans raise the restrictions. They lower them if the West Germans behave well. What "behaving badly" and "behaving well" mean is how much, and on what terms, the West Germans are willing to extend credit to the East Germans. In July 1984, for example, a deal was struck between the two Germanies in which West Germany made a private bank loan to East Germany, guaranteed by the West German government, estimated at $330 million. The government-guaranteed loan is subsidized, of course, since the risk element to the banks, and therefore the interest they must charge, is reduced.

What the West Germans are reported to have received in return is the following:

—the continued dismantling of the deadly, booby-trapped, automatic firing devices along East Germany's walled and fenced frontier with West Germany;
—a reduction of the mandatory foreign exchange required of West German visitors to East Germany from 25 to 15 deutsche marks;
—possibility for 5,000–10,000 more East Germans to emigrate to West Germany in 1984.

In New York City, we call this kind of deal "the protection racket"— in West Germany, they call it *Östpolitik*.

IT'S BIGGER THAN BOTH OF US

The desire for détente is so strong in the Federal Republic that it transcends political parties and ideological allegiances. "Despite a change in rhetoric, there has been a truly remarkable continuity in *Deutschlandpolitik* from the social-liberal to the conservative-liberal coalition governments," writes Timothy Garton Ash, editorial writer for *The Times* of London, in *The New York Review of Books*:

> The Christian Democrats came into office swearing they would be tougher about linking new credits to concessions from the Honecker regime in East Germany (*Gegenleistungen*), but in practice they have carried on much as their predecessors did. When I asked Herr Heinrich Windelen, the Minister of Intra-German Affairs... what concessions his government had won in return for approving two further billion Deutsche marks credits, he said the GDR had speeded up border crossing procedures for transit traffic between West Berlin and West Germany, and reduced the amount that West German pensioners have to exchange into East German marks for every day they spend in the East.[10]

Even the harshest of Germany's Soviet critics have done an about-face and now embrace détente as if they had invented it. "Most remarkable is the *volte face* of the most intemperate right-wing critic of the social-liberal *Ostpolitik*, Franz Josef Strauss; for today, it is Strauss who arranges new credits for Erich Honecker," Ash notes with obvious *schadenfraude*.[11]

In June 1983, Strauss organized a loan to East Germany, estimated at $358 million, through a private consortium of banks but guaranteed by the West German government. Although this loan did not officially carry political strings, it probably was more than coincidence that shortly after the loan was made, an unprecedented number of East Germans emigrated to West Germany. The Bonn government estimated that 30,000 East Germans moved to the West from January to May 1984, more than four times the number in all of 1983. In May 1984, however, the East German government slammed the door shut again, undoubtedly to squeeze more money out of the pocketbooks of their West German cousins. It worked, and will work again, so long as the West Germans are willing to pay—and there are no signs at present that they are not willing.

Not only do the West Germans allow themselves to be black-mailed into making subsidized loans to the East Germans, but they actually have been purchasing political prisoners from the East for the past two decades. Since the 1960s, about 22,000 political prisoners have been purchased by the West Germans, but their exact cost is a matter of some mystery. In a book on the subject, French journalist Michel Meyer reckoned that by 1976, Bonn had paid 761 million West German marks for about 11,000 prisoners. This would mean 1.5 billion West German marks, or $54 million, at the current rate of exchange for the 22,000.[12]

Timothy Ash claims the Bonn government presently pays $15,000 to $25,000 per head. "Honecker can export his dissidents in hard currency—a trick that General Jaruzelski [of Poland] can only dream of," notes Ash. "During the last two years this has been a highly cost-effective way of bleeding the independent 'peace groups' in the GDR. There are now more Jena 'peace activists' in West Berlin than there are in Jena."[13]

Erich Mende, who initiated the plan to buy political prisoners from East Germany twenty years ago, has changed his mind and now is against the purchases. "We are removing so-called oppositional elements and normalizing the coercive Communist state," he said. "We are sterilizing resistance to the Communists."[14] The West Germans also are making political repression in East Germany profitable—a practice which can only encourage further repression in the East. The more arrests the East Germans make, the more political prisoners they can sell to the West. So sure are the East Germans of West German "Dane-geld," that West German payments in raw materials like oil and copper are said to be taken into account in the East German five-year plans.

Should the West become alarmed at the increasing incidence of West German subsidies to their poorer cousins on the other side of the Berlin Wall? Is there reason to be concerned that, over the years, West German private investment, bank loans, and outright gifts from individuals and church groups have underpinned East Germany's singular prosperity within the Warsaw Pact? Ash writes:

Direct payment of more than one billion Deutsche marks a year from the Federal Republic, favorable credits, and the GDR's "secret membership" in the EEC have helped it to maintain its place among the world's top ten industrial nations, and a better level of consumer supplies than its Eastern neighbors. The contrast with impoverished Poland is a source of national pride among ordinary East Germans.[15]

Complacents argue that for every apparent negative that takes place in the West, there is a corresponding positive for the West taking place in the East. They point out that while the United States agonizes that closer relations between the two Germanies is neutralizing West Germany, Moscow is similarly concerned that East Germany is being drawn out of the Soviet camp by "revanchism" (the Soviet term for German unification). As evidence they offer the alleged fact that fears of East German revanchism led the Soviet Union to cancel East German leader Erich Honecker's planned 1984 trip to West Germany, and attacked the Federal Republic for using an "economic lever" to separate East Germany from its Communist brethren.

Only the excessively innocent, however, could believe that Moscow is not extremely pleased with West German use of its so-called "economic lever." The Soviets gain enormously from it. While the precise details of the Byzantine economic relations between East Germany and the Soviet Union are clouded in shadows, the basic relation between the two is clear enough. According to John Tagliabue, writing in *The New York Times*:

> Economically, resource-poor East Germany sends a steady stream of high-quality goods, including machinery and electrical equipment, to Russia, despite high prices it pays for Soviet fuel and raw materials. East Berlin also gives immense aid to pull Poland from the brink of bankruptcy. At the May (1984) meeting of leaders of COMECON, the Soviet-led economic community, East Berlin pledged even closer cooperation during the next five-year plan, 1986–90.[16]

West German subsidies to East Germany, then, wind up either propping up the Soviet puppets in Poland or financing the excessively high price East Germany must pay for Soviet raw materials.

The Soviets, while blustering and warning the West Germans not to get any false ideas about buying German reunification, are laughing all the way to the bank.

Honecker's scheduled trip to West Germany thus appears to have caught the Kremlin between two conflicting forces. Economically, the trip promised to yield the Soviets substantial benefits; politically, however, the Soviets feared that other East European nations might use the East German leader's trip as a lever to put greater distance between themselves and Moscow. If East Germany could have an additional degree of freedom in their foreign policy, they could argue, why couldn't they have the same? Apparently Moscow was sufficiently concerned with the political ramifications of Honecker's trip that they were willing to forgo its economic benefits. What the forced cancellation of the Honecker trip demonstrated above all, however, is that the East German leader does what Moscow tells him to do. Those who see West Germany's move away from the United States being matched by a parallel movement of East Germany away from the Soviet Union have another thought coming. As far as the Soviets are concerned, German neutralism is a one-way street going West to East.

GERMAN NATIONALISM TAKES A LEFT TURN

Despite Moscow's heavy-handed blow to West German hopes for closer relations between the two Germanies, neutralism remains a potent force in West German politics because of its strong identification with German nationalism. "If German nationalism is reviving," writes Peter Bender, West German political commentator and neutralist, "it is because we have the feeling that our country has become the training ground for a battle with which the Germans themselves have less and less to do."[17] Hellmut Diwald, professor of history at the University of Erlangen, asks: "What does Germany, what do the Germans, have to do with the motives, arguments, and interests of the two rivals? The U.S. and the Soviet Union each claims that it alone guarantees our security. A security that consists of being exposed as a Central European nuclear battlefield, to certain destruction."[18]

There are essentially two reasons why many West Germans do

not feel themselves to be participants in the East-West struggle. One is ideological; the other, an implication of their defense dependence on the United States.

The East-West struggle is to a large extent an ideological conflict between two political models of the future: some version of Marxist-Leninism on the one hand, and some version of democratic capitalism on the other. The West Germans, who have opted for social democracy during the past decades, find it difficult to relate to this struggle. The goal of the social democratic "elite" in Northern Europe has not been merely to create a bigger and better welfare state. It has been to create a new man—a "social democratic" man—whose personality is defined exclusively in terms of group norms and who is thus impervious to individual economic incentives. Irving Kristol writes: "Social democratic parties in Europe are 'movements,' not merely political parties in the bourgeois-parliamentary sense. Their mission is to create a new social order, based on a new way of life, not merely to govern well."[19]

As the enormous growth of the underground economy in the social democracies demonstrates, the social democratic elite obviously has failed in its mission. Individuals are no more group-oriented in the social welfare states of Northern Europe than they are in more capitalistic societies. This creates a dilemma for the social democracies that Kristol sums up as follows:

> European social democracy can govern democratically, but it cannot move the nation to socialism. Should it try to institute "true socialism," it would have to dissociate itself from bourgeois, parliamentary democracy, with its free, frequent elections, and move at least part way along the path designed by Marxism-Leninism. Unwilling to do either, it expends its energy in half-heartedly undermining capitalism and in half-heartedly opposing Communism. Meanwhile, the polity as a whole has no clear ideological self-definition by which to take its bearings in a world-wide ideological conflict.[20]

A lack of ideological self-definition is only part of the reason why many Germans do not feel themselves to be participants in the East-West struggle. Another part is that a foreign power, not the West Germans themselves, bears ultimate responsibility for their nation's defense.

As I wrote in *The Wall Street Journal* (March 1984): "Relying on a foreign power for defense has created the illusion among a good many Europeans that the East-West struggle has little to do with them; that it is a conflict between two superpowers with Western Europe caught in the middle."[21] Michael Howard, of Oxford University, argues that Europeans have been distanced from the East-West conflict because "the defense of Europe has become perceived not as the responsibility of the Europeans but increasingly in terms of a system of 'extended nuclear deterrence' manipulated from the United States in accordance with strategic concepts with which few Europeans are familiar."[22]

Dominique Moisi claims:

> Europeans are aware that they are largely spectators to their own history. Strategically, they are deeply sensitive to their dependence on the United States—all the more so since they have started to question the credibility of the U.S. security guarantee. They know that if Europe is still at the center of world history, it is more as the main stake of the East-West competition than as an independent actor.[23]

And Gregory Fossedal makes the same point in *Policy Review*:

> We have, by failing to let the Europeans defend the Europeans, in some way eroded the European spirit. War will come at the whim of Washington and Moscow; London, Bonn, and Oslo can merely watch the tanks roll and weapons fly. Europe . . . cannot take war seriously—not because a war would not be catastrophic, but because Europe today is not in a position to significantly influence its outcome. The stronger the U.S. and USSR grow in relation to Europe—regardless of which is ahead—the greater the drive to neutrality. American firmness in a crisis, because it threatens to involve the allies, is as great a threat as Soviet adventurism.[24]

To increase European interest in who wins this grand "contest" between East and West, our allies must be made to feel more like players and less like spectators. The Pershing and cruise missiles deployed on European territory, for example, are not controlled from Europe—they are controlled from Washington. "Realizing that you have the cruise missiles and the Pershings on your territory, and knowing you have no say in the matter, really is too much," writes French general Étienne Copel.[25] Richard Pipes reports that 40 percent of West Germans unconditionally oppose the stationing of U.S. nuclear missiles on their soil regardless of how many such missiles the Soviets deploy and target on West Germany.[26] Many in this country considered this disinterest in nuclear balance shocking. But what percentage of Americans do you think would calmly accept German, French, or whatever foreign nuclear weapons on American soil without having ultimate control over their use, even if the foreigners paid for them? Not a very high percent, I dare say. It is quite likely the Germans will continue to feel like spectators to a very dangerous game being played in their own backyard so long as they lack control over the nuclear weapons deployed on their territory. Thus, one cost of keeping German fingers off the nuclear control button has been the growth of West German neutralism.

NUCLEAR RECIPROCITY

The principle of "nuclear reciprocity"—that nuclear weapons on American soil cannot be pledged to the defense of any country that refuses to allow American nuclear weapons to be deployed on their territory—has great intuitive appeal. Why, after all, should the United States accept the risks of having nuclear weapons on its soil to protect other countries if these very countries are not willing to accept similar risks, and for the same purpose, by allowing American missiles on their soil?

America's allies can make a perfectly reasonable response to this question: that while the United States fully controls the nuclear weapons on its soil, its European allies do not control the nuclear weapons on their soil. This makes a critical difference both psychologically and politically. Nuclear weapons are sufficiently dangerous that the people who make themselves into nuclear targets by permitting deployment in their country should have ultimate control over their use. Europeans cannot be expected to accept willingly nuclear risks if they are not permitted to have nuclear control. Moreover, in the West German case, the problem is compounded because the foreign power to which the control of nuclear weapons is ceded is precisely the country that defeated them in

World Wars I and II. If it had not been for the United States, after all, Germany would be ruling the world today. This is a humiliation that cannot help but create deep resentment of the United States in the Federal Republic. And though the only way out of this dilemma is to give the West Germans control over the nuclear weapons deployed on their territory, the United States, supported by its allies, has not been willing to support a nuclear Germany.

Only West Germany, of all the alliance members, has been denied access to nuclear weapons. General de Gaulle fully understood the importance of nuclear weapons to the overall well-being of a modern nation-state. Nuclear weapons, according to de Gaulle, are essential if a nation is to have the political prestige and diplomatic status required to pursue an independent foreign policy. For this reason, the development of an independent French nuclear force was given top priority by de Gaulle and continues to hold this priority under President Mitterrand.

The French, however, act as if what is good for France is even better if it is denied the Germans. The late French philosopher Raymond Aron wrote in 1966:

> If the possession of nuclear arms has all of the value which General de Gaulle attributes to it, why should the Germans accept indefinitely to remain an inferior nation and to be deprived of them? . . . France is in the process of adopting, with regard to the Federal Republic, the attitude which the United States and Great Britain adopted with regard to France ten years ago (in 1956). We are condemning the Federal Republic to a permanent discrimination. [27]

The French recognize that the denial of nuclear weapons to West Germany makes the Germans feel unsafe, as well as inferior, in the alliance. Former French president Valéry Giscard d'Estaing predicts "that West Germany might never feel safe in the world community until it has its own nuclear weapons." Comparing France to West Germany, Giscard said in December 1984, "We are not a probable nuclear target. We are able to inflict the same destruction on the Soviet Union." Germany, on the other hand, "is a target without a shield. We cannot let Germany remain in this posture for long or their support for the Western alliance will be destroyed." [28]

Critics of a nuclear Germany, however, point out that the Germans themselves do not want nuclear weapons. Theo Sommer, the West German journalist, argues that there is an "aversion to nuclear weapons" in Germany and claims "the bomb would tear the nation asunder rather than cement it."[29] Sommer is supported by public opinion polls in West Germany that consistently show the German people to be against nuclear weapons. Such expressions of aversion and disinterest, however, must be evaluated in the context in which they are professed. The Germans know the Soviets are vehemently opposed to their having nuclear weapons. Since the West German strategy for reunification has been to calm Soviet fears about what a reunified Germany would be like, nuclear weapons are seen as antithetical to the reunification objective.

The United States, of course, could have made it more difficult for West Germany to follow a reunification-through-neutralism policy by advocating nuclear weapons for the Federal Republic. But it decided to accommodate the Soviet interest in a nonnuclear West Germany by placing the Federal Republic under the American nuclear umbrella. Indeed, though the United States did not realize it at the time, accepting the responsibility for the Federal Republic's security objective has allowed German reunification to become *the* preeminent objective of West German policy. If there were no American defense guarantee, national security would be the paramount German objective *per forza*, and reunification pushed into the background. But when the United States tells the West Germans, "Don't worry about security, we'll take care of it for you," we free our allies to worry about other things that concern them. And the thing that concerns West Germans most is that Germany is a divided nation.

"The Germans have a good case for obtaining nuclear weapons," writes Johannes Gross, conservative publisher of *Capital* magazine. "Let us remember that the Federal Republic of Germany has signed the non-proliferation treaty, under American pressure, in exchange for assurances that our security would be guaranteed under the U.S. nuclear umbrella."[30] The Germans now can argue that since the American guarantee no longer is truly credible, West Germany no longer is obliged to meet its obligations under the treaty. After all, one of Germany's most profound political as well as military problems is that it is nuclear-naked in a world where nuclear weapons are king.

Some argue, of course, that German acquisition of nuclear weapons would be a provocative act. Indeed, the fear is that a nuclear Germany might be so provocative to the Soviet Union that it could cause the Kremlin to launch a preventive attack against West Germany. This argument is nothing less than "Better Red than Dead" in disguise. The credibility the U.S. nuclear guarantee may be dubious, but the Kremlin really does not know how the United States would react to a preventive strike against West Germany. The consequences could be quite disastrous for the Soviet Union. The Soviet leaders, famous for their caution, are interested in dominating the world, not destroying it. Moreover, when U.S. strategy toward the Soviets comes to the point where it dares do only what the Soviets can live with, it soon will find that the only thing the Soviets can in fact live with is a Washington, D.C., where the Red flag flies instead of the Red, White, and Blue.

The counterproductive effects of the American nuclear guarantee promoting West German neutralism not only relates to the Pershing and cruise missiles located on German territory, but to the long-range ICBMs that protect Germany from the United States. Because of the "trip-wire" strategy, the commitment of the ICBMs to European defense entails the physical presence of American troops on West German soil. While some West Gemans view these troops as their nuclear ace in the hole, others, still traumatized by their defeat in World War II, see them as an occupying army. "The Americans did a great deal for Germany," says Étienne Copel, "but that did not alter the fact that a lot of Germans perceived the American presence there as a kind of occupation. They have not forgotten they were defeated in 1945."[31]

According to Bruno Bettelheim, the noted psychoanalyst, American troops in Germany remind the Germans on a daily basis that they must now depend for their protection on the very same forces that defeated them in World Wars I and II.[32] Whatever the rational justification for their presence in the Federal Republic, on an emotional level the Germans see the U.S. troops as a continuing army of occupation that makes them into an inferior partner in the Atlantic Alliance. Rather than make the Germans feel more secure, the American troops make them feel more anxious and resentful.

H. Joachim Maitre, professor at Boston University, writes:

Scratch most Germans and you will find resentment. A resentment not over Germany's defeat in war or over loss of German territory, but over . . . the subdued role of today's West Germany in the world, in the United Nations, in the European Community and in the Atlantic Alliance. West Germany, Europe's remaining economic giant, is seen—deep down—by its citizens as a political and military dwarf, not allowed to play its 'proper part,' yet scolded for not pulling its full weight."[33]

"Resentment crosses all ideological lines in West Germany," claims Maitre. On the right, there is resentment of Germany's distinctly minor role in NATO's conventional force strategy, and "on the left, the 'peace movement' draws fuel from Bonn's limited authority in NATO's nuclear decision-making."[34] Addressing himself to NATO's deployment of Pershing II and cruise missiles in West Germany and the government's lack of veto power over their use, Helmut Gollwitzer, a pacifist theologian, comments: "The government has abdicated national sovereignty in a crucial sphere. If it is not driven from power by a public outcry, this only shows the extent to which Germans have had their backs broken by Hitlerism and defeat in 1945, by Marshall Plan extortion and fear of Russia."[35] Though the German theologian's equation of Hitlerism with the Marshall Plan borders on the fanatic, his fundamental argument remains sound: Nuclear weapons located on domestic soil should not be controlled by foreigners.

But what can the Germans do about the ambiguous role they play in the Western Alliance? All intelligent Germans know, or at least should know, that their status as the enemy in World War II has not fully worn off. That the stigma remains was made manifestly clear when recently, forty years after D-Day, German leaders were refused an invitation to participate in the D-Day commemoration ceremonies in Normandy, France. Referring to this snub of the Germans, most editorial comment thought it wiser to focus on the present than linger on the past. *The Times* of London wrote: "The D-Day celebrations commemorate the past but take place in the present, so they cannot be wholly insulated form today's reality."[36] Similar words were used by the *Sydney Morning Herald*: "Although the roles of Nazism should not be played down, this continuing preoccupation with World War II seems to ignore the realities of the 1980s. The opportunity to symbolically bury old enmities and recognize the reality of today has been squandered."[37]

What these editors fail to recognize, however, is that ambiguity *is* today's reality about West Germany. Despite the fact that the Federal Republic today stands totally committed to democracy, its commitment to the Western Alliance is not as apparent. The Germans themselves sometimes give the impression that they are uncertain where they belong and who their friends are. Given these perceived uncertainties, could there have been a more dramatic example of Allied insensitivity to the need to steer German nationalism away from neutralism and the left than the D-Day celebrations at Normandy? Where was the statesmanship that would have recognized that not inviting the German officials would only intensify German feelings of alienation from, and distrust of, the West?

Of course there remains ambiguity toward Germany in the alliance; the German record warrants that. But it is precisely because such ambiguity continues to exist that the United States should reassure the Germans that they belong on our side—not drive them out of the Western camp.

The Soviets have proved themselves quite adept at exploiting the current national identity crisis in West Germany to pull that country farther along the neutralist path. For example, the Kremlin has instructed East Germany to closely identify itself with the Prussian tradition. Under Marxist aegis, such unlikely figures from German history as Luther and Bismarck have been reclaimed, and a statue of Prussia's King Frederick the Great, damaged in World War II, has been restored to a pedestal under Erich Honecker's office window. These actions exert a strong cultural pull on many West Germans.

For its own part, West Germany finds it difficult to compete with East Germany as the legitimate heir to the Prussian tradition because, geographically, East Germany is situated where Prussia used to be and, racially, East Germany is more homogenetically Aryan. One of the consequences of West Germany's economic miracle, it should be remembered, has been a vast inflow of non-Aryan guest-workers from Turkey, Greece, Cyprus, Italy, and other countries to the point where, of the two Germanies, the West today is the more racially mixed.

Guenter Gaus, Bonn's chief diplomat in East Germany under former Chancellor Helmut Schmidt, wrote about German cultural identity and the East in his 1983 best-seller, *Where Germany Lies*. In discussing East Germany, Gaus makes a virtue out of living under totalitarian rule. He asserts the East Germans have retained a kind of "Germanness" that their Western cousins have lost. "People in the East kept what the West Germans gave up," laments Gaus.[38]

With this kind of frustrated nationalism holding sway among respected German leaders, it is not surprising that Ronald Reagan took the opportunity he missed at Normandy to mark the fortieth anniversary of the liberation as a day of reconciliation between old-enemies-turned-friends. "We who were enemies are now friends," declared President Reagan at the U.S. air base in Bitburg, West Germany. Unfortunately, the American President's reconciliation message was lost in the din over his visit to the military cemetery at Bitburg, which contains the graves of forty-nine Nazi Waffen SS troops. Admitting his mistake, the U.S. President said "Some old wounds have been reopened, and this I regret very much, because this should be a time of healing." The purpose of Bitburg, of course, was to promote German-American reconciliation, not to resurrect the Nazis.

In summation, the idea of keeping West Germany in a militarily inferior position by having a foreign power provide for its defense and basic security needs had considerable appeal after War II, given Germany's dubious historical record. And so long as the militarily "deprived" country remained economically immature and insufficiently rehabilitated in a political sense, the idea proved sound. But what is appropriate under one set of circumstances may not be appropriate under another. When West Germany's commitment to democracy could no longer be challenged and its economy became the strongest in Western Europe, it should have been obvious that unless there was an adjustment of its status as a militarily inferior nation, West Germany increasingly would feel estranged from those responsible for its condition and particularly from that country most responsible and upon which it was most dependent, the United States. The appeal of neutralism to the West Germans should have come as no surprise, though it did to many.

The American troops in the Federal Republic are very much a part of the West German neutralist syndrome. Originally, the troops were a symbol of U.S. commitment to protect Germany from a Communist invasion, but time has worn the symbol thin. Today the troops are no threat to the Soviets and no protection for Germany. Moreover, the troops reinforce the West German self-image as the inferior partner of the Western alliance by constantly reminding them that they are a defeated nation in which Americans, and other NATO partners, continue to have limited trust. If the United States treats the Germans like an inferior partner, we should not be surprised if they occasionally act like one. The best way the United States can maintain the loyalty of the Federal Republic to the West is to announce a phased withdrawal of its troops from West Germany.

7

France and the Balance of Fears

When the Reagan administration bowed to European demands to adopt a more accommodating attitude toward the Soviet Union during the Euromissile crisis, it was not the first time the weaker partners in the Western alliance were able to impose their will on the stronger one. In fact, it was the latest in a long series of such incidents. French frustration of American attempts to rearm Germany by the subterfuge of a European Defense Community in the 1950s is an early example of the European tail wagging the American dog.

THE FRENCH TROJAN HORSE

Though the Korean War took place in Asia, it destabilized Western Europe by raising demands in certain quarters on both sides of the Atlantic for German rearmament. The parallel between the two Koreas and the two Germanies, plus the fact that Soviet-sponsored North Korea had invaded American-sponsored South Korea, was not lost on the West Germans and many in the United States, who feared an invasion from the East. To protect themselves, the West Germans wanted weapons. But as much as the French and their backers in the United States feared the Soviets, they feared the Germans even more.

The fact that the early part of the Korean War did not go well for the United States and its South Korean allies intensified the problem of the demoralization of the West Germans. In Washington, there was considerable concern that unless the United States did something timely to bolster German spirits, West Germany would bolt the West and make a separate "peace treaty" with the Soviets. Though President Harry Truman and his secretary of state, Dean Acheson, were opposed to the idea of German rearmament at the time, they were both convinced by John J. McCloy, high commissioner in Germany, that the United States had to do something if West Germany was not to be "lost." What McCloy proposed was the formation of a "European Defense Force"—an army that would be under NATO command but consist of divisions from the various continental nations, including Germany.

The idea of a European Defense Force clearly was the outcome of what can be called the balance of "fears." That something had to be done in the way of German rearmament was dictated by fear of the Soviet Union. That German rearmament was to proceed within the context of a supranational European Defense Force— that is, without the emergence of a separate German army, general staff, and defense ministry—was dictated by concern about German rearmament.

The main supporter of a European Defense Force in Washington was the U.S. State Department, which generally took the position that France should set the pace for the integration of Germany into the West. Its main detractor was the U.S. Defense Department, which wanted the Germans rearmed. When President Truman proclaimed that the United States would send additional divisions to Europe and appoint a supreme commander if, and only if, the Allies agreed to German rearmament, the European Defense Force appeared to be a dead letter. But the French were able to thwart American plans to rearm Germany by themselves proposing the formation of a European army.

On October 24, 1950, French Prime Minister René Pleven proposed the creation of a European army, with a united defense ministry and budget. Though the Pentagon saw the French proposal for the stall it was, the Truman administration, wedded to its objective of containment of the Soviets and feeling pressure from American isolationists to withdraw our troops from Europe, was very anxious for an agreement that would both allow more troops to be sent to Europe and provide some compromise measure for German rearmament. This gave the French the opening they were looking for. McCloy, who originated the idea of a European Defense Force in the United States, arranged a meeting between NATO Supreme Commander General Dwight Eisenhower and Jean Monnet. Once the prestigious general threw his full support behind the renamed European Defense Community (EDC), there was little that the Pentagon could do but relent in its opposition to the plan. Historian Thomas Schwartz writes, "By the September 1951 Washington conference, the EDC was a fundamental part of American policy, the only way to resolve French fears and the German demands. The EDC Treaty was signed in May 1952, along with agreements ending the occupation of West Germany."[1]

Though the EDC was inspired by a Frenchman, Jean Monnet, and proposed by the French foreign minister, René Pleven, the French National Assembly refused to ratify the treaty. Many reasons have been given for the French failure to ratify: that Monnet and his allies were not sufficiently representative of French public opinion, that the Americans were forcing German rearmament on the French, that the French debacle in Indochina had created strong anti-American feelings, in France, and that reluctance of patriotic Frenchmen to merge their army into a European force had grown since the idea first took shape. However, the most important reason the French failed to ratify the treaty was that the EDC was against France's economic interest. Acceptance of the EDC by France would have meant the surrender of substantial defense subsidies the United States had chosen to bestow upon her.

Daniel Lerner, a professor at the Massachusetts Institute of Technology, showed he understood this essential point when he analyzed why the EDC had failed:

> The "European" solution had been highly publicized and approved in this country; but scant attention was paid to the "national" solution and its appeal to very many Frenchmen. Few understood

that it was precisely the American guarantee which gave France *security at minimal cost* and made possible the rejection of EDC on rational grounds of self-interest.... For it was clear among French political leaders that the EDC, while presumably requiring no formal increase in France's military budget, would by remilitarizing Germany put them in a competitive position that inevitably would divert large shares of their limited resources to military purposes. Hence it seemed to them unreasonable to demand French expenditures for a defense *which was already guaranteed*—and which a French contribution could not significantly improve.[2] [Emphasis added.]

It should have been clear to American officials that the Pleven plan was merely a stalling tactic designed to postpone the day West Germany would be rearmed. But it was not until 1969, twenty years after Pleven had proposed his plan, that former Secretary of State Dean Acheson publicly admitted he had been duped. According to Acheson, the EDC was "a politically impossible and militarily unfeasible subterfuge for preventing German rearmament, designed for infinite delay."[3] The reason the French were able to get away with this subterfuge was the difference in the "balance of fears" between the United States and France at the time.

So long as U.S. fear of the Soviet Union was greater than that of Germany, then France, whose balance tilted in the opposite direction, had considerable leverage over U.S. policies. In particular, the French could oppose U.S. plans to rearm Germany with impunity. For example, when the Truman administration threatened to undertake an "agonizing reappraisal" of its relations if France rejected the EDC, the French simply thumbed their noses at the U.S. President and rejected the EDC anyway. The French knew a bluff when they heard one.

"'Agonizing reappraisal' failed because it was a bluff, and was widely recognized among Frenchmen as a bluff," wrote Daniel Lerner.

Reappraisal implied that the [American security] guarantee might be withdrawn and France left defenseless or, perhaps worse, dependent upon a European defense system based in Germany. The implication was that the French would have no alternative but to ensure their security by ratifying EDC. Instead, some French spokesmen turned the threat into a boomerang by reaching for the other horn of the dilemma, namely, by a campaign for negotiations guaranteeing its security by agreement with the Soviet Union. (An extremist minority in the Assembly even took up the Communist slogan of a *renversement des alliances*.)⁴

The end result of the EDC incident was that France was able to delay German rearmament for five years, and when German rearmament finally did take place, it was within the context of NATO, with substantial American troops stationed in Europe to reassure the French that history would not repeat itself for a third time within the century.

"AGONIZING REAPPRAISAL" AND THE NUNN AMENDMENT

The French have an expression that the more things change, the more they stay the same. Nowhere is this more apparent than in the Western alliance. Thirty years after the EDC failed, the United States once again is undergoing an "agonizing reappraisal" of the role U.S. troops should play in Western Europe, and once again the French are using the idea of a "European" solution to stall the threatened withdrawal of U.S. troops. *Plus ça change, plus c'est la même chose.*

Today, America's "agonizing reappraisal" of its defense support of Western Europe is based on two separate, but related, problems—the low nuclear threshold and burden-sharing within the alliance. The European strategy of the United States maintaining the burden of defending the West has meant a severely limited European conventional defense posture. This, in turn, has lowered the nuclear threshold to unacceptable levels. The Reagan administration has chosen to downplay the importance of these problems because of its concern about European acceptance of the Pershing and cruise missiles. But Senator Sam Nunn (D-Georgia) has sponsored an amendment in the U.S. Senate that proposes 90,000 of the 360,000 American troops in Europe be withdrawn within five years unless the European allies increase their conventional forces. The Senate voted on the amendment in June 1984. Even though the Nunn Amendment was opposed by President Reagan, Defense Secretary Weinberger, Secretary of State Shultz, NATO Supreme Commander Rogers, and U.S. NATO Ambassador to Europe Abshire, it was narrowly defeated by a margin of 55 to 41.[5]

Unlike the failed Mansfield Amendment of the 1970s, the purpose of the Nunn Amendment was not to remove U.S. troops from Europe. Rather, it was to increase the nuclear threshold by inducing Europe to add to its conventional forces. Senator Sam Nunn argues that "we are getting too little a conventional defense and too low a nuclear threshold for the billions of dollars we are putting into NATO."[6] Unless the Europeans are willing to raise the nuclear threshold by building up their conventional forces, Nunn reasons, the United States should at least trim its costs.

Though the chief concern of the Nunn Amendment is to increase the nuclear threshold, the senator from Georgia wants this done by increased European, not American, efforts. An essential part of the Nunn Amendment, therefore, is to ensure that Europe adopts a defense posture more in keeping with its economic resources. The "burden-sharing" aspect of the amendment proved extremely popular even among senators who chose to vote against it.

Former Senator John Tower of Texas voted against the amendment but said during the Senate debate, "I think we all agree that we are not satisfied with the current level of NATO burden-sharing. We do not believe that our allies are doing what they should do, or what they are capable of doing, given their resources."[7] Senator Richard Lugar of Indiana also voted against the amendment, but said, "I share with [Senator Nunn] some of the frustration and concerns in achieving a more equitable sharing of the defense burden by our NATO allies."[8] Senator William Cohen of Maine said, "I find myself in a rather unusual position, agreeing with the essence but opposing the action. I do that principally because of timing."[9] After the Nunn Amendment's defeat, the Senate adopted an alternative amendment sponsored by Senator Cohen by an overwhelming margin of 94 to 3. The Cohen Amendment calls on the Europeans to spend more for their own defense without the threat of troop withdrawal.[10]

THE FACTS OF DEFENSE BURDEN-SHARING IN NATO

Are American senators being fair to the Europeans? Is it true that the Europeans are not pulling their weight in the alliance? To evaluate the defense effort of the Western Alliance countries, the U.S. Department of Defense has constructed a statistical index comparing defense contributions on the one hand, with ability to contribute on the other. In Table 7.1, column 2 indicates GDP share, column 3 indicates defense-spending share, and column 4 indicates "defense effort" as shown by the ratio of defense-spending share to GDP share—all for the year 1984. The United States ranks first in GDP share (the share of U.S. GDP in total NATO plus Japan's GDP), first in defense-spending share (the share of U.S. defense spending in total NATO plus Japan's defense spending), and first in defense effort. The U.S. ratio of defense-spending share to GDP share is 1.45. This means that the U.S. defense contribution was approximately 45 percent more than in proportion to its ability to contribute. A ratio of 1.0 indicates that contribution and ability to pay are roughly in balance.

According to these statistics, Japan is the biggest defense free-rider of all. Its defense spending share to GDP share is only 0.22— that is, its contribution is 78 percent less in proportion to its ability to contribute. The list of countries, from least defense effort to most, are Japan, Luxembourg, Canada, Denmark, Italy, Norway, the Netherlands, Belgium, Portugal, West Germany, France, Turkey, United Kingdom, Greece, and the United States.

A similar statistical exercise was performed by the U.S. Defense Department to ascertain defense manpower effort by the NATO countries. In Table 7.2, column 1 indicates population share, column 2 indicates active defense manpower share, and column 3 indicates defense manpower effort as shown by the ratio of active defense manpower share to population share. The list of countries from least defense manpower effort to most are Japan, Luxembourg, Canada, Denmark, the Netherlands, Italy, United Kingdom, Portugal, Germany, Belgium, Norway, France, the United States, Turkey, and Greece. If reserves are included as well as active defense

TABLE 7.1 *Ratio of Defense-Spending Share to GDP Share, NATO Countries, 1984*

RANK	GDP SHARE		DEFENSE- SPENDING SHARE		DEFENSE-SPENDING SHARE/GDP SHARE: RATIO	
1	US	44.50%	US	64.73%	US	1.45
2	JA	16.32%	UK	7.28%	GR	1.43
3	GE	8.83%	GE	6.70%	UK	1.18
4	FR	7.03%	FR	6.56%	TU	1.12
5	UK	6.16%	JA	3.65%	FR	0.93
6	IT	4.77%	IT	2.87%	GE	0.76
7	CA	4.40%	CA	2.17%	PO	0.75
8	NE	1.79%	NE	1.29%	BE	0.75
9	BE	1.08%	BE	0.81%	NE	0.72
10	DE	0.77%	TU	0.75%	NO	0.69
11	NO	0.74%	GR	0.67%	IT	0.60
12	TU	0.67%	NO	0.51%	DE	0.54
13	GR	0.47%	DE	0.42%	CA	0.49
14	PO	0.28%	PO	0.21%	LU	0.28
15	LU	0.04%	LU	0.01%	JA	0.21

Source: "Report on Allied Contributions to the Common Defense," a report to the U.S. Congress, Caspar W. Weinberger, Secretary of Defense, Department of Defense (March 1985), pp. 19–21.

manpower, the U.S. drops from third to eighth (column 4).

Table 7.3 shows the "real" increase in defense expenditure (money defense spending less inflation) made by each NATO country for the years 1980–84. This period is very important since, in 1978, the European countries pledged to increase their real defense spending by 3 percent per annun. In 1980, only 6 out of 14 countries met or bettered the target; only 7 out of 15 countries (Spain included) met the target in 1981 and 1982; in 1983 only 5 out of 15 met the target; and in 1984 8 out of 15 met the target. In 1983–84, the following countries met the target both times: the United States, Canada, and Luxembourg. The following failed to meet the target in either 1983 or 1984: Denmark, France, West Germany, Greece, and Portugal. Three European countries—Belgium, France, and Denmark—actually reduced real defense spending in 1984.

Although the Nunn Amendment was defeated (tabled, but not killed) it had a significant impact in both Europe and the United States. *The Washington Post* warned that those who would simply

TABLE 7.2 *Ratio of Active Defense Manpower to Population Share, NATO Countries, 1984*

POPULATION RANK	SHARE	ACTIVE DEFENSE MANPOWER SHARE	RATIO: ACTIVE DEFENSE MANPOWER/ POPULATION SHARE	RATIO: ACTIVE AND RESERVE DEFENSE MANPOWER POPULATION SHARE
1	US 31.38%	US 39.73%	GR 1.85	NO 7.26
2	JA 15.92%	TU 10.70%	TU 1.67	GR 4.13
3	GE 8.22%	FR 8.78%	US 1.27	DE 2.22
4	IT 7.60T	GE 8.15%	FR 1.20	NE 1.92
5	UK 7.54%	IT 6.73%	NO 1.14	GE 1.92
6	FR 7.29%	UK 6.71%	BE 1.07	BE 1.72
7	TU 6.40%	JA 3.21%	GE 0.99	FR 1.35
8	CA 3.33%	GR 2.44%	PO 0.94	US 1.07
9	NE 1.92%	NE 1.59%	UK 0.89	TU 0.96
10	PO 1.35%	CA 1.48%	IT 0.89	PO 0.81
11	GR 1.32%	BE 1.41%	NE 0.83	IT 0.77
12	BE 1.32%	PO 1.27%	DE 0.74	UK 0.41
13	DE 0.68%	NO 0.63%	CA 0.44	CA 0.14
14	NO 0.55%	DE 0.50%	LU 0.35	JA 0.04
15	LU 0.55%	LU 0.02%	JA 0.20	LU 0.00

Source: "Report on Allied Contributions to the Common Defense," a report to the U.S. Congress, Caspar W. Weinberger, Secretary of Defense, U.S. Department of Defense (March 1985), pp. 19–21.

brush off the amendment as "impatient talk that true friends can withstand and ignore" are making a big mistake:

> They should consider that in the name of alliance solidarity and a strong defense, they are feeding political poison to NATO. They are supplying the European political leadership with new excuses to continue sloughing off its most vital responsibilities. They are keeping NATO's defense dangerously and precariously balanced on a nuclear threat that the alliance understandably fears and has no faith in. They are inviting the day when the real isolationists in the United States will start putting in their amendments. The Nunn amendment failed this year. Next year, if things have not improved, it should pass.[11]

The Nunn Amendment shocked many Europeans who know Senator Nunn as an articulate and loyal supporter of NATO who

TABLE 7.3 *Growth in Total Defense Spending* of NATO Countries, Percent Change from Previous Year in Constant Prices (excluding inflation)*

Country	1980	1981	1982	1983	1984 (EST)
Belgium	1.9	0.9	−3.3	−1.2	3.1
Canada	5.1	3.1	4.9	6.9	6.0
Denmark	0.7	0.6	−0.3	0.8	−0.6
France	3.7†	3.9†	1.4†	1.5†	−1.1†
Germany	2.3	3.2	−0.9	0.9	0.2/0.9
Greece	−9.4	22.8	−1.0	−8.2	8.2
Italy	4.9	−0.5	3.1	2.5	4.0/7.2
Luxembourg	16.3	4.8	3.9	3.5	3.1
Netherlands	−2.1	4.2	1.6	0.3	4.7
Norway	1.8	2.7	4.1	4.0	1.0/3.5
Portugal	6.0	1.2	0.6	−2.5	−5.7/−2.6
Turkey	2.0	1.8	4.6	−4.4	3.2
United Kingdom	2.8	1.4	6.0	0.5	6.7
United States	4.9	4.7	7.6	7.4	4.8
Non–U.S. NATO‡	2.6	2.9	2.3	1.1	2.7/3.3
NATO Total‡	4.0	4.1	5.8	5.3	4.2/4.3

*All of the figures depicted in this table are based on the NATO definition of defense spending and are the best estimates that can be made on the basis of information now available.

National fiscal years correspond to calendar years except as follows: Canada and the UK (April–March), U.S. (October–September); Turkish data through 1981 are based on a March–February fiscal year; in 1983, Turkey converted to a January–December fiscal year.

†DOD estimate

‡ Non–U.S. NATO and NATO totals reflect weighted average growth rates developed using 1983 constant prices and 1983 exchange rates.

Source: "Report on Allied Contributions to the Common Defense", a report to the U.S. Congress, Caspar W. Weinberger, Secretary of Defense, U.S. Department of Defense (March 1985), p. 53.

had strongly opposed the Mansfield Amendment to unilaterally reduce the level of American troops in Europe. They also were shocked by the obvious popularity of the amendment, which clearly would have passed had it not been for some heavy lobbying efforts against it by the Reagan administration. The administration apparently did not want to "reward" the European governments that had just accepted the Pershing and cruise missiles with its support of the amendment. The West German newspaper *Die Welt* writes:

> Democratic Senator from Georgia Sam Nunn enjoys, despite his youthful age, the reputation of "elder statesman." If he, the NATO friend and versed expert in this matter, initiates a motion demanding the withdrawal of U.S. troops, and if the alliance partners will not do more for their own defense, all alarm bells should begin to ring in Europe. It is unimportant that his motion was rejected. Nunn wanted to create a new awareness. He achieved what he wanted. Both houses will deal with the matter in September.
>
> The United States is tired of hearing anti-American statements while at the same time helping to finance European defense with expenditures that increase its own debts. Nunn is frustrated by the indifference of Europeans, and particularly the Germans.
>
> The defense minister will be facing difficult hours. Now he must show strength and convince the chancellor and the cabinet that greater efforts are necessary. Those who know the United States also know that what is happening there now is only the beginning.[12]

The Federal Republic's defense minister, Manfred Worner, obviously did not take the advice of the *Die Welt* editors to heart. On a public relations visit to the United States shortly after the defeat of the Nunn Amendment, Worner lambasted the United States with standard defense free-rider rhetoric: "If you threaten us with a withdrawal of part of your troops, to whose benefit is that? The Soviet Union's. It is entirely the wrong signal to send the Soviets."[13] Worner also said U.S. critics of allied spending levels should drop the notion "that you are doing us a favor" by stationing U.S. troops and weapons in Europe. "We are also doing you a favor," he said. "The United States without Europe would lose the base of its world position, perhaps even the bases of its own freedom."[14] What Worner forgets is that while Western Europe may be America's first line of defense against a possible Soviet onslaught, it is Europe's last. The United States has the option to pull out of Europe; the Europeans do not.

Just as Senator Nunn's amendment should be taken as a serious warning to Europeans that America's tolerance of transatlantic inequities in defense burden-sharing is wearing thin, Mr. Worner's unrepentant free-rider response also should remind Americans that European resistance to increases in their defense spending are not to be underestimated. The European bag of threats and excuses is rich and varietal:

—We don't have the money;
—We already pay our fair share;
—The Soviets are not a threat, so why waste the money on defense;
—The Soviets are a threat, but the West is already spending exactly the right amount on defense;
—The low nuclear threshold is good because real deterrence against a Soviet invasion rests on threat of rapid nuclear escalation;
—If you pressure us to pay more, the Soviets will gain from the breach of transatlantic unity;
—If you don't do as we say, we won't let you defend us;
—If you don't do as we ask, we will be put out of office and our successors will be even worse;
—If we pay the money it will create anti-Americanism because it will be understood that we paid under American pressure;
—We may not pay what we should in financial terms, but there are heavy political and psychological burdens caused by the American troops stationed in Europe.

THE KISSINGER PLAN

Some months before the Nunn Amendment was voted on by the U.S. Senate, Henry Kissinger published an article in *Time* magazine advocating changes in the Western system of security similar to those proposed by Senator Nunn. Like Nunn, the former secretary of state is concerned that the low level of European spending on conventional forces has lowered the nuclear threshold to a dangerous point. He wants the Europeans to build up their conventional forces and, failing that, argues that the United States should redeploy up to half of its ground level forces in Europe over a five-year period. Dr. Kissinger writes:

If Europe by its own decision condemns itself to permanent conventional inferiority, we will have no choice but to opt for a deployment of U.S. forces in Europe that makes strategic and political sense. If nuclear weapons remain the ultimate deterrent to even conventional attack, a gradual withdrawal of a substantial portion, perhaps up to one-half, of our present ground forces would be a logical result.[15]

Increased European defense spending to build up their conventional forces reflects the basic thrust of the Kissinger proposals—the "de-Americanization" of European defense, of what he—and the Europeans—call "Europeanization." To this end, Kissinger suggests that tradition be countervened and a European be named as Supreme Allied Commander Europe (SACEUR). On the other hand, Kissinger argues that NATO's secretary-general, who is responsible for running the alliance's political machinery, be an American whereas in the past he has been a European. Finally, Dr. Kissinger advocates that

Europe should take over those arms-control negotiations that deal with weapons stationed on European soil. The INF negotiations with the Soviets (for intermediate range missiles) and the MBFR negotiations (for conventional forces) have heretofore been conducted by American delegations. Both of these negotiations should "Europeanize" as quickly as possible with a European chairman, an American deputy, and a mixed, though predominantly European, delegation.[16]

The problem with the Western Alliance, according to Dr. Kissinger, is its lopsided nature. "Existing arrangements are unbalanced," writes the former secretary of state.

When one country dominates the alliance on all major issues—when that one country chooses weapons and decides deployments, conducts the arms-control negotiations, sets the tone for East-West diplomacy, and creates the framework for relations with the Third World—little incentive remains for a serious joint effort to redefine the requirements of security or to coordinate foreign policies. Such joint efforts entail sacrifices and carry political costs. Leaders are not likely to make the sacrifice or pay the cost unless they feel responsible for the results.[17]

AMERICAN TROOPS AND FRENCH FREE-RIDING

The European country that has been most responsive to the "agonizing reappraisal" of U.S. troops in Europe is France. Though it is not widely understood in this country, French defense policy critically depends on the presence of U.S. troops in West Germany. Our troops serve two important functions for France: (1) for historical reasons, they reassure the French that the West German armed forces pose no threat to them, and (2) they serve as a tripwire for the American nuclear guarantee. Even though the French have their own independent national nuclear force (the *"force de frappe"*), its effectiveness depends largely on America's nuclear commitment to Europe.

That such a commitment to the defense of Western Europe is critical to the basic parameters of French defense and foreign policy was made clear in 1983 by France's then–foreign minister Claude Cheysson. Mr. Cheysson wrote in *The Wall Street Journal*:

> Despite major changes in the international scene over the past 34 years none of the reasons that made the Atlantic Alliance necessary have lost their value. As then, the peoples of Western Europe and those of North America are linked by the same concept of society, the same respect for man, his freedom, and his rights. As then, the future of the U.S. is irrevocably linked to that of European countries. As then, the European countries cannot by themselves secure the defense of their "space." As then, the presence in close proximity of powerful Warsaw Pact armies and the Soviet nuclear forces gives rise to a link of security across the Atlantic.[18]

It may strike some Americans as ironic that the French, whose devotion to the concept of national independence is second to none in Europe, should argue so forcefully for extensive American military intervention in Western Europe. The truth, however, is that French independence not only is consistent with America's special commitment to the defense of Europe, but critically depends upon it.

The French are great believers in the trip-wire strategy. So long as there have been sizable numbers of American troops in West Germany, France has felt sufficiently sure of the American nuclear commitment—and the stability of the Western security system— to pursue an "independent" (of the United States) foreign policy; to withdraw its troops from NATO's military command; and to play the Kremlin card for what it was worth—all the while hypocritically criticizing West Germany for not being "European" enough because of its close links to the United States. This is the essence of Charles de Gaulle's foreign policy. The irony of the "independence" de Gaulle gave France is that it critically depends on a properly functioning system of Western security. So long as this system remains intact, the French can free-ride on it to shape a "global role" for themselves. Notwithstanding the fact that they have withdrawn from NATO's military structure and forced NATO's SHAPE headquarters out of France, the French stake in a healthy NATO is enormous.

Senator Nunn's agonizing reappraisal of U.S. troops in Europe threatens to pull the rug out from under Gaullist "free-riding" strategy. Moreover, the French fear that growing neutralism in West Germany will strengthen the hand of NATO's enemies in the United States, who will be able to argue, more convincingly than ever, that those who are not willing to defend themselves are not worthy of American assistance. The result could be a U.S. troop withdrawal that would "decouple" the American nuclear arsenal from the defense of Europe. French President Mitterrand is doing his best to prevent this.

It should come as no surprise, then, that despite dire predictions of pundits that ideological differences would turn French-American relations sour in the 1980s, socialist François Mitterrand and capitalist Ronald Reagan see eye-to-eye on such bottom-line foreign policy issues as the dangers of European neutralism, the installation of American Pershing and cruise missiles in Western Europe (other than in France, of course), and the need for the West to adopt a tougher stance toward the Soviet Union. The current French president has not been as independent from the United States as were his more conservative predecessors, Georges Pompidou and Valéry Giscard d'Estaing, not because as a Socialist Mitterrand is more suspect, but because he perceived the Western security system, upon which France's global role critically depends, to be faltering.

The first initiative taken by President Mitterrand to rescue the West's security system was to personally intervene in the West German debate over the Pershing and cruise missiles and argue in favor of their acceptance. In January 1983 the French president asked for, and received, an invitation to address the German Parliament on the dangers of splitting the United States from the defense of Europe. According to John Vinocur's report in *The New York Times*,

> Mr. Mitterrand said in substance that the debate on deploying American medium-range missiles in Europe was less one of numbers than of political will, with the essential test for the Atlantic Alliance being its ability to stop an attempt to "decouple" the United States and Western Europe. Although he never used the word neutralism, Mr. Mitterrand attacked all those who would bet on decoupling and said they were the people who risked creating an imbalance of forces that would threaten peace. [19]

The French president agreed with the Kohl government of West Germany, and with President Reagan, that NATO's system of nuclear deterrence alone safeguarded peace, that it worked only when there was a nuclear balance, and that the balance had been upset in Europe by the numbers and quality of Soviet missiles.

THE EUROPEAN PILLAR

At the same time that François Mitterrand successfully used his influence to convince the Germans to accept the Pershing and cruise missiles, the French president, in close cooperation with his German counterpart, Chancellor Helmut Kohl, took a second initiative to strengthen what is being called the "European pillar" of the Western Alliance. "The 'European pillar,'" explains Chancellor Kohl, "refers to the image of a bridge which crosses the Atlantic and includes the United States and Canada. A bridge needs to be anchored at each end. It's up to us Europeans to ensure that it is anchored on this side of the Atlantic by closing ranks and becoming a full partner with the U.S."[20] What this means in plain English is that President Mitterrand and Chancellor Kohl are afraid that the United States may pull out of Europe, and want to reassure the

Americans that defending Europe is not a waste of U.S. taxpayers' money.

The institutional setting chosen to strengthen the European pillar of the alliance is the Western European Union (WEU), a thirty-year organization once intended to serve as a watchdog over West German rearmament. The choice of the WEU, dictated by the French, was both delicate and inspired. There is, of course, within NATO a Euro-group that was especially set up to look after European regional interests in defense policy. But as Kurt Becker wrote in *Die Zeit*, "France has no intention of joining the Euro-group. It doesn't want to give rise to the slightest suspicion that it might want, in however roundabout a manner, to rejoin NATO's military organization."[21] The European Economic Community, another likely candidate for European defense cooperation, also was ruled out by the French because of the presence in the EEC of Greece and Denmark. The leadership of both these countries could be expected to obstruct efforts to build up European defense. The Danes long ago narrowed their interest in defense to appeasement, while Greece, under its present viciously anti-American prime minister, Andreas Papandreou, has become the Trojan horse of the Western Alliance.

Since pursuit of European defense cooperation through "living" institutions proved inconvenient for one reason or another, the French decided to pursue it through one that was "dead." Back in the 1950s, when the ill-fated European Defense Community failed to get off the ground in 1954, the WEU was established as an interim step in a process of bringing West Germany and Italy into the North Atlantic Treaty Organization. Germany's renunciation of the manufacture, possession, and use of atomic, biological, and chemical weapons forms part of the WEU treaty, as did the Germans undertaking to limit their conventional armament and arms product and to permit verification on both counts as part of their WEU obligations. Though the WEU still exists—its members include Great Britain, the Netherlands, France, Italy, West Germany, Belgium, and Luxembourg—the organization has been moribund for many years as NATO took over all of its important functions. For the French, the WEU was the right institution at the right time and in the right place. It excluded those who needed exclusion, it is totally separate from NATO, and it is ad hoc.

In June 1984, seven foreign ministers of the WEU met to establish certain themes that would define the future activities of the group. Four themes were described as under discussion. They included a threat assessment relating to Europe, taking in its long-term military situation (including the development of weapons in space); analysis of crises in the Third World; strengthening transatlantic dialogue; and cooperation in the development of arms production. "Of all the four policy areas which the foreign ministers have identified for further study," writes *The Financial Times*,

> the most accessible to agreement (at least in principle) is that of armaments cooperation. All European governments face serious cost escalation in modern weaponry; none of them can afford to develop the most sophisticated systems on their own; all of them face domestic pressure to reduce dependence on nuclear weapons by strengthening conventional deterrence; and the high-tech systems which would fit this bill would be horrendously costly.[22]

The point of the armaments cooperation initiative is to reduce Europe's dependence on armaments manufactured in the United States.

A similar motive lies behind the French proposal for a "European space community," put forward by President Mitterrand in a speech before the EEC Council of Ministers at The Hague in February 1984. "For Europe to be capable of launching into space a manned station, enabling it to observe and transmit information and therefore counter any eventual threat, would be a major step towards its own defense," President Mitterrand argued. "A European 'space community' would, in my opinion, be the most appropriate answer to the military realities of the future."[23] What President Mitterrand failed to say is that the French nuclear force needs the help of aeronautical spying devices to make it effective and that, at present, the French are dependent on American spy satellites. A European space community would reduce, and perhaps eliminate, that dependency.

Replacing American spy satellites with European ones is but one factor behind France's enthusiasm for a European space community. The French are convinced that the development of high-tech industries is critical to the economic salvation of France—and the cream of the high-tech industries, in their view, is the defense industry. The growth of a European high-tech defense industry is desired, therefore, not only for reducing defense dependencies on the United States but for its spillover effect on nondefense industries and French economic growth in general. If this appears to some American observers as protection through subsidization, so be it. It is far healthier for Europe that it spend its public monies subsidizing its own defense and reducing its dependence on the United States than spending it on the usual gamut of nonproductive welfare-state programs.

The truth of the matter is that it is highly unlikely that Europe will make the necessary expenditures to develop high-tech conventional weapons unless European business and labor profits from it. Though the U.S. government taxes its citizens to provide defense goods that benefit the Europeans, European politicians are loath to reciprocate by taxing Europeans to make defense expenditures that give work to American workers and make profits for American capitalists. This may not be fair, but it is fact.

There may be insufficient economic incentive at present for Europeans to make the necessary expenditures on technologically sophisticated conventional weapons, given American dominance of the high-tech defense industry. Why spend European money, the argument goes, when Silicon Valley (California) or Cambridge (Massachusetts) gets all the profit? Put those defense profits and defense jobs into Hamburg (Germany), Toulon (France), Turin (Italy), or Manchester (England), on the other hand, and European attitudes toward defense spending may very well change. This is why the development of the Western European Union along the lines suggested by President Mitterrand is worthy of support. By putting more European profit and jobs into European defense, the WEU could strike a blow against Europe's anti-defense attitudes.

While a step in the right direction, Mitterrand's initiative to further Franco-German arms coordination and the development of a European-based, high-tech conventional arms industry are likely to satisfy neither Senator Nunn nor the U.S. Senate with respect to raising the nuclear threshold and burden-sharing in the alliance. For one, the proposals do not meet the senator's specific concerns about Allied understocking of ammunition and inadequate bunkers for U.S. aircraft positioned on European airfields. More important, Europeanization so far has been little more than words; what Mitterrand had done in fact is cut, not add to, France's conventional forces. In slighting conventional weapons and emphasizing nuclear deterrence, Mitterrand's defense policy closely resembles that of de Gaulle.

In a 1983 reorganization of the French military, for example, the army was cut from 312,000 to about 290,000 men. "Equipment rather than men" was the slogan used to justify the cuts. But, as reported by *The Economist*, the savings will mainly go to pay for France's nuclear forces rather than to any improvement in the army's nonnuclear equipment. The latter is reported to be distinctly ragged, particularly in France's huge reserve force. According to *The Economist*'s military correspondent, "There is no ground for optimism about the future of nonnuclear forces. After years of tight-fistedness, the army's budget got a boost in 1981 and 1982. But the 8.3 percent increase in 1983 outlays represented a cut in real terms, and real spending in 1984 will be no higher."[24]

THE SCHMIDT PROPOSAL

Not only are the French, under Mitterrand, less willing to increase their own conventional forces, but they also have shown themselves to be unwilling to allow West Germany to pay for a conventional arms buildup in both France and the Federal Republic in exchange for an extension of French nuclear deterrence to the Germans. This became apparent when the French refused to even discuss the far-reaching proposals of ex–West German Chancellor Helmut Schmidt for Franco-German military cooperation.

With the mantle of state and party leadership removed from his shoulders, Helmut Schmidt obviously feels freer to express his own views and opinions on world matters. In an article written for *The New York Review of Books*, Schmidt reveals himself to be a member of the "dependency corrupts" school of thought. "Dependency corrupts," writes Schmidt, "and corrupts not only the dependent partners but also the oversized partner who is making decisions almost single-handedly."[25]

According to Schmidt, Europe needs an amplified voice in the alliance. And this requires closer cooperation between France and Germany. "Europe's further evolution depends in the first place on trust and cooperation between the French and the Germans," writes Schmidt.

Unless both the political and military quantity of this cooperation is improved, an autonomous "European pillar" of the Atlantic Alliance (as Kennedy puts it) is hardly conceivable. Together, Paris and Bonn hold in their hands the design for that pillar. Valéry Giscard and I had it in mind to establish a considerably closer link between, on the one hand, France's nuclear power and its conventional army and, on the other, conventional German military forces and German economic power. This goal today is a task for Mitterrand and Kohl. By comparison with that mission, the settlement of squabbles over EC budgets and contributions to the Common Market's farm pool are routine problems which every couple of years have to be tackled anew.[26]

Two reasons explain why Schmidt and Giscard left the thorny task of Franco-German military cooperation to their respective successors. First, during the 1970s when the two were in power, German neutralism was not the problem it is today. Second, during that same period, confirmed American atlanticists like Senator Nunn and Henry Kissinger were not advocating U.S. troop withdrawals from Europe unless the Europeans made more of the contribution to raising the nuclear threshold. Now that he is out of power, however, Schmidt admits that "most of the European governments rely much too much on American nuclear weapons, and that most of them neglect their own conventional defense...[and] both the United States and the Europeans now put an unsuitably high value on nuclear deterrence." He also admits the probability that "a new American generation, inexperienced in international affairs, could react to a continuation of European neglect by withdrawing a considerable part of the American military forces from Europe."[27] (Parenthetically, does Schmidt here really mean "inexperienced in international affairs," or does he mean a new American generation whose experience in international affairs has made it less concerned with Europe and more with other parts of the world?)

In any case, what Schmidt does see clearly is that a better balance of conventional forces is required in Europe if the old continent is to avoid being abandoned by the United States. Schmidt writes:

It isn't necessary to be able to place in the field a West German soldier for every Soviet soldier. The defender can make do with a certain numerical inferiority. But an improved military equilibrium in fact requires that the military equipment of the French reserve troops be improved. It also requires more British reserve forces. . . . We need a strengthening of the conventionally usable German air force, and more conventional munitions for the German army. Under such qualitatively and quantitatively improved conditions, a partial withdrawal of American troops would, by the way, not necessarily be a misfortune: the Europeans would be playing a role of their own.[28]

Less than a month after *The New York Review of Books* article appeared and one week after the U.S. Senate narrowly defeated the Nunn Amendment, Schmidt made a truly remarkable speech before the German Parliament urging that France and West Germany undertake a "major security initiative" to effectively merge their armed forces and sharply curtail Western Europe's military dependence on the United States.[29] Schmidt also suggested that France swallow its national misgivings "to extend the tasks of its autonomous nuclear force to include the protection of Germany." So imaginative were the proposals of the politician-out-of-power that one French critic wondered out loud: "Could the exercise of power and the exercise of imagination be incompatible?"[30]

Delivering his appeal during a parliamentary debate over the European summit in Fontainebleau in June 1984, Schmidt said France and Germany could, by mobilizing reserves, field thirty divisions that would be "sufficient to defend the western part of Europe and deter any attack." While acknowledging that Europe would still need the American nuclear umbrella, Schmidt said "the upgraded presence of 30 French and West German divisions would be the most practical way for Europe to assume greater control over its own defense and permit a considerable reduction in American army units."

The former chancellor said it would take up to five years to equip the divisions with enough weapons and munitions to form a credible deterrent against possible attack by the Soviet Union and its Warsaw Pact allies, and Schmidt suggested that much of the expense probably should be borne by the Bonn government. He said that if France would extend its nuclear shield to protect Germany, then Germany "would have to put its capital and financial strength into the other parts of the program."

One advantage of his plan, according to the former chancellor, is that it would raise the nuclear threshold. The emphasis on defending Europe with improved French and German armies and diminished U.S. help would mean "the nuclear threshold really would be raised and that nuclear war in Europe would be made less likely." Another sanguine repercussion of the plan, he claimed, could be the revival of strong public support for defense spending once Europe seized the initiative and took greater control of its own security. "If Paris and Bonn should decide on such reforms," Schmidt said, "35 years after the founding of NATO, the opinion polls show that two-thirds of the public in France would react positively and about three-quarters of the German people would be in favor."

Now, if President Mitterrand's interest in constructing a European pillar of the alliance was sincere, Paris should have given the Schmidt proposals the serious consideration they obviously deserved. "At first glance, the proposals have a lot to offer to France," notes international relations expert Dominique Moisi:

> At a time when West Germany and France are engaged in a joint effort to reactivate the military dimension of their collaboration, Mr. Schmidt's ideas are a leap toward a European defense for Europe. They acknowledge the possibility for France to play a world role as leader in a French-German tandem. They express evident skepticism as to the future credibility of the U.S. guarantee for Europe. Last but not least, they very specifically exclude the possibility of the Federal Republic having even indirect access to nuclear weapons, through a veto right or a dual key to the French nuclear arsenal. The recognition of France's world role, the diffidence vis-à-vis the United States, and the maintenance of the non-nuclear status of the Federal Republic should satisfy France's Gaullist tradition.[31]

There is, however, another Gaullist tradition in France, called "tactical maneuver," in which the late French president excelled. The initial French interest in the European Defense Community in the early 1950s was a tactical maneuver to postpone German rearmament as long as possible. One suspects that present French interest in building up the European pillar of the alliance also is a tactical maneuver to postpone the withdrawal of American troops from Europe as long as possible. If this is indeed the case, the proposals of Schmidt undoubtedly constituted an embarrassment to the Mitterrand government, if only because they were a serious attempt to come to terms with a problem the French apparently are not quite ready to come to terms with. Stony silence is an apt description of how the French government reacted to the Schmidt proposals. It neither embraced them nor attacked them. It simply ignored them.

THE FRENCH REVISIONISM

Though the basics of official French defense policy have changed very little under Socialist Mitterrand—faith in the deterrent value of the *force de frappe* backed up by American-based, long-range ICBM missiles; a refusal to build up France's meager conventional forces; and a profound skepticism of military cooperation with West Germany—there is a new revisionism gaining credibility in France that threatens the entire Gaullist defense edifice. This new French revisionism has a most unlikely spokesman in Yves Montand, the popular French actor and chansonnier. For decades, Montand was an outspoken and influential Communist fellow traveler. Today he remains as outspoken, influential, and popular as ever, but instead of flacking for the Communists and the Soviet Union, he now opposes them with the same passion he brings to his famous songs.

In April 1985, Montand narrated a feature film on French television which portrayed a Russian invasion of Western Europe by conventional forces only. The action in the film begins at 3 A.M. on June 12, 1985. Russian tanks invade West Germany and—meeting no resistance—in one day are at Bremen, the next day in the Ruhr, and during the night between the fifteenth and sixteenth of July, they enter France near Sedan. Montand asks the following question of his audience: "With the Soviets at the doors of Paris, what could the French president do?" Dare he risk what Albert Wohlstetter refers to as "the dying sting"—putting the *force de frappe* into action, with the virtual certainty of a fearful nuclear response by the Soviet Union? Or does he instead open the doors of Paris to the tanks coming from the East?

Montand's film, *Facing War*, had a simple message: Europe, thanks to a long period of peace, lives in the mistaken conviction that war no longer is possible. It believes that nuclear deterrence—mutual assured destruction—is sufficient to guarantee peace. It has lost the notion of its own danger and, faced with an invasion by conventional means and incapacitated by fear, it would be unable to decide what to do.

Because Montand believes that a conventional invasion of Western Europe is more credible today than in the past, he argues that a re-evaluation of France's emphasis on nuclear weapons to the detriment of its conventional forces is necessary. If President Reagan's Strategic Defense Initiative is put into effect by the United States, France, with an essentially useless *force de frappe*, will find itself more isolated than ever. Montand further argues for more intensive military cooperation between the European countries: a common defense strategy that will make Europe more solid, more strong, more united, and better armed—the third global superpower. The Soviets were so outraged by the Montand television spectacular that, for the first time in history, they formally protested a television program to the French foreign office.[32]

While Yves Montand has become the spokesman for the new French revisionists, the originator of many of the ideas contained in the television program is Étienne Copel, former chief of the French air force and author of the 1984 French best-seller *Winning the War*. In his book, General Copel puts forward the thesis contained in Montand's television film: that the danger of a conventional attack of Western Europe is growing, that the best deterrent is not nuclear weapons but strong conventional forces, and that French military cooperation with West Germany is necessary. Indeed, General Copel favors cooperation with the Germans to the point where he would be willing to send West Germany neutron bombs should the Federal Republic be attacked. "I do believe," said Copel, "that at the request of the German chancellor, we French could send neutron bombs to them to halt an attack on German territory." In addition, the French general favors development of a rapid deployment force by France because "it will allow us, in case of an attack at any place in Germany, to send in reinforcements fast."[33]

The new French revisionists challenge Gaullist defense orthodoxy on a number of critical points. First, the revisionists emphasize conventional weapons, while the Gaullists favor nuclear weapons. Second, the revisionists champion a European approach to defense by comparison with the France-only approach of the Gaullists. The most fundamental challenge levied at the Gaullist establishment by the revisionists, however, is the definition of the enemy. French revisionists are sufficiently anti-Soviet to have been called "Reagan's mouthpiece" in France. Gaullists, on the other hand, always have been confused as to who France's real enemy is. According to Jean-François Revel, "hatred of the United States," under de Gaulle, "became stronger than fear of control by the Soviet Union." In his book *How Democracies Perish*, Revel scores points when he criticizes de Gaulle's "odd foreign policy that consisted mainly of fighting his own allies instead of combating the common exterior danger the Alliance was formed to guard against."[34]

CAN A EUROPEAN DEFENSE WORK?

The new revisionists in France, former Chancellor Helmut Schmidt of West Germany, and others argue for a more intensive military cooperation between France and Germany to increase the military security of Western Europe. An important question raised by this line of argumentation is whether such cooperation is possible so long as American troops remain in Europe.

Zbigniew Brzezinski, President Carter's national security adviser, thinks the American troops in Europe constitute a serious obstacle to the emergence of the autonomous European defense entity he favors. "Europe must be prodded if it is to move in the direction of increased military cooperation," says the former national security adviser.

> Left as it is, Europe's cultural hedonism and political complacency will ensure that not much is done. Even the modest 1978 NATO commitment to a three percent per annum increase in defense expenditures was not honored by most European states. America should, therefore, initiate a longer-term process to alter the nature of its military presence in Europe gradually, while making it clear to the Europeans that the change is not an act of anger or a threat... but rather the product of a deliberate strategy designed to promote Europe's unity and its historic restoration.[35]

Brzezinski thus adds his voice to the growing chorus of experts calling for the withdrawal of American troops from Europe.

Brzezinski is undoubtedly correct that without the catalyst of an American troop pullout, European military cooperation is likely to remain but another entry on the long list of European "cooperative efforts" that fail to materialize. The reality of Europe, after all, is division, not unity: The European peoples are divided by different cultures, different languages, different religions, and different economic interests. Moreover, historical antagonisms have separated one country from the other. The French and the English have traditions of animosity going back hundreds of years. The same can be said for the French and the Germans. The Italians and Germans do not always get along with one another either. And the Belgians can't even get along with themselves. Only the ignorant would deny the dissonance and discord that has existed between the Europeans in the past, and undoubtedly will continue to exist in the future as well.

Can it be said, then, that the nations of Europe are so hopelessly divided that they cannot make common cause with one another under any circumstances? Of course not! Those who preach the lessons of history should remember that mutual distrust between France and Great Britain did not prevent the two nations from joining forces to defeat the Kaiser in World War I and Hitler in World War II. Nor did mutual national antagonism prevent the Germans and Russians from joining forces to defeat Napoleon, and so on. By themselves, national differences and traditional antagonisms are bad predictors of how disparate and desperate nations will behave in any given situation. If history does have a message for us, it is that despite differences and antagonisms, the European nations can come together when there is a common interest to do so. The coalescing force in European politics most often has been the existence of a common enemy.

Since the Soviets are the common enemy today, the question arises as to why the European countries remain disunited. The answer is that Europe's gross defense dependence on the United States has voided the common danger that, in the absence of America's defense commitment to Europe, could unite the separate European nations in common cause against the Soviets. Unwisely, the United States has pacified Europe to outside threats and thus removed the potentially congealing element from European politics.

Should that pacification be discontinued, however, the political unification feared by the Kremlin, and hoped for by the United States, could come about.

The argument that Europe's severe defense dependence on the United States is responsible for European political disarray is exactly the opposite of what the defenders of the status quo in NATO believe. Their position is that American troops in Europe have pulled the Europeans together, not pushed them apart. Former Secretary of State Dean Rusk, for example, was quoted as saying in 1967 that "the presence of our forces in Europe under NATO has also contributed to the development of intra-European cooperation.... Without the visible assurance of a sizable American contingent, old frictions may revive and Europe could become unstable once more."[36] In 1984 the idea of America as pacifying Europe's *internal* tensions and antagonisms was resurrected by West German journalist Josef Joffe, who argues for the continued presence of U.S. troops in Europe on the grounds that "the postwar West European system has not only been stable, but ultra-stable. While some hundred wars and civil wars have battered the rest of the world, Western Europe has remained a solitary island of peace. ... NATO's detractors ignore the central role America has played in pacifying a state system that almost consumed itself in two world wars."[37]

At the very time Joffe published his article "Europe's American Pacifier," extolling "cooperation between ancient regimes as having become routine within the expanding framework of the European Community," this same community was coming within a hairbreadth of total collapse because of a vicious squabble over contributions to the EEC budget and farm subsidies. Thus, his argument that U.S. troops in Europe have proved a congealing force must be looked at with considerable misgiving.

Here's what European "cooperation" looked like in the spring of 1984 when Joffe published his article. After the Athens summit of European leaders failed, in December 1983, to resolve British complaints that it was paying more than its fair share to Common Market budgets, Prime Minister Andreas Papandreou of Greece, who was chairman of the meeting, said the heads of government could not agree on anything despite six months of preparatory work. *"We were not able to reach a unanimous position on a single issue."*[38]

(Emphasis added.) President Mitterrand predicted that "Europe will become nothing more than an unfinished construction site" if the dispute continued.[39] He also spoke of the possibility of a "two-speed Europe" or a "Europe with variable geometry," expressions which have come to mean accepting a division between those Common Market countries that want to move toward more political cooperation and those—like Britain or Denmark—that have considerable reservations about increasing the community's powers.[40] Here was the Common Market on the verge of breaking up, and Joffe whistles in the dark about today's Europe being "ultra-stable" simply because the European countries have not as yet gone to war with one another.

While the French president was putting Britain and Denmark in the same boat, Denmark's Prime Minister Paul Schluter wanted no part of Margaret Thatcher. He attacked the British prime minister for being "un-European" and unwilling to compromise.[41] Thatcher, for her part, described other European leaders as "ostriches" for not realizing the need for changes in the Common Agricultural Policy, and claimed Britain was "the only member truly concerned about the Common Market's long-term future."[42] After the second attempt to resolve the budgetary dispute ended in failure in March 1984, President Mitterrand said, "The Europe of Ten is not dead, but it has received another wound, and the more wounds it gets, the worse its health becomes."[43] Chancellor Kohl described the entire Brussels meeting as a "regrettable and depressing experience."[44]

Though the dispute finally was settled at the Fontainebleau summit of June 1984, six months of failure had left deep scars. To many, the dispute over Britain's demand for a $1.3 billion rebate seemed petty. Indeed, the Brussels summit broke up with only a few hundred million dollars separating the parties. Yet, it was precisely that Europe could come that close to the brink over such relatively small sums of money that proved so disturbing to those who would like Europe to be more than a congeries of nation-states. One such person is Flora Lewis, who writes in *The New York Times*:

> There is no longer a single European leader who can speak to, or for, more than his own country, see beyond the national borders. This is the late President Charles de Gaulle's "Europe des Patries."

It is based on nations, all right, but it has lost the way to being Europe. Without bold new political action, a noble historical experiment will fade away.[45]

The bold new political action that can save the "noble historical experiment" is for Europe to eliminate its defense dependence on the United States. It is only by facing up to such "big problems" as the independence of European defense—and the independence of European foreign policy—that Europe can avoid being condemned to an infinite horizon of "petty quarreling," to quote the term President Mitterrand used to describe the recent Common Market disputes. "Mr. Mitterand is right that the European community needs a new heave to get itself out of the rut of 'petty quarreling,'" wrote *The Times* of London. "It needs a new sense of purpose to enable it to grapple with the much larger problems facing it, particularly in matters relating to defense. It is absurd that Europe should be as dependent as it is on American protection and American weapons."[46]

8

Ill Fares the Welfare State

Western Europe not only is dependent on the United States only for its defense and national security; it also is dependent for its massive welfare state. Indeed, the two dependencies are closely related. When the U.S. government declared it would defend Europe no matter what, it gave the Europeans a blank check which they made out to their own welfare state, not European defense.

Table 8.1 documents the changes that took place in European public expenditure between 1955–57 and 1974–76. In the Organization of Economic Cooperation and Development (OECD) countries of Europe, for example, nondefense government consumption rose 4.2 percentage points of gross domestic product (GDP). Government spending on education, health, housing, roads, etc., is defined as nondefense public consumption. Transfer payments are a separate item; they were the fastest growing item of public expenditure during this period, rising 8.5 percentage points of GDP. If transfers are added to government consumption, their sum is welfare-state expenditure. This increased by an enormous 12.7 percentage points of GDP, while OECD Europe defense spending

137

actually *decreased* by eight-tenths of 1 percentage point of GDP between 1955–57 and 1974–76. Thus as Europe's welfare-state expenditures soared during this twenty-year period, Europe's defense spending languished. The reason is the U.S. nuclear shield.

TABLE 8.1   *Changes in Major Components of European Public Expenditure, 1955–57 to 1974–76 (percentage points of GDP at current prices)*

| | GOVERNMENT CONSUMPTION | | TRANSFERS TO | | INTEREST ON PUBLIC | GROSS |
	TOTAL	DEFENSE	TOTAL	HOUSEHOLDS	DEBT	INVESTMENT
France	0.3	−2.1	6.9	6.7	−0.1	1.4
Germany	7.8	0.2	4.4	3.4	0.7	1.2
Italy	1.8	−0.5	10.6	9.7	2.0	0.4
United Kingdom	4.9	−2.4	6.8	5.2	0.4	1.3
OECD Europe	5.0	−0.8	8.5	7.4	0.6	(1.1)

Source: OECD, *Public Expenditure Trends* (Paris, 1978).

To many persons in the United States, particularly those of a leftist persuasion, the building up of Europe's welfare states has not been an evil thing. They see the welfare state as taming a corruptible capitalism at home and as a bulwark against communism abroad. Indeed, the idea of the welfare state being "the middle road" between capitalism and communism has been fashionable among anti-Communist leftists since at least the end of World War II. The eminent philosopher Sidney Hook, whose understanding of—and hostility to—communism stands second to none, likes to quote the statement attributed to Lenin that capitalists would sell the Communists the rope with which they would do the West in. This is undoubtedly true: Stricter controls over East-West trade in capitalist countries most definitely are in order (see below). But what Professor Hook and other distinguished Social Democrats fail to realize is that the welfare state also would sell Communists the rope, but would sell it to them at a subsidized price. The idea of combining welfare statism at home with anticommunism abroad has proved to be a grand illusion.

EUROPE'S MALAISE AND THE WELFARE STATE

The welfare state was viewed by its architects as a mechanism for combining growth with social justice. While the private economy provided the economic growth, the government was to provide social justice in the form of increased public health, public housing, public education, and other social welfare goods. After a successful start in the 1950s, cracks in the wall began to appear as the growth of social-welfare spending, and the ever-increasing tax bill that went with it, proved difficult to contain. The more these economies spent for social welfare goods, the greater the demand to create even more social spending, and so on. Moreover, the character of the welfare state was undergoing metamorphosis during the 1960s and 1970s. Instead of the mere provision of such social goods as public roads, housing, and health, egalitarian concerns began to strongly influence welfare-state taxation and labor market policies. The result was an increasingly distressed economy whose growth could not keep up with the demands made on it for social welfare goods.

TABLE 8.2   *Average Annual Growth Rates of Real Gross Domestic Product: Selected Industrial Countries (in percentages)*

COUNTRY	1960–70	1970–80
United States	4.3	3.0
United Kingdom	2.9	1.9
Japan	10.9	5.0
France	5.5	3.5
West Germany	4.4	2.6
Sweden	4.4	1.7

*Source:*World Bank, *World Development Report* (Washington, D.C.: 1982).

Three factors, in particular, can explain the malaise presently affecting Europe's welfare state. First, the 1970s was the decade of egalitarian policies. The failure to produce a new "social solidaric" citizen in the welfare state has meant that egalitarian policies have had counterproductive results. Second, the trend toward extending political rights into the economic arena has damaged the economic

growth of the welfare economies. Finally, the extraordinary increase
in the 1970s of the "wage gap"—the difference between what business firms pay for labor and what monies workers actually receive
—has resulted in a reallocation of the welfare economy's labor resources from the more productive private sector to the less productive public domain.

The essential failure of the European welfare state has been its
inability to produce a new social solidaric citizen—insensitive to
individual economic incentives. The most convincing evidence of
this is the extraordinary growth of the "underground," or "black
market," economy. If the welfare-state citizens were really social
solidaric, they would not run to the underground economy to evade
high taxes and egalitarian policies; rather, they would gladly submit
to them.

The welfare state's failure to desensitize its citizens to individual
economic incentives—at a time when social democratic regimes
have ruthlessly pushed through their egalitarian policies—has had
two major consequences: (1) the economic base of the welfare society
has been badly damaged, and (2) the welfare state has become
demoralized.

So far as the economic base is concerned, the result of a tax-
subsidy structure that attempts to equalize net incomes (after taxes
are taken out and subsidies added to earned incomes) and a solidaric
wage policy that equalizes the wages for skilled and nonskilled
workers, has been that citizens work less, they make otherwise
irrational investment decisions, they switch labor from high-
productivity to low-productivity uses by do-it-yourself, they fail
to develop skills, and they use tax-evading barter instead of more
efficient methods of exchange. Naturally, the consequences of these
measures have dampened the economic growth of the welfare economy upon which all social spending ultimately must depend.

Egalitarianism is preached, but not practiced, in the welfare state.
The hypocrisy of the welfare state leadership would be greatly
reduced if policies were adjusted to the true character and needs
of the people, rather than attempting to adjust the people to the
policies. Like the Communists in Russia and China, and the Nazis
in Germany, Social Democrats in Northern Europe have tried to
create a new man and failed. The sooner the Social Democrats

come to terms with this fundamental truth, the faster the crisis in the welfare state will be resolved.

Another factor responsible for the European welfare-state crisis is the extension of political rights into the economic arena. Citizens of those states today believe they have a right not only to freedom of speech, press, and assembly, but also to a job—(1) in the industry of their choice, (2) at the geographic location of their choice, and (3) at an income that permits politically determined minimum consumption standards. Equal political and economic rights go hand in hand in the welfare states of Northern Europe.

To secure citizens their "economic rights," government often must subsidize both labor and capital in low-productivity uses. Workers believe they have a right to particular employments even if these jobs are not economically viable without subsidization. Subsidies to inefficient private firms constituted an increasing portion of public expenditure in the welfare state during the 1970s. Such subsidies negate the ability of the marketplace to allocate resources efficiently. One cost of workers' "rights," therefore, is an inefficient allocation of resources.

Of course, once workers realize that government will guarantee their jobs by subsidy, all incentives to increase productivity and restrain wage demands go by the board. The willingness of government to save jobs *creates* the need for it to do so. Governments can tie all the productivity and wage restrictions they want to their bailout packages—workers and management will flout these restrictions so long as they know that government will relent once the crunch comes. The destructive dynamic of job subsidization has helped undermine the economic base of the welfare economy.

If there were no taxes and social security charges, the wage received by the worker—for his own consumption and savings—would be equal to the cost of the wage to the firm employing the worker. But firms must pay social security charges and payroll taxes on workers' services. These create a gap between the disposable wage which workers receive and the cost of that disposable wage to the firm. This gap is called the "wage gap," also known as the "Laffer wedge."

The wage gap is not limited to social security charges and payroll taxes; income taxes and sales taxes also are involved. Although workers are legally responsible for their personal income taxes, the economic burden of the income tax increasingly has been shifted onto the firm because powerful trade unions in the welfare state have been able to bargain for net-of-tax wages. The result has been that labor has been made artificially expensive for the firm. The wage gap in the European welfare states is extraordinarily high. Precise measurements are not available, but some imprecise ones performed in Sweden by the Swedish Employers Confederation give a clue as to the possible extent of this gap in the welfare state.[1]

In 1987 it was estimated that the marginal hourly disposable wage (net of taxes) for a white-collar worker in Sweden was 14 Swedish crowns per hour. The cost of this 14-Swedish-crown-wage *to the firm* was estimated at 68 Swedish crowns per hour. The difference—the wage gap of 54 crowns—went to the government in the form of taxes of one sort or another. What this extraordinary statistic means is that Swedish firms must pay 5 crowns to a Swedish worker to increase his or her disposable income by a mere 1 crown. No wonder the black market for labor services to evade taxes flourishes in the welfare state!

The substantial increase in welfare-state taxes during the 1970s has meant a substantial increase in the wage gap. This has affected the economy in essentially two ways: by an "income transfer effect" and by an "incentive effect."

The increase in the wage gap in the 1970s promoted an income transfer from business profits to government. Because of the different ways the funds are used—by private business firms on the one hand and the government on the other—the income transfer effect has slowed the growth of both private investment and labor productivity in the past decade. Instead of being used to enhance labor productivity, business profits have gone to government, where they have been spent on day-care centers and subsidies to inefficient firms. An important reason for the economic problems of the European welfare state therefore has been that funds that should have been used for private investment to enhance labor productivity have gone instead for public consumption and programs that subsidize labor in low-productivity uses.

The increase in the wage gap also has an incentive effect, making labor services artificially expensive to business firms. This has negatively affected overall productivity in the economy by reducing the demand for labor in the private sector. Given the government's full-employment commitment, however, the displaced workers must be given government jobs even though government often has no useful work for these people to do. Unemployment is hidden in the welfare state. But hiding unemployment does not make it cost-less; it simply changes the form in which the costs of unemployment manifest themselves. Instead of idle workers at home, there are useless workers on the job.

A final factor behind Europe's economic malaise in the 1970s was increased economic rigidity caused by welfare state programs that reduce the flexibility of the economy. In a sense, the economy is like the human body. Both are subjected to periodic external shocks, and both can experience breakdowns as a result of these shocks if their internal adjustment mechanisms are not functioning properly. Social policies that discourage labor mobility, subsidize inefficient firms, equalize wages for skilled and nonskilled workers, etc., inhibit the economy's internal adjustment mechanisms.

The costs of "rigor mortis ockonomikus" often are not apparent until there is an external shock to the economy. Then, instead of taking the shock in stride, the economy simply keels over like an old man who is punched in the stomach. During the 1970s, the "punch" the oil-consuming nations had to absorb was a dramatic increase in the price of oil. The response of three different countries, or groups of countries, to the oil shock can be compared: the welfare states of Northern Europe, the United States, and the economies of the Pacific Basin region—Taiwan, Singapore, South Korea, etc.

Of the three, the economies that did least well were those of Northern Europe. Indeed, the European welfare states have yet to get over the oil shock. The United States did better than the North-ern Europeans because its economy is less welfare-oriented, thus more flexible. The countries that did best, however, were those of the Pacific Basin region. Judging by growth rates of exports and economic productivity, the Pacific economies—which import all their oil but lack extensive welfare programs to rigidify their econ-omies—barely seem to have noticed the oil shock. This line of reasoning suggests that it was not the oil shock *per se* that con-tributed to Europe's economic malaise, but Europe's inability to adjust to it.

THE ANTI-DEFENSE STATE

Europe's welfare state, though bad for Western Europe, has been extremely good for the Soviet Union. By slowing down Europe's rate of economic growth, the welfare state has restrained U.S. allies from spending more on their national defense. To demonstrate the relation between slower growth and defense spending, the case of Sweden is instructive. Sweden is an example of a welfare state *par excellence*. It also is a non–NATO country that allocates a good amount of its resources to defense. Between 1950 and 1969, for example, the Swedes spent between a low of 4.3 percent to a high of 5.7 percent of their gross national product on defense. The average through 1966 was well over 5 percent. During this period, Sweden spent more on defense on a per-capita basis than all other countries in the world except Israel, the United States, and the U.S.S.R. on a per-capita basis.[2]

Slower growth in the 1970s, however, has forced Sweden to cut into its defense expenditures. When Sweden's economic growth rate dramatically fell from an average annual real rate of 4.4 percent in the 1960s to 1.7 percent in the 1970s, the country's defense spending as a share of gross national product dropped from the high 4 percent level to just below 4 percent.[3] Correlation does not prove cause and effect, of course, but when asked to explain the reason for the decline in defense spending, Swedish officials invariably point to the poor economy.[4]

Not only has slow growth reduced the resources available for defense, but it has created a welfare constituency that is hostile to defense spending. The headlines of a recent issue of *This Week in Germany* read: "Union Institute Says Military Spending Harms Social Welfare." The Dusseldorf-based Economic and Social Science Institute of the Federation of German Trade Unions brought attention to the fact that West Germany's 1984 budget called for a 3.2 percent hike in defense expenditures. "The labor group perceives a causal relation between this expansion of military costs and the recent curtailment of social welfare expenditures."[5] Welfare institutions see defense spending as reducing the welfare budget on a dollar-for-dollar basis whereas if growth produced new dollars to spend, welfare budgets would not have to be reduced to accommodate an arms buildup. Slow growth, in other words, has made defense spending more competitive with welfare spending than it need be. Though it was not planned that way, the welfare state has become the "anti-defense" state.

The competitiveness of defense spending with welfare spending induced by slow growth is an important factor behind Europe's intense interest in arms control negotiations with the Soviet Union. Increasingly, arms control negotiations are seen as weapons to save social welfare programs. Without arms control agreements, the fear in Europe is that defense spending will have to increase. This raises serious questions about the national security implications of slow growth: Slow growth puts inordinate pressure on welfare economies to reach arms control agreements with the enemy to avoid domestic welfare cuts *regardless of the national security implications of such potential agreements*. Moreover, this pressure is asymmetrical as between Western democracies and the Soviets, who, though they have worse growth problems than the United States, do not face the pressure from welfare or consumer constituencies to reach arms limitation pacts. The argument that the capitalistic economies can win the arms race because of their better growth potential is true but probably irrelevant. The omnipresent welfare state will not let the capitalistic economies win.

The welfare state also has important implications for the low nuclear threshold in Europe. The American nuclear guarantee created the low nuclear threshold by permitting the Europeans to build up their welfare states instead of their conventional forces. In a very real sense, NATO created Soviet conventional force superiority in Europe. The Europeans know that if the Soviets were to use conventional forces to invade Western Europe, the doomsday decision of whether to push the nuclear button or surrender would have to be made in a very short period of time, perhaps within seventy-two hours of an invasion. If they wanted, U.S. allies could buy more time for themselves—they could increase the nuclear threshold by adding to their conventional strength. But apparently Europeans prefer to live with a low nuclear threshold than give up part of their welfare state to finance the increase in military spending that reducing the nuclear threshold requires. It is ironic that those who accused the United States of increasing the threat of nuclear war for trying to put the Pershing and cruise missiles in Europe are the very same people who refuse to relinquish some of their social welfare programs to raise the nuclear threshold and reduce the nuclear threat!

So great is European resistance to scaling down the welfare state that even the promise of ridding the world of nuclear weapons is opposed because they would then have to increase their defense expenditure on conventional weapons. For example, the Europeans oppose President Reagan's Strategic Defense Initiative because neutralizing the importance of nuclear weapons implied by strategic defense would magnify the importance of Soviet conventional superiority in Europe. According to *The New York Times*, "Should a reliable shield be developed against nuclear missiles, European officials fear a conventional war might become more likely, setting off a conventional arms race and subjecting Europe to the risk of devastation by conventional arms."[6] Perhaps it is true that strategic defense could set off a conventional arms race, but what the Europeans really fear is not devastation by conventional war but the expense of building up their conventional forces *to deter* such devastation. The evidence builds that Europeans fear reducing their welfare states more than they fear nuclear weapons.

THE SIBERIAN NATURAL-GAS PIPELINE

One of the many effects of slow economic growth is to put disproportionate pressure on particular sectors of the private economy. The capital goods industry, for example, was very hard hit by the economic malaise of the 1970s. As noted above, it is quite common for these battered industries to receive help from government. Sometimes this help can be of enormous benefit not only to the recipient industry, but to third parties as well. Unfortunately, the Soviet Union often has been the third party who has benefited greatly from such welfare-state subsidization programs.

The most notorious case where this occurred was the Siberian natural-gas pipeline. The basic international economic transaction involved in the pipeline deal was that Europe imported natural gas from the Soviet Union, and in return exported pipeline, compressors, turbines, and valves to the Soviets. Gordon Crovitz, former

Wall Street Journal European editorial page editor, pointed out at the time:

> The Germans have been in the forefront of the pipeline project. A consortium led by Deutsche Bank AG provided one-third of the project's long-term credits. Much of this went to pay for the pipe and compressor stations sold by Mannesmann AG. These loans are supposed to be repaid from the proceeds of gas sales by Ruhrgas, a German and U.S.–owned supplier that will buy 30% of the gas from the pipeline. This sort of agreement is old hat to the Germans, who have conducted several such "gas for pipe" deals since the early 1970s.[7]

It is important to realize that the pipeline deal never would have gone through had it not been for the subsidy element. The Soviets are a high-cost supplier of natural gas; other, cheaper sources of energy were available to the West Europeans. To make it profitable for the Soviets to export their gas, the West German government had to subsidize capital equipment to the Soviets through a complicated financial scheme. German banks lent more than $1 billion to the pipe manufacturers. Hermes Credit Insurance Company, an arm of the West German government, guaranteed these loans, thus making the real interest rate fall well below the market rate. The German manufacturers, in turn, lent money to the Soviet Union to buy the equipment, charging only 7.8 percent when the market rate for West Germans at the time was 11.5 percent.[8] According to a Dutch Economics Ministry estimate, each percentage point of subsidized interest was worth nearly 5 percent of a contract's value.[9] Apparently even these subsidies were not enough for the inefficient Soviets. There is widespread evidence the Soviets used forced labor to build the pipeline.[10] Thus, subsidies on both labor and capital were required to make it profitable for the Soviets to export natural gas at prices that covered their cost of production. The West German taxpayers provided the capital equipment subsidies, the Soviet "slaves" provided the labor subsidy.

The West German government was by no means the only West European government to subsidize the pipeline deal. Indeed, one reason the Germans agreed to the 7.8 percent rate was to compete with the French, who secretly offered the Soviets this extremely favorable rate to get their business even though French domestic rates were at 16 percent at the time and the OECD rate for the Soviet Union was at 11 percent.[11] The sluggish domestic economies of the European nations apparently made the vast Soviet market even more attractive to the Europeans than ordinarily would have been the case.

Why did the West European governments, in contradiction of sound economic practice, bargain to import natural gas from the high-cost source of supply rather than a low-cost one? Moreover, why did they force European consumers to pay unnecessarily high prices for their energy when lower prices for a comparable quality of energy were readily available? *The Wall Street Journal* writes: "If the gas pricing contracts were understood by the man in the street, Europe would be awash in a consumer revolt. . . . Europeans have given the Russians below-market loans for the privilege of buying above-market energy."[12]

The answer provided by Crovitz is détente. "European governments," writes Crovitz, "agreed to unfavourable terms with the Soviets not out of economic shortsightedness, but out of blinding respect for the major precept of detente—that trade would tame the Soviet beast."[13] True enough; the pipeline deal clearly is part of the overall European strategy of Soviet appeasement. But there is another important aspect of the deal that warrants discussion, if only because European governments define "economic shortsightedness" somewhat differently from Crovitz.

Economists know that economic change affects the public in two separate, though related, ways: as producers of goods and services, and as consumers. For reasons that are not altogether clear, welfare-state governments tend to discount consumer interests, considering only how a deal like the Siberian gas pipeline affects producers and workers. Moreover, government tends to be overly concerned with the direct and identifiable aspects of the deal, overlooking indirect and diffuse effects that can adversely affect the economic well-being of producers and workers in industries other than the one that is directly impacted.

The Siberian natural-gas pipeline deal is a classic illustration of the "under-class" role played by consumers in the welfare state. Domestic producers of pipeline equipment and their employees were subsidized at the expense of energy consumers and taxpayers. According to an official of the AMRO Bank in the Netherlands,

"The whole point of the pipeline was to give work to European exporters, and the gas itself was less important."[14] A member of the West German Economics Ministry concurred that "jobs were the main consideration."[15] When welfare state officials force consumers to subsidize the faltering pipeline business by paying higher prices for energy than necessary, they do not consider this to be "economic shortsightedness." It is simply the way welfare states do business.

The truth of the matter is that the Soviet pipeline deal probably had as much to do with increasing employment and profits in a severely depressed European industry as it did with paying tribute to the Kremlin. The Soviets provided a market for the pipeline equipment that the Europeans needed to prop up their faltering industry. Without the Soviets, it would have been much more difficult for the European governments to subsidize the pipeline industry. True, the West German, French, and British governments could have given the targeted industry direct subsidies from tax funds. But tax funds have been scarce lately in Europe, and forcing consumers to pay higher prices than they otherwise would is a less obvious way to subsidize. This made the pipeline deal politically more palatable—at least in Europe.

In the United States, on the other hand, the Reagan administration tried to countervene the Siberian gas pipeline deal by threatening the Europeans with economic sanctions. This approach did not work for a variety of reasons. First, the Europeans undermined the moral basis of the administration's case by arguing that if Reagan could lift the Carter embargo on U.S. grain exports to the Soviet Union, it had no right to embargo their exports of pipeline equipment. The administration might have countered that since the United States spends so many billions of dollars each year for their defense, the Europeans have no right to subsidize and otherwise enrich the enemy from whom they seek protection. But it did not!

A second reason the Reagan threat did not work was that the administration was very anxious for the Europeans to accept the Pershing and cruise missiles. With this kind of leverage over the Reagan administration, it was highly unlikely the Europeans would sit still for the imposition of economic sanctions against them by the United States. The administration belatedly got the message— either drop the sanctions threat or we reject the missiles—and after thoroughly embarrassing itself, it was forced to back down. Had Reagan quietly assured his European counterparts that unless they backed out out of their gas pipeline deal with the Soviets his administration would support the Nunn Amendment the next time it came up in the Senate, chances are the Europeans not only would have accepted the missiles but would have accepted Reagan's views on East-West trade as well. Once again the European politicians demonstrated they understood the use of leverage better than their American counterparts.

EAST-WEST TRADE CANNOT BE FREE TRADE

The pipeline controversy not only highlighted transatlantic differences on East-West trade, but raised the issue of what trade policy a Western nation should follow in its relations with the Soviet Union and its East European empire. In particular, the question arose as to whether the economists' predilection for free trade should be applied to commerce with political enemies as well as with friends. Responses to this question generally range between two extremes: Fervent anti-communists favor extremely limited trade with the Soviets because they seek to deny Moscow the economic benefits and discount the economic gains that trade bestows on private Western interests; whereas fervent free-marketeers favor trade with the Eastern bloc because they discount the effect free trade has on building up the enemy, focusing instead on the economic gains East-West trade bestows on the Western private sector. Neither extreme appears desirable as a basis for setting national trade policy with communist countries.

The theoretical case against free trade with the East European bloc is based on the defense feedback effect. The standard international trade models that prescribe free trade as the best policy implicitly assume that the economic gains made by one trading partner have no adverse repercussions on the other. This assumption is not met, however, when the two trading countries are political and military enemies. The economic gains made by the Soviets, because they fuel their military machine, impose a defense cost on the Western trading partner. Hence, the collective interest in defense expenditure must be balanced against the private interest in profitable exchange to determine the optimal amount of trade. The free market alone will not give the proper signals in this case.

For example, the real cost to the United States of exported grain to the Soviets cannot be measured solely in terms of market price, as when trade is with a friendly or politically neutral country. Instead, measurement of the cost must take into account the military hardware produced by the Soviets with the resources freed from the development and production of agricultural machinery that the Soviets would be forced to make if they had to produce their own grain. The defense feedback cost of the grain sales, then, is the cost the United States bears to counter the increase in Soviet military hardware facilitated by the grain sales. If these costs are under-estimated (as when cost is measured solely in terms of the market), too much East-West trade will take place and the collective interest in defense will not be adequately served. If they are overestimated, too little trade will occur and the private interest in profitable exchange will be shortchanged.

Which type of error—too little Soviet trade or too much—is likely to occur if the Europeans were to bear their fair share of the Western defense burden? Ironically, it can be argued that the United States would be likely to err on the side of too much trade and Western Europe on the side of too little. The reasons for this relate to differences in the economic structures of the United States and Western Europe. The United States has a tradition of a competitive market economy, modified to some extent by government regulation. The Europeans, on the other hand, believe more in state-directed economies, modified to some extent by the need to compete in world markets.

The tradition of a strong private sector and a relatively weak public one in the United States means that private companies that do substantial Soviet bloc business are likely to push for increased trade and ignore the defense feedback costs. Indeed, many argue that this presently is the case in the United States and that this country trades too much with the Eastern bloc. Conversely, the existence of a strong public and a relatively weak private sector in Western Europe means that if Europe were to assume the full cost of its own defense, consciousness of the defense feedback costs of East-West trade would keep trade levels down. This implies that the collective interest in defense could be adequately served in

Europe once the allies assume more of the costs of their own defense. The Europeans, in other words, have the way if they have the will. And if defense free-riding were eliminated, they would have the will as well.

THE COMMON AGRICULTURAL POLICY

A further example of a European welfare-state policy wherein the Soviets have benefited because they provide an important market for the Europeans is the Common Agricultural Policy (CAP) of the European Economic Community. The basic objective of the CAP is to raise the incomes of European farmers above their competitive levels. Though there are several ways to accomplish this, the EEC government has chosen to increase prices of agricultural goods to EEC consumers. While this raises producers' incomes, it also gives them artificial incentives to increase output. And unless government is able to eliminate these surplus agricultural products from the marketplace, the subsidy scheme will fail because the jacked-up prices will not be maintainable.

To validate the higher prices, therefore, the EEC has had to buy surplus agricultural products on the open market at inflated prices. Farm subsidies presently take two-thirds of the Common Market's budget of $21 billion. And since the subsidization procedure is an ongoing process, the problems and cost of storing the surplus agricultural goods is substantial (storage costs today run more than total agricultural subsidies in the early days of the EEC). It is logical to assume that in the absence of a credible solution to the storage problem, the costs of storage would become so great—and be such a political embarrassment—that the entire CAP edifice of subsidy would collapse.

This is where the Soviet Union comes in. The European authorities have found it convenient to reduce their storage costs (and thus save the CAP) by dumping the surplus agricultural goods induced by the artificially high food prices in the Soviet Union. The Soviets buy their goods at below-cost prices—that is, below the European costs of production, not the Soviet costs (which are much higher). This is the economic reward that accrues to the Soviets from a domestic subsidization process that might collapse without them. In the topsy-turvy world of subsidy, the Soviets support Europe's CAP as much as the CAP supports the Soviets.

Yet another example where the Soviets benefit from being a market for subsidized goods is export credit subsidies. Exporters in Western countries often argue that they have a special case for subsidization because an "export surplus"—exports being greater in value than imports—is good for the economy of the country. This myth is an outgrowth of the old mercantilistic idea that the wealth of a nation is defined by its stock of precious metals, and that an export surplus (an outflow of goods) leads to an inflow of precious metals. However, in his classic work, *The Wealth of Nations* (1776), Adam Smith made the infinitely sensible suggestion that rather than being defined by its stock of precious metals, the true wealth of a nation was given by the standard of living of its citizens. Smith then proceeded to argue that the living standard was independent of whether the nation's production was for domestic consumption or for export. He convinced most modern economists, who, following Smith, believe that an export surplus is neither inherently good nor bad.

Modern economists, however, do not dictate economic policy. In most countries of the West—and particularly those where government intervention in the economy is routine—exporters make use of the old mercantilistic myth to obtain subsidies from obliging government officials. These subsidies can be paid directly from the public treasury, but more often they are effectuated in an indirect "back door" manner. One of the preferred ways government does this is to give loans to consumers in foreign countries at a subsidized rate of interest, conditional on the loans being used to purchase the country's exports. This results in an income transfer from local taxpayers to foreign consumers. The subsidy also increases the exports of the subsidizing country above the level that would have occurred in its absence.

The Soviet Union and Eastern Europe have been important beneficiaries of Western export credit subsidies. Keith Crane and Daniel Kohler made a study for the Rand Corporation that estimated total export credit subsidies—direct and indirect—received by the Soviet Union and the Warsaw Pact countries in 1981 from the OECD countries, including the United States. Direct export credit subsidies came to $1.2 billion, of which $500 million went to the U.S.S.R. and $620 million to Eastern Europe. Indirect export credit subsidies came to $1.5 billion, of which $250 million went to the Soviets and $1.25 billion to Eastern Europe. The subsidy grand total for this one year alone thus was $2.7 billion.[16] Clearly, the Communist stake in the export subsidy practices of Western countries is quite substantial.

CONCLUSION

The cases of the Siberian natural-gas pipeline, the European Common Agricultural Policy, and export credit subsidies render a very important insight into the nature of the welfare state. Far from being a middle road between capitalism and communism, the welfare state is destroying the economy of the former while subsidizing that of the latter. In fact, a complex and dangerous relationship has been spawned between the welfare state and the Soviet Union. As part of its normal way of doing business, or should one say, subsidizing business, the welfare state is rendering an enormous economic advantage to the Soviet Union. This is not *exclusively* a matter of political tribute and Europe's détente-as-defense strategy. It also relates to the continued viability of the welfare state subsidization structure itself.

9

Japan: King of the Free-Riders

he first part of this book is concerned with America's European allies. We now turn attention to U.S. allies in the Pacific.

Indeed, in many respects Japan and West Germany are quite similar. Both countries were defeated in World War II. Both were demilitarized after the war. Both continue to eschew nuclear weapons, preferring to be protected by the American nuclear umbrella. Both have been politically rehabilitated. Both made exceptionally strong economic recoveries during the post–World War II period. And both continue to spend relatively small amounts of their substantial economic products on their own defense. Our two former enemies today are among the world's richest nations, yet both show little inclination to end the defense dependency on the United States that is their, and the American, legacy of World War II.

THE EXCEPTION THAT PROVES THE RULE

In Europe, being rich and militarily vulnerable has resulted in economic and political appeasement of the Soviet Union. West Ger-

157

many has been contrasted with France to show that the greater the defense dependence on the United States, the greater the appeasement. If this logic is extrapolated to the case of Japan, one would expect the island nation off the North China coast to be an even greater devotee of détente and appeasement than West Germany. This is because Japan is much more dependent on the United States for its national defense.

As a percentage of the country's gross national product, Japan's postwar defense spending reached a peak in the postwar period in 1955, when it totaled 1.78 percent of GNP. The ratio fell below 1 percent in the mid-1960s and has remained there ever since. This is not a happenstance, but a conscious act of Japanese policy. In theory, Japan's "one-percent rule" has been aimed at rectifying fears that Japanese militarism would again run rampant in the Pacific. In practice, it has proved a convenient excuse for Japanese politicians to use against Washington, which wants to cut down on U.S. defense subsidies to Japan. Japanese politicians argue that they would like to oblige the United States by spending more on their own defense, but domestic political considerations prevent it. The West Germans, it should be noted, spend three and one-half times the proportion of their economic product on defense as do the Japanese.

Clyde Haberman, *The New York Times* correspondent in Japan, claims some Japanese take a cost-effective approach to their relations with the United States. "Why do more for the world than necessary, they ask. Japan, they argue, has managed to get by with the best possible defense policy: Somebody else pays for it, namely the United States, which also tends to shape and worry about foreign policy for them, too."[1]

What makes the Japanese case particularly interesting is that despite the presence of several key factors that led to appeasement of the Soviet Union in Western Europe—extreme dependence on the United States for defense coupled with reduced credibility of the American nuclear guarantee, meager self-defense forces, and the economic wherewithal to buy off the Soviets—the Japanese have not as yet adopted a détente-as-defense strategy toward the Soviet Union. Even in the best of times, Soviet trade has not exceeded more than about 2.5 percent of Japanese total trade. Japan has been particularly wary of increasing its trade with the Soviet Union in the energy area. This is really quite extraordinary when one considers that Japan must import all its oil from abroad and the Soviets have precisely the raw materials the Japanese need.

An example illustrates the extreme reluctance of the Japanese to get involved with the Soviets in energy projects. In 1974 the Soviets asked Japan to help them build a trans-Siberian railway (the Baikal-Amur Mainline). Its purpose was to transport Russian oil to Japan, but the railway had obvious strategic possibilities as well. It is interesting to compare the Japanese response to the Soviet offer with that of the Europeans, who helped the Soviets build their Siberian natural gas pipeline. One influential Japanese newspaper wrote at the time of the Soviet request: "Our country's security is guaranteed by the U.S. nuclear umbrella, and it would be wrong for Japan to draw hasty conclusions concerning cooperation in the construction of a Trans-Siberian railway by ignoring the U.S."[2] The Europeans, who also benefit from the U.S. nuclear umbrella, not only ignored the United States, but defied its ally. Despite American threats of economic sanctions against European firms that helped build the pipeline, the Europeans nonetheless went ahead with the project.

Part of the reason Japan refused to help the Soviets build the Baikal-Amur Mainline is economic in nature. The Japanese feared unilateral actions by the Soviets (reductions in the agreed-upon rate of oil to be exported to Japan) that would reduce their rate of return on the investment. They also objected to the long-term and low-interest deferred payment schedule demanded by the Soviets. But the primary reason Japan turned the Soviets down was strategic. The Baikal-Amur Mainline would have enhanced the Soviet military strength in North Asia and increased the military threat to Japan. It also would have increased the Soviet military threat to Red China at a time when both the United States and Japan were seeking better relations with Peking.

The economic and strategic considerations of the European gas pipeline deal were analogous to those of the Baikal-Amur Mainline. The Europeans were aware of the danger of unilateral Soviet actions that would reduce the deal's economic benefits to them. The Soviets demanded—and received—subsidized interest rates from the Europeans. The Siberian natural-gas pipeline also had strategic implications damaging to the West. It gave the Kremlin a "gas lever" to use against the Europeans.

In at least two ways the Baikal-Amur Mainline made even more sense for the Japanese in 1974 than did the Siberian pipeline for the Europeans in 1984. In 1974 the Japanese were in a much tighter pinch for energy than the Europeans were in 1984, the year cracks began to appear in OPEC and energy prices dropped substantially. Moreover, the opposition of the Nixon administration to the Baikal-Amur Mainline was not nearly as strong as that of the Reagan administration to the Siberian natural gas pipeline. The Japanese, in other words, had more reason to go ahead with the trans-Siberian railway than the Europeans did with the Siberian natural-gas pipeline. The fact that the Japanese refused the Soviets, and that Europeans accepted them, indicates the difference détente plays in the foreign policies of these two U.S. allies.

Further evidence of the Euro-Japanese difference in détente policies relates to support for U.S. initiatives to punish the Soviets for their imperialistic policies in the Third World. The Soviet invasion of Afghanistan has been the most explicitly imperialistic act the Soviet Union has committed in recent years. To protest the invasion, the Carter administration imposed sanctions on the Soviets, including the boycott of the Moscow Olympic Games. "Japan's position was considerably more cooperative with the U.S. policy than that of key West European countries," writes Gerald Curtis in *Foreign Affairs*.

> In addition to forcing the Japanese Olympic Committee to boycott the Moscow games, the government brought a halt to most trade talks then on-going. Negotiations relating to fourteen projects valued at $4–5 billion were suspended, new Japanese plant exports to the USSR virtually ceased, and a freeze was put on new loans through the Japanese Export-Import Bank for exports to Moscow on a deferred-payment basis.[3]

Unlike Europe, Japan put its money where its mouth is.

Despite radically changed perceptions in Japan of American economic and military strength during the 1970s—that the United States no longer could be depended on to underwrite a stable international currency system, to guarantee Japanese access to energy and raw materials, or to secure Japanese political interests in a stable political order—the Japanese did not make détente their second line of defense against the Soviets. The mere presence of an incentive to practice détente does not guarantee a strong response to the incentive. Economists use the term "elasticity" to denote the response of human behavior to a given incentive. The greater the elasticity, the greater the expected response and vice versa. As economists use the term, elasticity is a general concept applying to a wide range of diverse phenomena.

If elasticity is to be useful in the attempt to predict, rather than merely categorize, human behavior, its determinants in any particular case must be discovered. This is a question of why a given elasticity is high, low, or medium. Several factors explain why the European response to the incentives to adopt a détente-as-defense strategy has been greater than the Japanese response.

The most important is that the Soviets are much more of a conventional military threat to Western Europe than Japan. Because Japan is an island nation, a Soviet conventional attack would require an amphibious landing with substantial air support. National security expert Henry S. Rowen, of the Hoover Institution, writes:

> This Soviet threat has not alarmed Japanese or American planners. Almost all of the Soviet divisions are on the Chinese border, and the Soviets' simultaneous amphibious capacity in the region is only about 4,000 men. Soviet tactical-air offensive strength has been sharply limited by short-range aircraft and poor air-to-ground missiles. To invade successfully, the Soviets would have to establish a strong beachhead, gain air superiority, hinder the movement of Japanese troops, damage U.S. forces in the area, and block U.S. reinforcements. The prospects must look unpromising. The odds are high that the Soviets would find themselves in a prolonged and highly dangerous conflict with both Japan and the United States, and Moscow's worries over its differences with Peking make such an attack even more remote.[4]

The situation in Western Europe is far less optimistic. The Soviets could send a massive force of troops and tanks across the West German border that, at current Western conventional troop strength levels, would force the allies either to capitulate or push the doomsday button in a matter of days. Because of NATO's weakness in conventional forces, it has to rely on nuclear weapons. On the other hand, the Western Alliance is still capable of countering Soviet conventional forces in East Asia, as Henry Rowen makes clear. This has further contributed to the Japanese unwillingness to exercise the nuclear option. What this means, of course, is that the advent of U.S.–U.S.S.R. nuclear parity has made the Europeans feel less safe vis-à-vis the Soviets than it did the Japanese.

A second factor that accounts for the absence of a Japanese "détente as defense" strategy is the strong antipathy felt by the Japanese toward the Soviet Union. Public opinion polls consistently show the Soviet Union to be the country most disliked by the Japanese people. "Anti-Soviet sentiment in Japan is strong," writes Gerald Curtis, "and it is growing."[5] Historically, this antipathy can be traced to the Russo-Japanese War (1904–05). In modern times the central issue that divides the two peoples is Soviet occupation of the so-called "Northern Territories." Public opinion polls show that 92 percent of the Japanese people consider this occupation to be the most important foreign policy issue facing the island nation.

Japan's official position regarding the Northern Territories is summed up by a Ministry of Foreign Affairs publication:

> The Northern Territories are still under illegal Soviet occupation, and this is the sole unsettled issue left for Japan resulting from World War II. This issue has delayed conclusion of a peace treaty with the Soviet Union. . . . The Japanese people remain strongly attached to these integral parts of Japan's national territory, and the attachment can only be strengthened in years to come.[6]

The Northern Territories comprise the islands of the Habomai group—Shikotan, Kunashir, and Etorofu. These islands lie off the northeastern tip of Hokkaido, stretching in a northeasterly direction. The total land area of the Northern Territories is 4,996 square kilometers. They are reputed to be one of the three best fishing grounds in the world.

Extending northeast from the Northern Territories are the Kurile Islands. Japan obtained the Kuriles from Russia by treaty in exchange for Sakhalin in 1875. After World War II, in accordance with Article 2(c) of the San Francisco Peace Treaty, Japan renounced all rights, title, and claim to the Kurile Islands and to

Southern Sakhalin (which Japan obtained during the Russo -Japanese War). According to the Japanese, the term "Kurile Islands" in the peace treaty does not include the Northern Territories. They base this claim on the definition of the Kurile Islands used in the 1875 agreement and the Portsmouth Treaty of 1905, ending the Russo-Japanese War.

The Soviets have occupied the Northern Territories and the Kurile Islands since September 1945. During World War II, the Soviets honored their neutrality pact with Japan (signed in 1941) until the very last days of the war. Then, sensing Japan's eminent defeat, the Soviets rushed in and grabbed the Kuriles and the Northern Territories at the very last minute. The Soviet action left Japan doubly aggrieved: Not only did the Soviets violate the Neutrality Pact, but they did it to steal the Northern Territories. The Japanese have made it clear they have no intention of forgetting the disputed territories, which the Soviets now are using for military bases to threaten Japan. In 1981, Japan designated February 7 as "Northern Territories Day." The West Europeans apparently have let time erase the fact that Eastern Europe was illegally annexed by the Soviets. The Japanese have not—and apparently will not—let the same thing happen to them.

The Soviet grab of the Northern Territories has soured Soviet-Japanese relations to the point where Moscow gets a better press in the United States than it does in Japan. For example, when former Soviet Foreign Minister Andrei Gromyko sent Japanese Foreign Minister Shintaro Abe a telegram of congratulations on his sixtieth birthday, a well-known Japanese newspaper, *Sankei Shim-bun*, responded:

> Abe is the first foreign minister of Japan to receive such an "honor" from "Mr. Nyet." . . . After many years of experience with the Soviet pattern of behavior, one cannot ignore the rising suspicion that if the Soviet Union is happy, we have either failed or made a major concession.

> Talks between Abe and Gromyko on the occasion of Andropov's funeral and working-level Japanese-Soviet meetings held in March [1984], as well as other contacts, have made it abundantly clear that the new Soviet leadership has no intention of altering its Japan policy, which has been maintained since Brezhnev and Andropov.

The new Soviet leadership has flatly rejected all of Japan's demands regarding the return of the Northern Territories, the Japanese islands seized by the Soviets at the end of the second World War. At the same time, Soviet leaders have persisted in putting pressure on Japan to conclude various agreements, including a Good Neighbor Cooperation Treaty, "trust-building measures," and a nuclear non-use pact in place of a peace treaty.

Many signs have appeared since Chernenko took office, suggesting that the Soviet position toward Japan has even hardened. The Soviets have deployed more SS-20s in the Far East. The *Novorossiysk* is now cruising with the Pacific Fleet in addition to the *Minsk*, indicating that the USSR is instituting a two-aircraft-carrier system in the Far East.[7]

Soviet occupation of the Northern Territories not only feeds Japanese anti-Sovietism, but protects Japan from the neutralist disease—common in Western Europe—of feeling like a spectator to a superpower struggle being played out in one's own backyard. The Japanese very much feel like "players" in the East-West struggle because part of their country is illegally occupied by the Soviets. This has made a big difference in the way the Japanese react to Soviet provocations. For example, in 1983 when Moscow flew in 10 MIG-21s to replace out-of-date MIG-17s at its military base on the disputed island of Etorofu, the United States offered to deploy 50 F-16s at Misawa Air Base in Northern Japan as a countermeasure. The Soviets were so furious that the Japanese agreed to this, they threatened to move more of their European-based SS-20 missiles to Asia. "Moscow warned Japan that it could face a retaliatory strike more devastating than the 1945 atomic bomb explosions if it agreed to the deployment of more weapons aimed at the Soviet Union," reported *The New York Times*.[8]

The Soviets apparently forgot that the Japanese do not consider Etorofu a part of the Soviet Union. Compare this Japanese reaction to Soviet provocation with the European reaction to Soviet threats during the Euromissile crisis. The Japanese did not equivocate about deployment of the F-16s as the Europeans equivocated about deployment of the Pershing and cruise missiles. They welcomed the American planes because the F-16s were attempting to neutralize the Soviet presence in what Japan considers to be illegally occupied Japanese territory. Unfortunately, U.S. West European allies no longer consider Eastern Europe to be "illegally" occupied by the Soviets. If they did, neutralism would not be the problem it is today in Western Europe.

THE JAPANESE ECONOMIC IMPERATIVE

A third factor that explains why, in the face of incentives to pursue détente, the Japanese have refused to do so is the economic imperative of modern Japanese life. After their defeat in World War II, economic development took on a meaning for the Japanese far beyond the usual one of raising the material standard of living. The Japanese are a proud people who felt humiliated by their defeat in the war. If national pride and self-esteem were to be restored, it would have to be through achievements in economics, not war. Japan renounced the use of force in its so-called "peace" constitution of 1946. Though the constitution was imposed on Japan by occupying American forces, its antimilitaristic tone has had broad support among the Japanese people. Article 9, the famous "no war" clause, reads:

> Aspiring sincerely to an international peace based on justice and order, the Japanese people forever renounce war as a sovereign right of the nation and the threat of force as a means of settling international disputes.
>
> In order to accomplish the aim of the preceding paragraph, land, sea, and air forces, as well as other war potential, will never be maintained. The right of belligerency of the State will not be recognized.

One obvious implication of Japan's peace constitution was the assumption of responsibility for the defense of Japan by the United States. Concerned about Mao's victory in China, the United States chose Japan as a model of capitalistic development in the Pacific region. For their part, the Japanese worked hard at economic development not only for reasons of national pride and material reward, but because they wanted to give the United States a greater stake in their security. Japanese economic development thus came to be identified with Japanese national security in a way that is rather unusual.

So much attention in recent years has been placed on the competitive challenge of the Japanese economy to other industrialized countries that one sometimes gets the impression that Japan's economic success has been a negative development for the West. This could not be further from the truth. Japan's economy not only has been a force for prosperity, stability, and peace in the Pacific, but it has tied Japan to the United States in a way that virtually has made that island nation "détente proof." The close identification of national security with economic strength precludes Japan from offending the United States, the one foreign country upon which Japan's continued economic success vitally depends. The United States provides Japan with markets, technology, and a basic commitment to free trade. Even Japan's oil imports from the Middle East depend on American military strength to keep the sealanes open. If the United States were to turn against the Japanese, the island nation could hardly survive.

This is not the case with Europe. The Europeans are not as dependent on the American economy as are the Japanese. They trade with one another more than they trade with the United States. American military power is less relevant to their energy supplies than it is to Japan. Europe has North Sea oil and gas. The Europeans have not replaced a military imperative with an economic one. The identification of national security with economic strength is weak in Western Europe. If the Europeans can be said to have any imperative, it is a social welfare imperative—the movement toward equality of access to goods, the extension of political rights to the economic arena, the provision of social welfare goods, and so forth. As pointed out in chapter 7, Europe's social welfare imperative reinforces its demand for détente. Japan's economic imperative works in the opposite direction.

THE DEFENSE FREE RIDE: FOREIGN AID FOR THE RICH

The fact that Japanese defense dependence on the United States has not led to appeasement of the Soviets does not mean that U.S. defense relations with Japan have been problem-free. At the moment there are two outstanding defense-related issues that could fester if not properly attended to. The first relates to the economic aspects and consequence of the defense free ride; the second relates to the future role of Japanese militarism.

The essence of the defense free ride is that the United States provides a defense service for an ally which that country either cannot, or will not, provide for itself. Implicit in this transaction is a resource (or income) transfer from the United States to the recipient of the defense service that is analytically equivalent to foreign economic aid. In the recipient country, the aid appears as a saving of resources that otherwise would have been spent on defense. In the United States the aid shows up in the defense rather than the economic assistance budget. No resources actually flow from country to country, but the effect of the defense free ride is the same as if they had. It is possible to have the United States provide the defense service without the resource transfer element only if the recipient country makes a compensatory transfer of resources back to the United States, that is, only if it returns the foreign aid to the donor.

In the real world, defense free-riders do not return foreign aid—they spend the resources as they see fit. The social welfare imperative of Western Europe dictated that the resource transfer from the defense free ride be spent to enlarge the welfare state. Japan's economic imperative, on the other hand, dictated that the resources saved by Japanese defense free-riding be left in the private sector, to be used either for private consumption or private investment. In the early postwar years, the saved resources undoubtedly gave the Japanese extra room to pursue a high growth policy. Private investment could be increased without dramatically impinging on private consumption.

Little if any of the resources transferred to Japan from the United States went into Japanese social security spending until the 1960s. The low point of social security spending in Japan occurred in 1958. As is clear in fig. 9.1, social security represented approximately 8 percent of Japan's General Account Budget in that year; defense spending as well as educational and science promotion expense accounted for a greater proportion of the budget. From 1958 to 1967, however, social security expenditure rapidly increased in Japan. The crossover year for defense expenditure was 1960, and for science and education, 1964.

The second phase of rapid welfare-state expansion in Japan took place from 1973 to 1976. Social security increased from 14 to 20 percent of government expenditure during this period. It was in the early 1970s that the ruling Liberal Democratic Party (LDP) found itself losing voter support on the issue of the social costs of rapid economic growth—particularly environmental pollution and lagging welfare benefits compared with other industrialized countries. "By bringing welfare-spending up to the standards of other industrial states, the LDP hoped to neutralize the appeal of socialist and communist parties," writes Daniel Okimoto. "Although establishing causality is always difficult, the rapid expansion of welfare benefits appears to have helped the LDP halt the erosion of its popular base of support."[9] What all this means is that by the mid-

FIG. 9.1 *Defense and Other Expenditures as a Percentage of the General Account Budget*

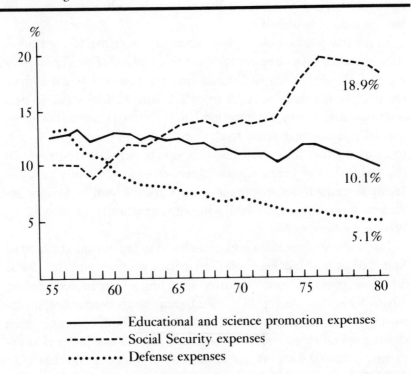

———— Educational and science promotion expenses

------- Social Security expenses

•••••••• Defense expenses

Source: Daniel I. Okimoto, "The Economics of National Defense," in *Japan's Economy: Coping with Change in the International Environment*, ed. Daniel I. Okimoto (Boulder: Westview Press, 1982), p. 247.

1970s, the Japanese consensus over the desirability of a pure economic standard had broken down.

The growing importance of Japan's welfare state raises serious questions as to the continued advisability of allowing the Japanese to defense free-ride on the American taxpayers. The free ride proved a wise expenditure of American tax funds so long as it helped sustain the best argument for capitalism that could be made in the Far East—the Japanese economy. Not only did the United States go "one up" vis-à-vis the Communists in the battle of ideas, but Japan's economic imperative proved an effective bulwark against Soviet expansionism in the Pacific Basin area.

Today, however, Japanese capitalism is not being sustained by American economic assistance via the defense free ride; Japanese state welfarism is. The United States is not—or at least should not be—attempting to make a case for the welfare state in the Pacific Basin. The geo-strategic importance of this area is based on its economic strength. Anything that threatens that strength—such as the attempt to imitate European and American standards of social security—threatens Western security. Moreover, given the close link that has been shown to exist in Western Europe between détente on the one hand and the welfare state on the other, the United States should be discouraging Japan's attempt to build up its welfare state, not bankrolling it.

Even if the economic growth and strategic aspects of the defense free ride were not of primary concern to the United States, there are fundamental issues of international equity involved that dictate the free ride be discontinued. Japanese politicians claim that Japan's huge current budget deficit prevents them from increasing defense expenditures. But the reason the Japanese have a huge budget deficit is due to excessive social security expenditures relative to tax revenues. Given the enormous U.S. budget deficit, the defense free ride has come to mean that the United States must cut its social programs so that the Japanese can maintain theirs (or, what amounts to the same thing, that the United States keep its budget deficit high so that the Japanese do not have to increase theirs). This is the epitome of "beggar-my-neighbor" policy. If Japan wants a large welfare state, Japanese citizens, not American citizens, should pay for it.

The Japanese claim that their "beggar-my-neighbor" budgetary policies are not motivated by selfish considerations, but are the unintended by-product of the nation's minimalist defense posture. That this is not a valid argument is apparent once it is realized that the United States can continue to provide its present level of defense service for Japan without the resource transfer effect if Japan would be willing to make a direct resource transfer to the United States as compensation for the indirect resource transfer made to them when the United States provides the defense service. The "compensatory resource transfer" would offend neither Japanese anti-militarism nor the U.S. taxpayer. Moreover, there is a precedent for a compensatory resource approach in the current U.S.–Japan arrangements. The United States returned Okinawa to Japan in 1971, but the Japanese reimburse the United States for the 25,100 U.S. marines stationed there to the tune of $1 billion per year. If this arrangement could be extended past compensation for the 49,500 American military personnel physically located in Japan to the entire range of defense services the United States provides Japan, the charge of free-rider no longer could be levied at the Japanese.

Some argue that full compensation to the United States for the extra cost Japan's defense imposes on this country would not involve large sums of money because Japan's "one-percent rule" exaggerates the actual extent of Japan's free defense ride. As far as the American nuclear guarantee goes, adding Japan to the nuclear umbrella's coverage certainly has had only a marginal effect on this country's strategic expense. And unlike the case of the Pershing missile, where we built the weapon specifically for the European theater, no nuclear weapons have been custom-made for Japan. Thus, the argument goes, if the United States were to reconsider its commitment to the defense of Japan, it would save few resources.

Where Japanese free-riding has cost this country, however, is not so much with regard to the defense of Japan itself but with the defense of the Pacific Basin region. Japan has become one of the world's leading economic powers, and certainly *the* top economic power in the Pacific Basin region. A country of Japan's wealth surely should play a more substantial role in securing the region in which it is located. "There is something unhealthy about a country as economically powerful and technologically advanced as Japan attempting to remain politically out of sight," Edwin O. Reischauer, the former U.S. ambassador to Japan, wrote in a Japanese magazine.

"This falsifies the real situation, creating confusion and suspicion among others and breeding resentments within Japan itself."[10]

Overseas critics, less friendly to Japan than Ambassador Reischauer, have grown weary of Japan's refusal to assume greater political and military responsibilities in the Pacific. "To critics," writes Clyde Haberman in *The New York Times*, "Japan is nothing less than sneaky. The country accumulates more and more money but does little to help maintain the very world order from which it prospers, they say. Specters of a new 'yellow peril' are raised now and again. Even good friends warn that Japan may have carried its role as an international Hamlet too far."[11]

In defense of Japanese behavior, Haberman claims that Japan has yet to figure out "how to become an active global force without scaring both themselves and everyone else to death." Japan's neighbors undoubtedly remember the "Greater East Asia Co-Prosperity Sphere"—the euphemism Japan employed to cover its imperialistic policies of the 1930s and 1940s. Theodore H. White, the Pulitzer Prize–winning American author, reminisces:

> The slogan was scrawled across the walls of all the regions I visited from Manchukuo to North China, down finally to Hanoi in 1940, when the Japanese took over Vietnam. And they meant to go further: to Thailand (with its tin), Malaya (rubber), Indonesia (oil and timber). The Japanese idea was simple: that Japan was the leader of East Asia, and so it should harness Asia, with its resources, its genius of mind, its hundreds of millions of people, and all would grow prosperous—Japan most of all.[12]

The United States thus has had to assume, and maintain, the responsibilities for securing the Pacific area that normally would fall to a country of Japan's wealth, but for Japan's malignant behavior forty years ago. At a minimum, the United States should be compensated by Japan for this service. It is an inherently inequitable arrangement that the Japanese get the benefits of a secure Pacific region without the economic costs they should, and would, be bearing had it not been for their warlike behavior forty years earlier. An even better solution than financial compensation would be for the Japanese to contribute ships, planes, and men to the defense of the Pacific Basin region. Though the United States might not cut down on the number of its ships and planes in the Pacific region in response, it should feel more comfortable than it does today about shifting parts of its forces to the Atlantic or Indian Oceans should the need arise.

"COMPREHENSIVE SECURITY"

To answer critics of their minimalist defense posture and one-percent rule, Japan has developed the concept of "comprehensive security." Based on the notion of an international division of security responsibilities and comparative advantage, comprehensive security argues that countries should specialize in those areas in which their comparative advantage lies. Because of its wealth, Japan could contribute to international security (for example) by giving economic aid to countries that are of strategic importance to the West. (Japan already has given economic aid to Pakistan on this basis.) Because of its geographic proximity to the Soviet Union, Japan also could contribute by gathering intelligence information on Soviet activities. "The KAL 007 incident," writes the Japan Economic Institute, "indicated that Japanese intelligence capabilities are far better than is generally assumed and that the United States can depend upon Japanese cooperation in this area where mutual security concerns are clearly at stake. Transcripts released in the days following the incident indicated advanced capabilities for ground and air monitoring of Soviet flights and communications."[13]

The notion of "comprehensive security" enjoys a considerable amount of support not only in Japan itself, but among Japan's neighbors in the Pacific region—South Korea, China, Taiwan, and so forth. These countries favor "comprehensive security" not only because of lingering fears of resurgent Japanese militarism, but, as Clyde Haberman notes in *The New York Times*, because they

> are not above playing on Japan's war-inspired guilt complexes to extract a little more aid.... When [Japanese Prime Minister] Mr. Nakasone went to South Korea and China, he bore considerable gifts in the form of direct assistance and loans. In a period of fiscal austerity, the [Japanese] Government has signaled out foreign economic aid as the one area other than defense spending that will escape severe budget cuts.[14]

The popularity of the comprehensive security concept in the Pacific Basin should not distract from the dangers it holds for the United States if it substitutes for a more active Japanese defense posture. Unless our economically-able allies pitch in and do their fair share of carrying the military burden of defending Western values in the Pacific, the United States will find its defense forces spread dangerously thin throughout the world. Indeed, several defense experts claim the United States already has reached that unenviable point. It must be remembered that while Japan has steadfastly retained its one-percent rule on defense spending, the Soviets have increased their presence in the Pacific Ocean from modest forces a decade ago to 825 ships of all descriptions, including ships and submarines with nuclear weapons, undertaken a major military buildup in the Northern Territories, and transferred SS-20s from Europe to the Far East. It is true that these developments have concerned the Japanese, but as yet they have done little to redress them.

If the Soviet military buildup in the Pacific continues, it is unlikely that Japan will be able to maintain its minimal defense posture, and it may even have to reconsider its antinuclear policies. Nuclear weapons, of course, have a special meaning for Japan. "As a result of Hiroshima, Nagasaki, and Bikini, Japan is the only nation in the world to have felt the horrible effects of nuclear weapons," writes Kei Wakaizumi of Kyoto Sangyo University. "Naturally, the Japanese hate the weapons even to the point of neurosis and this is a powerful deterrent to any consideration of national nuclear weapons."[15]

As a result of its distaste for nuclear weapons, ex-Prime Minister Sato enunciated three "nonnuclear" principles in 1967: that Japan would not possess nuclear weapons, manufacture them, or allow their introduction onto Japanese soil. "These principles have been strongly supported by successive governments," according to the Japan Economic Institute, "and enhanced by Japanese ratification of the nuclear test ban treaty and the U.S. 'nuclear umbrella.'"[16] The third nonnuclear principle, which bars the introduction of nuclear weapons on Japanese soil, has conflicted with the American nuclear guarantee on several occasions. To implement the guarantee, American ships, presumably armed with nuclear weapons, sometimes operate in Japanese waters. When they do, antinuclear

Japanese protest their presence and stir up considerable anti-American sentiment. To this point, the Japanese government has not used the nonnuclear principle to keep the ships out, but the Reagan administration believes this might change if only because of actions like New Zealand's recent barring of American ships suspected of carrying nuclear weapons from its harbors.

The United States is in a very delicate position as far as Japan's nuclear policies are concerned. It is particularly unseemly of this country to openly protest Japan's third nonnuclear principle, if only because the United States is the country that used nuclear weapons against the Japanese. On the other hand, Japan must understand that it cannot indefinitely enjoy the benefits of U.S. nuclear protection without assuming certain nuclear risks. The reconciliation of these two conflicting forces via the device of the Japanese government "looking the other way" whenever U.S. nuclear ships enter their waters is hardly the solution required. Even the appearance of the United States pushing nuclear weapons down Japanese throats is unwise and strengthens the anti-American, anti-Western sentiments in Japan that the United States seeks to undermine. It is time the Japanese reconcile their legitimate need for nuclear protection with their unfortunate nuclear history.

While appropriate to the early postwar period, when memories of Japanese aggression and imperialism were fresh and the Soviet Union posed little threat in the Pacific, Japan's three nonnuclear principles have a distinctly outdated look about them. In today's world where the "balance of fears" in the Pacific Basin—of Japan on the one hand and the Soviet Union on the other—has tilted decidedly toward the Soviets, Japan's nonnuclear principles represent nothing less than an opting out of its responsibilities for the region's security. The doctrine of "comprehensive security" does more than merely accommodate antimilitarism, it encourages it by giving the nonnuclear principles, and other Japanese antidefense measures, a legitimacy they no longer deserve. Japan need not go nuclear at the present time, but to set the stage, at least the third nonnuclear principle should be rescinded. This would serve as a sign to Japanese and Americans alike that the post–World War II minimalist phase of Japan's military history is coming to a close.

Apart from its deleterious consequences for the security interests of the Pacific region, comprehensive security also holds an economic danger for the United States. The scheme to substitute economic aid for real defense has the earmarks of full-blown international redistribution-of-income in which the United States gives economic aid to Japan via the defense free ride, and Japan "intermediates" part or all of it to third countries in the Pacific region. Except in cases where an intermediary is needed for strategic reasons—where the United States wants to shield its identity—this arrangement makes little sense from the American point of view.

Most obviously, the purpose of United States defense support of Japan is not to give economic aid to such countries as South Korea, China, and Taiwan. Even if the United States wanted to help these countries, giving that aid via Japan means that Japan gets the *quid* for the American *quo*; also, that Japan defines the conditions for the aid. Japan could tie the aid to its exports, for example, so that comprehensive security becomes little more than a scheme by which the Japanese subsidize their exports with American money. The only positive aspect of comprehensive security for the United States is that the doctrine could be used to justify the negotiation of compensatory resource transfers to the United States from Japan in return for its defense support. In this case, the United States would send the Japanese the equivalent of economic aid through the defense free ride, but Japan would return it through direct transfers.

TRADE, THE DOLLAR, AND THE DEFENSE FREE RIDE

As the deficit in our trade balance with Japan reaches record levels, there is a growing tendency to blame the deficit on the defense free ride. The argument is that U.S. defense support for Japan has given Japanese industry an unfair competitive advantage over American producers, because the latter must pay taxes to pay for Japan's defense. Protectionists in the United States take this argument one step further: To neutralize the alleged unfair competitive advantage enjoyed by the Japanese, they advocate that the government place protectionist impediments against Japanese imports into the American market. That, they claim, would equalize the conditions of competition between Japan and the United States.

Public opinion polls show that a plurality of Americans believe that Japan has become economically strong because it has spent little on defense. Forty-three percent of the Americans queried think that spending relatively little on defense has helped Japan become strong economically, while 37 percent think that the level of defense spending has had little or nothing to do with Japan's economic success (20 percent had no opinion).[17] Of course, just because a plurality of Americans believe something is true does not necessarily make it true. All the plurality indicates is that the protectionists' argument that links Japan's economic success to its defense free ride should have considerable public support.

The first point to be made is that our record trade deficits are not only with the Japanese; we have a record deficit with the aggregate of all countries in the world economy. The reason we have a record deficit in our overall balance of trade is that there is a record capital inflow into the United States. It is an axiom of balance-of-payments adjustment theory that the balance of payments always balances. If we have capital inflow, we must have a trade deficit to balance it. A trade surplus, on the other hand, requires a capital outflow. The trade account adjusts to the capital account in our balance of payments, not the other way around.

Our record trade deficits are not caused by the unfair trading practices of our trading partners, but by the attractiveness of the U.S. capital market to foreign investors. The capital inflow is what has pushed the U.S. dollar to record levels. And the high (not overvalued) dollar in turn has made imports from all countries—and not only from Japan—relatively cheap in the American market. It is wrong to blame the Japanese for a "problem" that many feel is not a problem at all, and would not be the fault of the Japanese even if it were. The capital inflow has helped finance U.S. record budget deficits, and in so doing increased employment in the United States by keeping interest rates lower than they otherwise would have been. The high dollar also has kept U.S. inflation under control as the economy recovered from its recession.

It is true, of course, that to finance the resource transfer effect of the defense free ride, taxes on American citizens must be made higher than they otherwise would be. The protectionists are correct on this point. But there is absolutely no reason to believe that these additional taxes disadvantage American exports or subsidize Japanese imports—the implicit assumption of the protectionists' argument. On a theoretical level, the additional taxes might have such effects, but they could just as well be neutral with respect to international trade, or even subsidize U.S. exports and restrict U.S. imports.

The latter can be illustrated by a simple example. Suppose that the money the United States spends on Japanese defense is raised by an import tariff. In this case, the tax imposed on the American people to finance the resource transfer to Japan restricts U.S. imports. Neutralizing the trade effects of the defense free ride when a tariff is used to raise the money requires that the United States liberalize Japanese imports, not restrict them. In the United States the federal government depends primarily on the personal income tax to finance its expenditures. For the protectionists to make their case, they would have to demonstrate that the trade effects of the personal income tax restrict exports and/or subsidize imports. And even if this could be demonstrated, which it can't, the proper policy response would be to end the defense free ride rather than attempt to counter it by protection.

The truth, of course, is that the people who make the free-ride argument for protection have little interest in ending Japanese free-riding. Their real concern is in reducing competition in the American marketplace by keeping Japanese goods out, and to the extent that the free-ride argument helps their cause, they probably hope it continues. The free ride thus constitutes a threat to the American consumer as well as a burden on the American taxpayer. If U.S. protectionists prevail because of it, the American consumer will have to pay higher prices for goods that compete with Japanese imports than is necessary.

The Japanese do not need U.S. economic aid, but they do need U.S. markets. The pique many Americans feel about the free ride is being exploited by those who want to severely limit Japanese imports into the American market. Japan would be wise to renounce the aid altogether rather than give an undeserved semblance of legitimacy to the protectionists in the United States. The potential loss of a chunk of the American market must be worth more to the Japanese than the gains they enjoy from the defense free ride. Moreover, when one considers the negative effects the welfare state has had on the European economies, the gains from the free ride in building up the Japanese welfare state certainly should be approached with the utmost caution.

The defense free ride is only one among a myriad of phony arguments protectionists in the United States have been using in recent years to justify the exclusion of Japanese products from the U.S. market. Protectionists claim, for example, that the Japanese authorities are keeping the yen artificially low by comparison with the dollar so as to give Japanese goods an unfair advantage in world markets. "The government of Japan has been getting away with economic murder," writes William Safire. "Japan's currency is artificially rigged to make exports cheaper and imports more costly. Japan practices outrageous trade discrimination and pioneered domestic content legislation. Japan takes our nuclear umbrella for granted and benefits from its tiny investment in defense."[18]

Safire's attack on Japanese economic policies shows that even the normally clear thinking can get fog-bound when it comes to economic reasoning. If *The New York Times* columnist had checked the business pages of his own newspaper, he would have discovered that during the first Reagan administration the yen had risen against all major currencies except the U.S. dollar. This is not a case of the yen being low, but of the dollar being high. And while it is true that Japan maintains controls on its capital imports that tend to depress its currency, the very trade discrimination Safire refers to offsets this effect by reducing imports.

While the charge that "Japan's currency is artificially rigged to make exports cheaper and imports more costly" is pure hokum, it is true that Japan practices protectionism on a wide range of products—from medical equipment to communications satellites. In particular, Japan's refusal to open its markets to agricultural products has angered American farmers, prompting Bill Brock, the President's trade representative, to issue a "lower-your-trade-barriers-or-else" ultimatum to the Japanese. Senate Foreign Relations Committee members are even less diplomatic, and have at times demanded a 20-percent tariff on Japanese products.

Is it fair that Japanese producers have far greater access to American markets than American producers have to Japanese markets? When phrased this way, the question answers itself and provides the moral underpinnings for American "retaliatory" protection against Japan. Another—and from an economic point of view, more accurate—way of phrasing the question is as follow: Is it fair that American consumers have far greater access to Japanese goods than Japanese consumers have to American goods? The answer is that it is not fair to Japanese consumers but that is strictly an internal Japanese affair, in which the United States has little right to intervene. What is of American concern is the welfare of *its* consumers and, because U.S. consumers have wider access to foreign goods than Japanese consumers, the present international trading system treats Americans more fairly than it treats the Japanese. When viewed in this economically more relevant manner, American retaliation against Japanese protection makes no sense whatsoever.

Just as Americans have come to resent Japanese defense free-riding, the Japanese have come to resent the campaign by American protectionists to exclude Japanese products from the U.S. market. Akio Morita, chairman of the Sony Corporation, noted:

> Instead of treating Japan as a friend, the United States and Europe are ganging up on Japan...treating us almost as an enemy....I think Americans are too wrapped up in their own economic difficulties and frustrations to think about the impact of what they are saying and doing to their allies. This is causing a lot of trouble, not just in Japan, and it is eroding the very fabric of the free world.[19]

The point Morita makes, of course, is that "Japan-bashing" not only is bad economics, it is bad politics. It is simply insane to whip up anti-Japanese feeling and new yellow-peril fears in the United States for the profit of a relatively few domestic industries. Theodore H. White goes further than most in "bashing" the Japanese, equating Japan's present trade practices with their behavior at Pearl Harbor. "The superlative execution of their trade tactics may provoke an incalculable reaction," writes White, "as the Japanese might well remember the course that ran from Pearl Harbor to the deck of the U.S.S. *Missouri* in Tokyo Bay just forty years ago." He urges "the Japanese to remember that if peace is paramount, they need us to keep the peace more than we need them."[20]

White's point about keeping the peace probably is correct but it definitely is irrelevant. Regardless of which country needs the other more, the United States needs Japan—and needs it badly. The Pulitzer Prize winner needs to be reminded that today Japan is the most important U.S. ally in the Pacific. If the Japanese were to go as soft on the Soviets as the Europeans, the United States would be in deep difficulties. The Soviets are making a big play in the Pacific, building up their naval fleet, their air strength, and their nuclear capabilities. The United States needs Japan's help in combating this new Soviet threat. The Theodore Whites and William Safires apparently have gotten themselves into such a muddle about Japan's allegedly "unfair" trading practices that they have forgotten who the real enemy is in the Pacific.

CONCLUSION

The coalition of forces, both economic and military, for the preservation of the status quo in the Pacific Basin region is so formidable that, in the absence of some major foreign policy or economic shock its perpetration appears guaranteed. Even Japan's disinclination for détente conspires to leave well enough alone. The shock that could encourage both the Japanese to seriously reconsider its minimalist defense posture, and its neighbors in the region not to take umbrage at such a development, is a withdrawal of U.S. troops from Western Europe. Not only would this action challenge the fundamental assumption of Japanese defense policy—that the time horizon for free-riding is infinite—but it would create almost irresistible pressures in Japan to negotiate compensatory resource transfers with the United States to forestall similar withdrawals from Japan and the Pacific Basin.

Bickering and badgering the Japanese to increase their contributions to defense has not gotten the United States very far—except in the hard feelings department. Correctly using the leverage the United States has over Japan—without threats—promises to elicit more help and less resentment. A U.S. troop withdrawal from Europe could save the United States billions of dollars at the same time it helps its allies free themselves from their dangerous defense dependence on this country. The feedback effects on Japan of a troop withdrawal from Europe makes the case for a European withdrawal even stronger.

10

Withdrawing from Korea: The Right Thing for the Wrong Reason

On March 10, 1977, President Jimmy Carter was asked the following questions during a news conference at the White House:

Q. At the risk of oversimplification, sir, I believe I understand that during the campaign you proposed a gradual withdrawal of American ground troops from Korea.

A. Yes.

Q. Yet, after your revised budget went to Congress, the Army has gone to Congress and asked in fiscal 1978 for a doubling of military construction funds for Korea, and in the three ensuing years for more than $110 million for similar construction. How does that square with your withdrawal plans?

A. My commitment to withdraw American ground troops from Korea has not changed. I'll be meeting this afternoon with the Foreign Minister of South Korea. This will be one of the matters that I will discuss. I've also talked to General Vessey, who is in charge of our armed forces in South Korea.

181

I think that the time period as I described in the campaign months—a four- or five-year time period—is appropriate. The schedule for withdrawal of American ground troops would have to be worked out very carefully with the South Korean government. It would also have to be done with the full understanding and perhaps participation of Japan.

I would want to leave in place in South Korea adequate ground forces owned by, controlled by, the South Korean government to protect themselves against any intrusion from North Korea.

I would envision a continuation of American air cover for South Korea over a long period of time.

But these are the basic elements, and I'm very determined that over a period of time, as described just then, that our ground troops would be withdrawn.[1]

Nine years have passed since that press conference took place, and the American ground troops in South Korea proved to have a lot more staying power than the American president. Jimmy Carter no longer is in the White House—and today there remain 29,200 of the 33,000 American ground troops that were there in 1977 when Carter announced the withdrawal. Why did Carter want the troops out of Korea, and why did he fail? Are the lessons to be learned from Carter's failed pullback applicable to the broad spectrum of America's defense commitments, or are they specific to the nation that occupies the southern half of the Korean peninsula?

JIMMY CARTER'S "MORAL IMPERIALISM"

The major problem with the proposed pullout from South Korea was Jimmy Carter's reasons for doing it. Reportedly, the withdrawal was not the work of the President's foreign policy advisers, but was Carter's own idea. "On one side there is the President and on the other side there is everyone else," is the way one aide described the apparently fierce debate inside the White House over the Korean pullout. The then-president of South Korea, Park Chung Hee, personally rubbed Jimmy Carter the wrong way. Park abridged the freedoms of many Koreans. He persecuted and jailed his political opponents. And he bribed—or attempted to bribe—several members of the U.S. Congress to follow a more favorable policy toward his regime. President Carter decided that American power and prestige should not be identified with an authoritarian regime like Park's. Carter wanted South Korea to have a more moral government, and was willing to do all he could to help bring it about.

"The administration has started a thorough policy review of relations with South Korea," noted *The New York Times* in March 1977.

> The outline of the new policy is emerging, with options for specific decisions to be presented to President Carter shortly. Concern for human rights will be a priority item, officials said, and hearings in Congress will focus more attention on that issue.... Administration officials said that President Carter and Secretary of State Cyrus R. Vance expressed the administration's concern over continued violations of human rights in Korea to the visiting South Korean Foreign Minister, Park Tong Jin.[2]

Concern over the "human rights" policies of the South Korean government did not begin or end with Jimmy Carter. According to Robert E. White, ambassador to El Salvador during the Carter administration, the regime of the present South Korean President, Chun Doo Hwan, also "is intolerant of dissent and routinely treats political activists to harassment and imprisonment." The ex-foreign ambassador argues that "the fundamental error of the Reagan administration in South Korea is to identify United States power and prestige with the survival of a military regime dedicated to hanging onto power regardless of the people's will."[3] Robert E. White must have been one of Jimmy Carter's favorite ambassadors.

Whether merely a tactic to promote a greater sensitivity for human rights among South Korea's rulers, or an end in itself, Jimmy Carter's proposed pullout from South Korea is a textbook example of the moral isolationism that has plagued and, as Ambassador White's comment indicates, continues to plague the American Left. Although administration officials insisted at the time that Carter's attempt to disassociate the United States from the repressive policies of the Park regime was to be carried out in a way that "preserved the military balance on the Korean peninsula," in fact, strategic considerations played a distinctly minor role in the original decision to withdraw. Moral absolutists, like Jimmy Carter, want to disassociate this country from "immoral" allies no matter what the strategic implications of decoupling and no matter how immoral the opposition may be. Allies are written off simply because of Washington's dissatisfaction with their internal policies of repression.

In his memoirs of the Carter years, Carter's national security advisor, Zbigniew Brzezinski, recalls a speech Democratic candidate Jimmy Carter made at Notre Dame in May 1976, in which he quoted John F. Kennedy saying that we should not insist on identical governments or on all nations of the world accepting our standards exactly. "But," Carter added, "we cannot look away when a government tortures its own people, or jails them for their beliefs, or denies minorities fair treatment or the right to migrate or the right to worship."[4] When the President said in his inaugural speech that "our commitment to human rights must be absolute," he was expressing a moral absolutism that endangered the United States and its allies alike.

In Korea, Carter's moral absolutism led him to focus his indignation on the undoubtedly authoritarian regime in South Korea while ignoring the much more serious totalitarian regime that threatened it from the North. "The Koreans have never had a democratic or constitutional system," writes Masataka Kosaka, professor of international politics at Kyoto University.

> Viewed in this context, the dictatorship of Park Chung-hee in the South was very natural. Some U.S. observers may be impressed with the degree of pluralism in South Korea. Unlike their counterparts in North Korea, people in the South are at least willing to express dissent. But one should not mistake these factions for the kind of pluralism associated with a democratic system. Korea's tradition of authoritarianism poses a formidable obstacle to the establishment of a democratic system.[5]

"The Carter administration's policies concerning human rights in Korea also seem to be based on an insufficient appreciation of the realities of the Korean situation," writes Fuji Kamiya, professor of international relations at Keio University. "It is true that Park Chung-hee, like Kim Il-sung (the Northern leader), saw himself as a god. Both Koreas have felt that need for a dictatorial system. But it is inappropriate for Carter to expect the Koreans to practice democracy or to respect human rights as defined by the United States. Korean and U.S. standards simply are not the same."[6]

Many Americans, and not only Jimmy Carter, apparently have a great deal of difficulty accepting this point. "The American tendency towards universalism, toward the assumption that others think and behave just as we do, is utterly inappropriate when applied to foreign policy," argues Jeane Kirkpatrick, former U.S. ambassador to the United Nations. "When we project our own hopes and fears and goals on people from other civilizations, we may be projecting hopes and fears and goals that aren't there at all."[7]

Indeed, in pushing American moral standards of conduct upon the South Koreans, Jimmy Carter appeared to have forgotten the reasons American troops were in South Korea in the first place. The United States did not fight the Korean War to make South Korea's political system into a carbon copy of its own. Nor was the war fought to impose U.S. moral standards on South Koreans— "moral imperialism" was not, and is not, the basis of U.S. support. The only reason the United States entered the Korean War was to stop the Communists from imposing *their* system on the South Koreans. It is tantamount to a betrayal of the American soldiers who fought and died in Korea to have risked what they helped secure there—an independent South Korea.

Even though President Carter discounted the strategic implications of his order to withdraw American troops from South Korea over a five-year period, other, more sober, heads in Washington were deeply concerned about the effects withdrawal would have on the military balance in Korea. Would the South Korean army be able to deter an attack from the North without the help of American ground forces and the reduced overall U.S. commitment to the defense of South Korea that withdrawal implied? Or would the North Koreans find the Carter pullout too provocative to resist and thus launch a preemptive attack? The answers to these questions were by no means clear-cut and, by focusing his fire exclusively on the moral aspects of withdrawal, Carter ceded the strategic arguments to his opponents.

This proved to be a major political mistake. A February 1978 report to the Senate Foreign Relations Committee by two senators from Carter's own Democratic Party, Hubert Humphrey and John Glenn, was highly critical of the withdrawal plan and called for legislation requiring President Carter to give Congress full detailed military justification before each increment of his planned withdrawal. In April 1978, in a direct challenge to President Carter, the House Armed Services Committee voted overwhelmingly to prevent a "premature" withdrawal of U.S. ground forces from Korea. The coup de grace to Carter's plan, however, came from "new" U.S. army intelligence reports, which showed the North Korean army to consist of forty-one divisions instead of the twenty-eight divisions previously believed to exist. Though there was considerable suspicion at the time that estimates had been "cooked up" to thwart the President, they were nonetheless sufficient to put the troop withdrawal on hold until the 1980 presidental campaign. When Carter phased the controversial withdrawal over a five-year period, he gave his opponents in Washington the time they needed to defeat him—and defeat him they did.

THE STRATEGIC CASE FOR WITHDRAWAL

The ironic part of Carter's policies toward South Korea is that the President may have been right for wanting the troops out. The fact that Carter's proposed pullout was undertaken because of his dissatisfaction with the moral content of Korea's domestic policies does not mean that a strategic case for withdrawal could not have been made at the time. In fact, a compelling strategic case could have been made but wasn't. The most important element in the case for U.S. strategic restraint in South Korea is Korean defense free-riding.

Even though the South Koreans are technically still at war with North Korea and live under the threat of a military invasion on a daily basis, they spent only 6 percent of their gross national product on defense in 1982. This is an extremely small sum, especially since in that same year the North Koreans are estimated to have spent anywhere from 10 to 20 percent of their GNP on defense. To some extent, the disparity in defense-spending ratios between the two Koreas reflects the fact that South Korea has a higher level of economic output than the North, has a much higher economic growth, and also has a larger population. From 1970 to 1979, for example, the average annual growth rate in South Korea was 10.3 percent—an extraordinarily high figure compared not only to North Korea (which refuses to publish economic statistics), but to most countries in the Western world. Thus, while South Korea finances its military expenditures from its high economic growth, North Korea must have a high defense-spending/GNP ratio because its economic growth rate is so slack.

Excellent economic performance in the Republic of Korea explains part of its low defense-spending/GNP ratio, but does not explain it all. There is good reason to believe, for example, that the presence of American ground troops in South Korea encourages the South Koreans to keep the defense-spending ratio artificially low. American ground troops apparently play the same role in South Korea that they do in Western Europe. In both cases they are part of a "trip-wire" strategy to ensure American involvement should hostilities break out. With Uncle Sam's enormous defense facilities to back them up, South Koreans feel comfortable economizing on their defense, using the resources they save to build up their private economy. This is precisely the strategy Washington wanted the Republic of Korea to follow in the early days of U.S. support, because an economically strong South Korea was perceived as a means by which communism could be combated in the Pacific Basin region.

Empirical evidence supports the thesis that South Korea defense "free-rides" on the United States. From 1975 to 1979, for example, South Koreans maintained their defense spending/GNP ratio at a constant 5 percent figure. Between 1980 and 1982, however, the figure climbed to 6 percent—an increase of 20 percent. This sudden jump was not mere happenstance. "In response to a request from President Carter during his July 1979 visit to Seoul," writes Franklin B. Weinstein, "South Korean officials indicated plans to increase defense spending in 1980 by an extra one percent of GNP (approximately $500 million)."[8] Of course, by July 1979 the American withdrawal already had been suspended, so that the $500 million may be interpreted as the price the South Koreans were willing to pay to make sure the U.S. troops remained in place. Obviously, the South Koreans felt they were saving at least 1 percent of their gross national product by having the American ground troops in their country. In fact, they probably were saving much more. Israel, for example, whose geo-political situation bears several striking similarities to that of South Korea though it does not have the kind of U.S. defense guarantee provided South Korea, spent 35.7 percent of its GNP on defense in 1982.

Though the South Koreans clearly were thankful for the suspension of the American troop withdrawal, their reaction to Carter's original announcement in 1977 provides evidence that when the United States withdraws defense support from its allies—or at least announces it will withdraw over an extended period of time—rather than fall into a frenzy of appeasement and sue the enemy for peace, they rally behind their leaders and increase their military efforts. "The South Koreans adapted extremely well to the withdrawal decision," writes Makoto Momoi, professor of international relations at the National Defense College of Japan.

> The Seoul government responded to the withdrawal plan by moving to consolidate the populace behind President Park ... and by taking steps to accelerate the modernization of the Korean armed forces. Not only was the ROK's (South Korea's) Force Improvement Program stepped up, but there was a more rapid development of South Korean defense production capabilities, including substantial improvements in the capabilities for production of sophisticated arms. Equally important, the South Korean people demonstrated an increased willingness to bear sacrifice. Even opposition groups rallied to support the president on this issue. This left the South Koreans feeling stronger and more self-confident than before. Of course, the knowledge that U.S. troops were to be gradually phased out over five years rather than immediately pulled out, as had previously been feared, allayed feelings of uneasiness and resentment among the South Koreans.[9]

In fact, the South Koreans responded to the American troop withdrawal just as many opponents of withdrawal had feared—by building up their military strength. "Opponents of disengagement," writes Selig Harrison, "have argued that the South will react to U.S. withdrawal by accelerating its defense buildup, and that the accompanying anxieties will foreclose any peaceful dialogue with the North."[10] American "détente-niks," who want to keep South Korea dependent on the United States, hope that sooner or later the South will sue the North for peace out of weakness and despair. The American people should support withdrawal for the very same reason the détente-niks oppose it—because by bolstering the confidence and military capacities of the South Koreans, withdrawal will prevent the eventual collapse of their political will to carry on the struggle with the North.

A cripple needs a crutch for ambulatory purposes, but a crutch can turn an otherwise healthy person into a cripple. There is good reason to fear the crutch of American ground troops is turning the South Koreans into cripples. Although the South Koreans have an enormous economic advantage over the North, from a strategic point of view this is largely balanced by the distinct psychological inferiority complex suffered by the South Koreans vis-à-vis the North. "Even though the average standard of living in North Korea may be lower than the standard of living of South Koreans," writes former South Korean CIA Director Kim Hyung Wook, "I believe that the people of North Korea live with a greater sense of satisfaction. . . . The discipline and ideological zeal of the North Korean Communists is much stronger than that of the South Koreans. In fact, I feel that there is no comparison; the will of the North Koreans is almost 100 times stronger than the will of the South Koreans."[11]

The South Koreans suffer from a psychological inferiority complex and inadequate political will because they are constantly reminded of their extraordinary dependence on a foreign power for their survival by the presence of American ground troops in their country. According to Selig Harrison,

> The South's psychological malaise basically results from an angry ambivalence with respect to its dependence on the United States and its U.S.–promoted [economic] dependence on Japan. On the one hand, the U.S. presence is a constant irritant to nationalist sensitivities; on the other, there is a deep feeling that as one of those responsible for dividing the country, Washington has a responsibility to support Seoul until Korea is reunited on terms favorable to the South. Similarly, while the Japanese presence arouses bitter memories of the colonial period, there is a feeling that it is an unavoidable expedient in the South's contest with the North.[12]

The North Koreans, on the other hand, do not have foreign troops on their soil and they do not have to cooperate with their former colonial master "as an expedient in its contest with the South."[13]

Several commentators have noted the link between the presence of American troops in South Korea and South Korea's morale problems. Franklin Weinstein, for example, argues that

> maintaining U.S. forces in South Korea beyond the time when they are really needed may be damaging to the South Koreans. For example, whatever "psychological inferiority" the South Koreans may feel *vis-à-vis* the North will only be perpetuated by a continued U.S. presence. Such inferiority can be overcome only by showing that they can in fact stand without U.S. support. The U.S. military presence in Korea is easily exploited psychologically by the North Koreans. It causes considerable embarrassment and frustration for South Korean youth; it serves to buttress the North Koreans' claim to the mantle of Korean nationalism and their characterization of the southern regime as a mere puppet of the United States. Pyongyang can argue to its own populace and to receptive audiences in the Third World that the Seoul government would collapse if American military support were withdrawn.[14]

But American military support was withdrawn—at least, it was announced by the Carter administration that it would be withdrawn—and rather than collapse, the Seoul government actually was strengthened by the move. The prophets of doom were proved wrong about South Korea, just as they undoubtedly are wrong about the demoralizing effects American ground troop withdrawal would have on such European countries as West Germany. Indeed, the two Koreas provide an interesting parallel to the two Germanies. Both countries are split into Communist and non-Communist parts; both have a cultural need for reunification; and both have American ground troops stationed in the non-Communist part. However, while North Korea has no foreign Communist forces stationed on its soil, East Germany has substantial Soviet troops located inside its borders.

The analogy between the two divided countries is so close that the foregoing quote from Weinstein about the poor psychological effect American ground troops have on South Koreans can be restated almost word for word, substituting East and West Germany for North and South Korea at the appropriate points. Thus: The

U.S. military presence in "Germany" is easily exploited psychologically by the "East Germans." It causes similar embarrassment and frustration for "West German" youth; it serves to buttress the "East Germans" claim to the mantle of "German" nationalism and their characterization of the "Western" regime as a mere puppet of the United States. "East Berlin" can argue to its own populace and to receptive audiences in the Third World that the "Bonn" government would collapse if American military support were withdrawn.

KOREAN AND JAPANESE DEFENSE FREE-RIDING

An American troop withdrawal from the Republic of Korea (ROK) could kill two birds with one stone—it could end both Korean and Japanese defense free-riding on the United States. The Korean peninsula holds extreme strategic significance for Japan. That Korea is a divided country is a big strategic plus for Japan, just as the division of Germany is a plus for the Soviet Union. The reason is that the ROK itself is a potential military threat to Japan. Korea also serves as a vital barrier between Japan and its two principal enemies—China and the Soviet Union. If either of these two countries were to gain control over the Korean peninsula, Japan would have no choice but to rearm.

The strategic role Korea plays for Japanese security normally would impel Japan to take an active interest in Korean affairs. But the Japanese have been able to opt out of Korea by getting Americans to do their job for them.

> The role that the United States has played in the defense of Japanese interests [writes James William Morley of Columbia University] goes a long way to explain why Japan itself has been so slow to advance its own strategic interest in Korea in the postwar period. ... As a result, while the Japanese are extremely sensitive to developments in Korea—especially including any that may disturb the peninsula's tranquility—so long as the United States is ready and able to stand in the front line, they have preferred to stay in the rear.[15]

Morley continues:

> The logic of Japan's position is well explained by the so-called
> theory of collective goods. Both Japan and the United States have
> an interest in a favorably aligned Korea—or half Korea. Presumably
> each should share the burden for securing this *collective good* pro-
> portionately to the benefit each receives. It would, of course, be
> difficult to arrive at a common evaluation of such benefits, but even
> if one could, there is a powerful tendency for the United States to
> bear more, and Japan less, than what might be thought of as a fair
> share.... Given this power and the strength of its own interest in
> Korea, the United States has been inclined to act there—to the
> benefit of both the United States and Japan—whether Japan acts
> or not; and knowing this, Japan prefers to bear no more burdens
> than may be required to keep the United States fully committed.[16]

Japan's ability to free-ride on the United States in Korea has
been particularly convenient for the island nation, given that relations between those two nations have been extremely strained
since Korea gained its independence from Japan after World War
II.

> The Japanese attitude toward Korea [writes Morley] also finds
> its particular origins in the colonial experience, from which the Ko-
> reans emerged resentful that Japan had tried to subordinate their
> ancient civilization to its own, and the Japanese came out equally
> resentful that Korea was not more grateful for the contributions the
> Japanese felt they had made to Korea's modernization. Perhaps no-
> where in the world has the relationship between two countries been
> more poisoned by the colonial past.[17]

Selig Harrison appears to agree: "Given the depth of the bitterness
left over from the colonial period," he writes, "the potential for
future conflict between Japan and Korea would appear to be serious
under the best of circumstances. Colonialism aggravated what was
already an endemically difficult socio-cultural encounter between
Japanese and Koreans, touching off a psychological cycle of challenge and response that continues still."[18]
Given Japan's present antimilitary posture, the bitter aftermath
of the colonial period, and the resources Japan saves by letting

Uncle Sam assume full responsibility for the security of the Pacific Basin, it is apparent that maintenance of the status quo on the Korean peninsula is one of Japan's principal foreign policy objectives. In particular, the Japanese perceive American troops in the Republic of Korea to benefit them in a variety of ways. First, the troops help keep the North Koreans in check. Japan certainly does not want to see North Korea overrun the South. But just as a reunited Communist Korea ruled from Pyongyang would be seen as a severe danger by the Japanese, so would a reunited capitalist Korea ruled from Seoul. The Japanese are comfortable with the idea that the South Koreans are dependent upon, and therefore controlled by, the United States; they realize that the American troops restrain the South Koreans from attacking the North as much as they discourage the North Koreans from attacking the South. And if there is one thing Japan hopes to avoid, it is an outbreak of overt hostilities on the Korean peninsula.

"It is clear," writes Franklin Weinstein, "that the overriding Japanese interest in Korea is the avoidance of hostilities which would polarize the Japanese people and could lead to Japanese involvement in the conflict. Avoiding an 'explosion' on the peninsula is deemed even more important than preservation of a non-communist South Korea."[19]

The Japanese also are extremely concerned that South Korea does not obtain nuclear weapons, for a nuclear South Korea surely would deliver the coup de grace to Japan's antimilitary policies. Most experts are agreed that the Korean development most likely to lead to a military buildup in Japan, including the acquisition of nuclear weapons, is the development of an independent nuclear capacity by South Korea. Even the Soviet nuclear buildup in the Pacific is deemed less threatening to Japan by some than a nuclear South Korea. The Americans, Japanese reason, would help them countervene a Soviet buildup. But Japan could not use (or abuse) the excuse of containment of communism to get the United States to shield it from a nuclear South Korea. The island nation would be forced to deal with South Korea on its own.

The Japanese have been fortunate that the United States shares its objective of keeping South Korea nonnuclear. As in the cases of both Japan and West Germany, a critical reason the United States provides nuclear protection for the South Koreans is that it does not want them to provide nuclear protection for themselves—that is, the United States seeks to prevent nuclear proliferation. The conventional reason for being against nuclear proliferation is that it is said to decrease the probability of a nuclear holocaust. A less conventional reason why Washington favors nonproliferation is the mistaken belief that American nuclear protection gives the United States extraordinary control over the foreign and defense policies of the countries protected by it.

The danger to the U.S. from a policy of control through nuclear protection is that it can, and often has, led to anti-Americanism in allied countries. Ceding control over one's foreign and defense policies to the United States does not make the United States popular abroad. On the other hand, if the United States were to allow South Korea to have nuclear weapons, it is a virtual certainty that North Korea would get them too. The United States appears to have an unwritten agreement with the Soviet Union—one which the Soviets apparently have kept—that the United States will deny South Korea nuclear weapons if the Soviets deny them to North Korea, and vice versa. So long as the Soviets keep their part of the bargain, the United States should do likewise. The bellicose nature of the North Korean regime makes it imperative that it be denied nuclear weapons.

It may be argued in extension of this principle of reciprocal nuclear denial that the United States continue to deny nuclear weapons to West Germany as well as South Korea. The cases of the two Koreas and the two Germanies, however, are not parallel in this regard. The Soviets have an inordinate fear of a nuclear Germany. They are hardly likely to give East Germany nuclear weapons in response to a nuclear West Germany. Two nuclear Germanies, to them, would be worse than one.

A DIFFERENCE OF VIEWS

While the status quo of an American-enforced-and-financed stable equilibrium between two mutually offsetting parts of a permanently divided Korea is perceived by the Japanese to be in their national interest, the question for Americans is whether it is in our national interest as well. The conventional wisdom is to answer this question in the affirmative.

> When one does focus squarely on the Korean problem as such [writes Selig Harrison], it soon becomes clear that Japanese and U.S. interests are largely congruent. At present, the governing interest of both Japan and the United States in Korea lies in reducing North-South tensions and in preventing a renewed, large-scale military conflict in which either of the two countries could become even directly involved. This goal is linked to their broader mutual interest in the preservation of regional stability and the avoidance of conflict with China or the Soviet Union. For both Japan and the United States, the danger of renewed conflict in the peninsula poses a continuing threat to their efforts to improve relations with Peking and Moscow.[20]

Harrison's view on the congruency of U.S. and Japanese interests in Korea are mirrored by Japanese international relations expert Fuji Kamiya.

> Japanese and U.S. interests in Korea are essentially the same, particularly in the short run. But there are some differences. Japan tends to be more satisfied with the existing situation on the peninsula. The United States, as the Nixon Doctrine and Carter's withdrawal policy show, is unwilling to contemplate the indefinite continuation of the current U.S. military presence. It should, however, be possible to avoid a major split between Japanese and U.S. policies, since the Americans are likely to recognize that any rash change in the present situation would jeopardize the overriding U.S. interest in the maintenance of peace and the deterrence of armed conflict.[21]

How vacuous the conventional wisdom sounds when coming from these two distinguished experts. Of course, Japan and the United States are united in wanting to prevent a "renewed large-scale military conflict" on the Korean peninsula. What major country does not share in such a unity? What makes the two countries different, however—and what is critical for determining congruency of interest—is the price each is willing to pay for peace. According to Weinstein, "avoiding an 'explosion' on the peninsula is deemed even more important [by the Japanese] than preservation of a non-communist South Korea."[22] Selig Harrison writes: "Most

Japanese appear less fearful of an eventual communist triumph in Korea than of two possible outcomes. One would be a conflict entailing U.S. intervention that could, in turn, embroil Japan militarily. The other fear involves precipitate U.S. disengagement from the South that would not allow Japan time to reshape its approach to the peninsula."[23]

Unlike the Japanese, the United States never would sacrifice a non-Communist South Korea as the price for peace on the Korean peninsula. The United States made a blood commitment to the South Koreans, and a betrayal of that commitment would be a betrayal of the American soldiers who fought, and died, in the Korean War. This highlights a critical difference between Japanese and American long-run interests in Korea. U.S. interest in Korea is part of its global struggle to contain communism. The Japanese interest is a nationalist one—to contain the Koreans. Japan seeks to prevent a militarized and unified Korea—capitalist or Communist—that could threaten Japan. The United States would welcome a unified Korea, so long as it was capitalist and ruled from Seoul.

"A unified Korea, combining the economic and military power of North and South, could pose a formidable threat to Japan if it were to adopt a strongly nationalistic, explicitly anti-Japanese, attitude," writes Daniel Okimoto. "For this reason," explains the Stanford University political scientist, "some Japanese believe that their national interest will be best served if the Korean peninsula remains divided... perhaps on the pattern of the 'German solution.'"[24] The United States, however, should be extremely wary of imposing a "German solution" upon Korea. In West Germany, the permanent presence of U.S. troops has led to anti-Americanism, neutralism, and pacifism. The United States does not want this duplicated in the Republic of Korea. Moreover, it would be extremely demoralizing for South Korea if the best its principal benefactor wanted for it was permanent division. The long-run strategic objective of the South Koreans must be a united capitalist Korea under South Korean auspices; otherwise the West will lose South Korea just as it is currently in danger of losing West Germany.

Not only does Japan's nationalistic interest diverge from the U.S. ideological interest in Korea, but the two actually are in serious conflict with one another. Kim Il Sung has imposed a ruthless

Communist totalitarianism upon the people of North Korea. One would have to look far and wide to find a more fanatic, more aggressive, and more anti-American country. Yet despite North Korea's status as an incorrigible Communist puppet state, Japan has chosen to give it economic assistance. According to a report in *The Wall Street Journal*, North Korea has agreed to its first joint venture with Japanese companies: a chain of 31 department stores that sells Japanese consumer electronics, household goods, and clothing. "The arrangement," according to the press report, "is part of a push by long-isolated North Korea to open its doors to Western and Japanese capital and technology. Since the Korean War, South Korea's economic growth has been much faster than that of the North, and Pyongyang is trying to narrow the gap."[25] The question is why Japan is helping.

Profit clearly is not part of the answer. An official of the Asahi Trading Company, one of the two Japanese firms participating in the project, admitted that "the partners don't expect to make large profits from the venture, but hope to bring business acumen to North Korea and learn more about the country's consumer preferences." The North Koreans themselves undoubtedly were surprised to learn that they were even allowed to have consumer preferences. Why the sudden Japanese interest in North Korea? After all, the Communist government in Pyongyang has steadfastly refused to repay the several hundreds of millions of dollars it currently owes Japan. But according to the the *The Wall Street Journal* story, "the Asahi president said he wasn't concerned about North Korea's debt-repayment problem," even though the country for several years has been in arrears on its foreign debt, estimated at about $2 billion. Clearly, politics rather than economics is behind Japan's joint venture with North Korea.

As explained in chapter 8, Japan does not follow a détente-as-defense strategy so far as the Soviet Union is concerned. But they are following a variant of that strategy in North Korea. Japan apparently is willing to invest a certain sum of money in North Korea to "buy peace" on the peninsula. Thus, analogous to the situation in the Atlantic Alliance where the United States subsidizes the Western Europeans—who then turn around and subsidize the Soviets to "buy peace"—in the Pacific Alliance, the United States subsidizes the Japanese—who then subsidize the North Koreans.

Paying off the enemy with American money, however, is not the reason the United States formed either of these alliances. Washington should let Tokyo know that its business ventures in North Korea are not at all appreciated.

In addition to divergent long-term strategic interests in Korea, Japan and the United States also have conflicting economic interests in preserving a non-Communist South Korea. "South Korea's economy has not only 'taken off,'" writes Fuji Kamiya, "but the country is in fact already quite industrialized. In perhaps ten years [1990], South Korea will be one of Japan's strongest economic rivals. Indeed, this competition could lead to serious problems, because Korea and Japan—unlike the United States and Japan—have no reservoir of good feeling to fall back on when their economic relationship is strained."[26]

Some may argue, of course, that the emergence of South Korea as an industrial power directly threatens the United States as well as Japan. But the South Korean economy promises to be much more complementary to, rather than competitive with, that of the United States. Economic experts, like Gary Saxonhouse, predict that the expected surge in South Korean exports in the forthcoming years will not come at the expense of domestic U.S. production, but rather at the expense of Japanese exports. "South Korean exports," claims Saxonhouse, "may replace Japanese exports in overseas markets rather than compete directly overseas with import substitutes, because South Korea has moved away from the Japanese strategy of targeting exports at particular import substitutes abroad."[27]

Moreover, increased Korean exports will generate increased Korean income, which will be used in part to buy U.S. products. This means greater exports for the United States. And while it is true that increased Korean income will be offset by decreased Japanese income, because the Korean market is more open—that is, less protectionist—than the Japanese market, the net effect of the redistribution of income from Japan to South Korea should be distinctly positive for U.S. exports. South Korea also will give the United States the extra leverage it needs over Japan to open up its markets as well. "Why," we could ask the Japanese, "should we buy from you when we can buy from the Koreans, who at least reciprocate our purchases from them with purchases of their own from us?" Considering, then, the stiff economic competition that South Korea is likely to provide Japan in years to come, is it really surprising that Japan gives the impression that it would be willing to sacrifice South Korea to the communists as the "price for peace" on the Korean peninsula?

In summation, the burden of defending Japan from Korea clearly should be a Japanese burden, not an American one. U.S. interest in Korea simply is to prevent the spread of communism from North Korea to South Korea. But because containment of communism in Korea has what for the United States is the unintended side effect of stalemating Japan's potential enemy, the Japanese receive a substantial economic and strategic benefit from U.S. operations in Korea. This is the basis of Japan's free ride on the United States in Korea. When the United States bears the cost of enforcing the peace in Korea, Japan saves resources that it otherwise would have to spend to protect itself from its potential enemy.

PLAYING THE KOREAN CARD

How, then, can the United States get the Japanese to pay a fair share of the cost of maintaining U.S. troops in South Korea without resort to the kind of badgering and threats that, for example, have sullied U.S. relations with Japan over the issue of Japanese protection? The answer to the question of how the United States can "play the Korean card" to its advantage is that (1) Washington should announce an immediate and phased withdrawal of U.S. troops from South Korea and (2) adopt a policy of "wait and see" as to how the Japanese respond. If, as seems likely, the Japanese respond by offering to contribute to the costs of the U.S. military presence in South Korea in the event the United States should reverse its withdrawal decision, that offer can be considered without prejudice. If not, Japan can react to the "new South Korea"—unrestrained by the United States—in whatever manner it sees fit.

What better proof can there be that an American troop withdrawal from South Korea would be a good thing than that all of the "experts" are against the idea? William Watts, a public opinion analyst, took a sampling of forty-nine "unusually knowledgeable" individuals from the U.S. government, private business, labor, journalism, the legal profession, and the academic community— all experts

whose careers involve them directly with Korean affairs. If there is one factor that characterizes the perceptions of virtually all members of this specially chosen leadership group, [writes Watts] it is the remarkable unanimity of opinion held about the genuine importance of Korea, its economic well-being, and, in particular, *the guarantee of its security for U.S. interests* [emphasis mine]. . . . Any further withdrawal of the remaining U.S. ground forces from Korea is looked upon as a policy error of potentially disastrous proportions. *On this point, more than any other, there is almost complete agreement* [emphasis mine]. Troop withdrawals are seen as giving a dangerous signal to North Korea; in fact, seen as coming close to inviting Kim Il-sung to move South before he passes from the scene. In addition, the threat or actuality of further troop withdrawals is viewed as injecting unnecessary fears into the South Korean body politic, thereby increasing the potential for instability in that portion of the divided peninsula. *A continued U.S. troop presence, at about the present level, is endorsed by the overwhelming majority of this particular leadership group* [emphasis mine].[28]

The reader must be warned: When there is such unanimity of opinion among the "experts," you know they must be wrong!

U.S. withdrawal of its ground troops from South Korea, however, should be more than simply a strategy for getting the Japanese to compensate the United States for its security guarantee of South Korea. The reason is that containment of communism in the Pacific region requires that Japan be enticed out of its "anti-military" equilibrium to play a much more active military role in the Pacific. From the mid-seventies to the mid-eighties, the Soviet Union has greatly increased its military strength in the Pacific. According to James William Morley,

The Soviets have deployed at least one-quarter of their ground and air forces in the Far East, together with a theater nuclear complement of SS-20s and Backfire bombers. While ostensibly arrayed against China, these forces obviously could be turned toward the Korean front. The Soviet Pacific Fleet is being strengthened rapidly. With a tonnage larger than that of the U.S. Seventh Fleet and expanding access to port facilities in North Korea and Vietnam, it presents an increasingly destabilizing aspect.[29]

It is true, of course, that the United States remains the preeminent power in the Pacific. But it also is true that the United States no longer can bear the burden of containing communism without help from allies such as Japan.

> While U.S. interests remain global and its desire for leadership remains strong [writes Morley], it can no longer bear the bulk of the non-communist world's security burden as it has in the past. . . . But for more than a decade now it has been clear that beyond this hemisphere, in the *conventional defense* [my italics] of even regions of primary concern—including Northeast Asia, Western Europe, and the Middle East—the United States cannot adequately make up the shortfall of its allies and friends. . . . It is time that each of us in the southern coalition faced the obvious: in the immediate future, a balance of forces in Northeast Asia can only be secured by a systematic buildup of our conventional power there. . . . But the continuing growth of Soviet power in Northeast Asia and the Northwest Pacific requires that Japan's minimal contributions be upped if the security of Korea is not to deteriorate below a level commensurate with Japan's vital interests.[30]

What all this comes down to is that so long as the military balance in the Pacific remained comfortably in favor of the United States, Japan's anti-military, defense free-riding policies could be tolerated. The United States could afford whatever benefits accrued to Japan from its mini-defense policies because it did not need Japan's military help to secure the Pacific. Today, the situation is different in two important respects. First, because of the extraordinarily rapid economic growth of both Japan and the "Gang of Four"—South Korea, Hong Kong, Taiwan and Singapore—the West has more to lose by an expansion of Communist influence in the Pacific Basin region. This area is the future economic breadbasket of the Western world. Second, because of the deteriorating military balance in the region, the probability that the breadbasket may be lost has increased. America cannot afford to ignore this increase in both the costs and probability of expanded Communist influence in the Pa-

cific Basin. Policies that were appropriate in the earlier era of un-
doubted Soviet weakness have become dangerous in today's world
of growing Soviet strength.

Many foreign policy experts, however, do not appear to have
noticed that we have moved from one era to another, and continue
to offer yesterday's solutions to today's problems. According to
Selig Harrison, "defenders of the U.S. presence in Korea contend
that a U.S. withdrawal would lead to a militarized, possibly nuclear-
armed, Japan."[31] Unlike Jimmy Carter, who, in urging withdrawal,
was right for the wrong reasons, these spokesmen for the status
quo, in urging that the United States remain in Korea, are wrong
for the right reasons. Of course, it is true that a "U.S. withdrawal
would lead to a militarized, possibly nuclear-armed, Japan." But
this is a reason why withdrawal should be supported, not one why
it should be opposed. The militarization of Japan is needed to
correct the deteriorating military balance in the Pacific. Thirty or
so years ago, it was proper to support Japanese pacifism. Today,
it is folly.

CONCLUSION

Jimmy Carter's disdain for the domestic policies of Park Chung
Hee has given U.S. troop withdrawal a bad name. It has reinforced
the perception of troop withdrawal "as punishment" and obscured
that of troop withdrawal "as cure." If the United States were to
pull back its troops from South Korea or, say, from Western Europe,
it should do so to help its allies shake off the debilitating syndrome
of defense dependency and weakness—not to punish them because
they are judged to have behaved in an unacceptable manner. Allied
resentment of dependence must not be replaced by an equally negative resentment of the United States for abandonment. When the
time comes for withdrawal, whether or not the allies feel abandoned
will depend to a large extent on U.S. motives or, more precisely,
on allied perception of U.S. motives. In the final analysis, this is
why doing the right thing for the wrong reason turned out as badly
for Jimmy Carter, and the United States, as doing the wrong thing.

11

Facing the Soviet Threat in the Third World

T he confrontation between the United States and the Soviet Union in the Korean War was but a single episode in the ongoing struggle against Soviet imperialism in the Third World. Though the Soviets lost the Korean War, in recent years they have made enormous gains in extending their influence in the poorer countries of the world.

> As a result of the Kremlin's efforts over the past decade [writes Charles Wolf, Jr., of the Rand Corporation], the Soviet imperium now includes Angola, Ethiopia, South Yemen, Vietnam, Laos, Cambodia, Benin, Madagascar, Congo-Brazzaville, Afghanistan, Nicaragua, Syria, and Libya, in addition to its previous satellites, allies, and associates in Eastern Europe, Cuba, and North Korea. . . . While there have been some Soviet losses and setbacks (e.g., Somalia and Egypt) during this period, there is no question that the gains and extensions of the Soviet empire have vastly exceeded the losses and retrenchments.[1]

One reason the Soviets have attained critical influence over the foreign and domestic policies of the aforementioned countries has been their ability to split the opposition to their Third World imperialism. Japan, for example, is the very model of a rich, democratic nation dedicated to the proposition that it should not do anything to defend freedom beyond its borders. As far as Western Europe is concerned, the threat of a Soviet military invasion has effectively neutralized European opposition to Soviet expansion in the Third World. The fact that the United States stands virtually alone among the Western powers concerned with growing Soviet influence in the Third World, and willing to do something about it, makes the adoption of a unilateralist foreign policy by this country all the more urgent.

THE SECRET OF SUCCESS

The success of the Soviets in extending their influence in the Third World is due not only to their ability to neutralize the opposition, but to superior tactics as well. Unlike the United States, which has allowed American combat forces to be used directly in the attempt to contain communism in the Third World on several occasions—Vietnam, Korea, and Lebanon, to name but three—the Soviets rarely allow their troops to be used directly in combat. "Soviet troops are generally only a final, and usually disfavored, resource," writes Charles Wolf, Jr., "whose use is confined to such exceptional circumstances as Afghanistan."[2] The Soviets, in other words, do not have a knee-jerk, "send-in-the-marines" mentality. When "marines" are required, the Kremlin is smart enough to send in the other guys' marines, not their own.

According to Wolf,

> the Soviet Union has developed an artful and complex network of cooperating "fraternal" communist states (e.g., Cuba, Vietnam, East Germany, North Korea, and Nicaragua), as well as supportive non-communist states and entities (e.g., Libya and the Palestine Liberation Organization, PLO). These participants perform military as well as non-military roles *and* provide contributions in forms that vary in different contexts and "projects." Although precise operational details are—unsurprisingly—shrouded in secrecy, orchestration is provided by the Soviet Union, which also pays most of the bills.[3]

The Soviet "takeover network" can be thought of as a set of triangular relationships with the Soviets occupying one corner of the triangle, the Soviet proxy nation at the second corner, and the local Communists in the country of conflict at the third corner. An example could be the Soviet Union, Cuba, and Angola. The Soviets provide Cuba with infrastructure, weapons for the military operations, and economic aid. Cuba, in turn, sends combat forces and military weapons to local communists in the country of conflict. Should the local Communists prevail, the Soviet Union receives a variety of benefits from the new member of its empire, including access to its troops for use as proxy troops in other countries targeted by the Soviets as takeover candidates. Should the Communists lose, on the other hand, the Soviet leaders do not have to face the kind of trouble at home and embarrassment abroad that U.S. leaders faced after defeat in Vietnam or, more recently, the fiasco in Lebanon when 250 U.S. Marines were killed.

The advantages of the Soviet indirect approach to subversion abroad by comparison with America's more direct approach to countering it are many. First, domestic support for participation in the hostilities is likely to be greater, and approbation in case of defeat less, when one's own troops are not directly involved in the fighting. Second, a proxy nation has more flexibility putting troops into, and pulling them out of, conflict areas than a superpower has. This reduces substantially the potential for defense free-riding by locals under the Soviet system. If local Communists in the country of conflict attempt to free-ride on the proxy nation by doing less as the proxy does more, the proxy may simply withdraw its troops. Third, the indirect approach is less likely to lead to a superpower nuclear confrontation. This gives the proxy nation additional degrees of freedom to act by comparison with a superpower. Fourth, in a dispute that takes place in a Third World country, it is more useful, for propaganda purposes, for another Third World country to intervene than the superpower itself. It is somehow less offensive to Third World opinion when black Cubans rather than white Russians intervene in places like Angola.

The example *par excellence* for demonstrating the superiority of the Soviet tactics for extending their influence in the Third World is Vietnam. In retrospect, the biggest mistake made by the United States during the Vietnam War may have been the massive use of

American ground troops in the actual fighting. This undermined support for the war at home, encouraged the South Vietnamese to let the Americans do their fighting for them, and gave the North Vietnamese a tremendous propaganda victory. It is sometimes argued that the United States had to intervene directly because the North Vietnamese were too tough an adversary for the South. But if the United States had done in Vietnam what it did in El Salvador—namely, help the locals help themselves rather than fight their battles for them—the outcome could have been much different.

COPYCATTING THE SOVIETS

The Soviet use of substitute forces to extend their influence in the Third World has been so successful that some leading anti-Communist strategists in the United States are openly advocating that the United States copycat the Soviets by developing an American network of "cooperative forces" to assist "genuine and legitimate movements within the Third World seeking to achieve liberation from communist imperialism and totalitarianism." According to Charles Wolf, Jr., who favors the use of American substitute forces abroad,

> the purpose of these forces would be to contain or reverse communist imperialism in the Third World, and to further the mutual interests of the U.S. and its cooperators in the development of more pluralistic and more open political systems in the Third World. The proposal entails selective, measured, and increased U.S. assistance—rhetoric as well as programmatic—to the indigenous forces of nationalism, independence, and pluralism which currently, as well as potentially, offer resistance to the communist empire of the Soviet Union and its principal associates. It is worth noting that six resistance movements are currently active in communist or "fraternal" socialist countries, namely, Angola, Mozambique, Afghanistan, Cambodia, Ethiopia, and Nicaragua.[4]

The mere mention of Nicaragua should flash a warning signal that beating the Soviets at their own game may be difficult indeed. The Soviets clearly plan to make Nicaragua into a second Cuba.

All the necessary ingredients are in place: the Sandinistas' inherent anti-Americanism, a weak Nicaraguan economy, and a "fraternal" relationship between Nicaragua and Cuba. Not blind to this fact, the Reagan administration has been trying to counter the Soviets by making the Nicaraguan rebels—known as "Contras"—into a U.S. "cooperative force" to neutralize the Sandinistas. For this purpose, Ronald Reagan asked Congress to approve $14 million in aid to the Nicaraguan rebels. Even though our failure to deal with the Sandinistas indirectly through substitute forces means that a more direct approach may have to be effectuated later on, the U.S. Congress initially refused the Reagan administration's request for funds. Had Daniel Ortega, the Sandinista leader, not embarrassed the U.S. Congress by running off to Moscow (presumably to negotiate an arms deal) the moment after it turned down the President's aid request, there would have been no American assistance for the Contras. But Congress reconsidered when Ortega's Moscow trip gave credence to the charge that it is "soft on communism," and agreed to fund $23 million for "humanitarian" purposes only. If Congress refused to support the concept of American cooperative forces in this case—where the danger is so close to home and the lessons of Cuba so unambiguous—can it realistically be expected that Congress ever will support this concept?

The White House, too, must shoulder some of the blame for Congress' initial failure to approve the $14 million in aid to the Nicaraguan rebels. In the aftermath of the President's defeat on this issue, informed voices have indicated that the outcome on Capitol Hill could have been different had Reagan been more forceful in dealing with Congress. For example, the nationally syndicated columnist George Will, no enemy of Mr. Reagan, publicly criticized the president for his failure to go to the people directly to explain why the Contras need—and deserve—American support.[5] Some Republicans in Congress, according to Suzanne Garment in *The Wall Street Journal*, complained they did not get strong enough White House support on the Contra vote.[6] The bottom line of Congress' initial turndown of aid to the rebels appears to have been that, for one reason or other, the President was reluctant to fully use his political capital to ensure passage of the aid bill.

The reasons for this can only be guessed, but certain factors appear to have influenced the president's decision not to go all the way on aid to the Contras. At the same time that Congress voted down the $14 million aid bill (May 1985), President Reagan was battling Congress to get his proposed federal budget adopted. In particular, Reagan was fighting off Democratic attempts to scale down his request for increased military spending. The President and his advisers may well have considered the battle over the budget to be more important than the battle over aid to the Contras. Just as Congress faces trade-offs when considering how to spend the public's money, the President faces trade-offs on how to "spend" his political capital. The more political capital spent on one item, the less he has to spend on others.

The specific problems Reagan faced with Congress over aid to the Nicaraguan rebels illustrates a more general point of why any attempt on the part of the United States to copycat Soviet use of substitute forces is likely to prove ineffective. Just because a given strategy works for one person, or nation, does not mean that it will work for another. Different nations have different traditions, institutions, and cultures that make them more or less suited to different types of activities. In economics, this is called "the principle of comparative advantage." There are several reasons for believing that while the Soviets have a "comparative advantage" in using substitute forces to further their imperialistic ambitions, America's comparative advantage in countering them lies elsewhere.

First, U.S. political institutions have been built on the principle of decentralized power. The Founding Fathers were sufficiently concerned that no man—or groups of men—gain excessive influence over public affairs that they put into the Constitution the principle of separation of powers: that there be three branches of government—executive, legislative, and judicial—and that each branch should be dependent upon, and thus checked by, the other. This is an optimal system of government for an isolationist society concerned with maximizing the individual freedom of its citizens. For a society concerned with developing a network of cooperative forces to thwart an enemy abroad, however, it is inferior to the centralized and secretive Soviet system.

Reflecting on Soviet success in the use of substitute forces, Charles Wolf, Jr., notes that "these imperial operations have been undertaken, with rare exceptions, selectively, flexibly, adroitly, cautiously, and deliberately." Wolf finds "the success of these operations

profoundly puzzling, because flexibility and adroitness are not char-
acteristic of the Soviet system or its leadership, which are more
typically associated with rigidity and regimentation."[7] But the success of the Soviets in developing cooperative forces abroad should
not really come as a surprise.

Once the Soviet decision-makers make up their minds to act, for
instance, there is no analogous institution to the U.S. Congress in
the Soviet Union to frustrate their plans. The trade-off problems
Reagan faces with the Congress to get his program through have
no counterpart in the Soviet system. Perhaps even more important
for the Soviet success with substitute forces is the fact that the
Kremlin is able to work in secret. The doctrine of public account-
ability does not exist in the Soviet Union, and Moscow is not
confronted by a free press determined to expose, and undermine,
each and every covert activity taken by the Kremlin. This gives
Moscow an enormous advantage over Washington so far as freedom
of action in foreign policy is concerned.

In summation, the fact that the Soviets have had considerable
success in extending their influence in the Third World through
use of substitute or cooperative forces does not mean that the United
States will have equal success in countering this influence by copy-
ing them. Soviet institutions are structured to give their leaders
maximum flexibility and resources to pursue subversion abroad;
American institutions are structured to restrain our leaders from
unduly restricting the rights and freedoms of individual citizens.
Playing the Soviet game with American institutions and attitudes
makes about as much sense as would playing the American game
with Soviet institutions. If the United States is to effectively counter
the Soviets in the Third World, the game it plays must be its own.

IS ECONOMIC AID THE AMERICAN GAME?

If the Soviet Union has a comparative advantage in the use of
substitute forces to further its imperialistic ambitions, does the
United States have an analogous comparative advantage in the use
of economic aid to counter the Soviets? At first glance, the answer
to this question appears to be in the affirmative. The United States
clearly is a wealthier country than the Soviet Union. If it has a

comparative advantage in anything, it would appear to be in economics. Certainly the United States can afford to give more economic aid to poor countries than can the U.S.S.R.

Another reason why the comparative advantage of the United
States appears to be in economic aid is the success of the Marshall
Plan. There can be no doubt that the Marshall Plan was an important factor in helping the European economies get back on their
feet again after World War II. Because of this, many argue that
what worked in Western Europe also would work in the Third
World. The idea that a Marshall Plan for the Third World is—or
perhaps should be—the American answer to the Soviet challenge
in the Third World certainly is a widely held one. But like many
widely held ideas, it happens to be incorrect.

This is truly a pity, because the vast wealth of the United States
would make it relatively easy for this country to defeat communism
if the solution to Soviet expansion in the Third World was that
simple. However, two leading international economists, Gottfried
Haberler of Harvard University and Lord Bauer of the London
School of Economics, argue that the success of the Marshall Plan
was a unique occurrence not likely to be duplicated in today's poor
nations. "It is one thing to assist a war-ravished industrial country
put its economy back on its feet," writes Haberler, "and it is an
entirely different thing to help a less-developed, backward country
change its way of life and modernize its economy."[8] Lord Bauer
states that "the success of the Marshall Plan in the early post-war
years is frequently invoked in support of wealth transfer to the
Third World. This analogy is altogether misleading. The damaged
economies of Western Europe had to be revived, not developed. As
was evident from pre-war experience, the personal, social, and
political factors congenial to economic achievement were present."[9]

Few economists, even those who favor economic aid, argue that
aid can substitute for what Peter Bauer calls the "personal, social,
and political factors" necessary for economic development. What
they do argue, however, is that aid is better than nothing—that it
can provide relief for people who suffer from extreme poverty and
that this, too, is important in the fight against the spread of communism. This argument is misleading for two reasons. First, economic aid seldom reaches the poor people for whom it is intended.
Because economic aid is given for the benefit of poor people does

not mean that the poor actually receive it. The reason is that the aid must be intermediated, and what happens in more cases than not is that the intermediary—the government—confiscates all or part of the aid for itself.

The tragedy in Ethiopia is a case in point. One has to be hard-hearted indeed not to be deeply moved in that poverty-stricken North African country. What did it matter if Ethiopians were Communists, capitalists, or whatever? These people are dying a most horrible death before our very eyes—indeed, even as we sat in the comfort and security of our living rooms viewing them on television. Who was not moved to dig into their pockets to give, and give generously, in the face of such calamity?

It goes without saying that all three U.S. television networks— CBS, NBC, and ABC—assured their viewers at the time that the deaths they were viewing on the screens were due to famine—a natural not man-made calamity. But according to a group of concerned physicians, Doctors Without Borders, "more Ethiopians were dying as a result of the policies of their Government than as a result of famine." Their report, entitled "Mass Deportations in Ethiopia," says that as many as 300,000 people are likely to die in the forced re-location from North to South, a death rate of 20 percent. The information in the Report came largely from relief workers and Ethiopian refugees in the Sudan.

According to a story in *The New York Times*, "the doctors' report says that thousands of people have been resettled 'at gunpoint,' that families have been separated, that food and blankets from abroad have been 'used as bait' and that conditions during transport and in the resettlement areas have led to widespread disease and death."[10]

While Ethiopian officials claim that resettlement was necessary because the dense population of Ethiopia's northern plateaus had exhausted the land, informed sources contend that the true purpose of the program is to depopulate the northern areas where anti-Marxist rebel groups receive active support from the masses and set up Government-dependent colonies and Soviet-style collective farms in the new areas of settlement.

Doctors Without Borders calls the re-location program "one of the most massive violations of human rights we have seen" and notes that it is "being carried out with funds and gifts from international aid."

Some days after Doctors Without Borders released their report, *The Wall Street Journal* published the following editorial: "French relief workers were touring Washington last week with awful news that had already been reported by eyewitnesses from the U.S. Agency for International Development. The Ethiopian government's year-old 'relocation program,' now greatly stepped up by the military Dergue, or junta, and its Russian patrons, has already claimed the lives of 20 percent of its targets, a death toll of some 100,000. It shapes up as a mass extermination in the order of the Khmer Rouge killing fields and the deportation of Armenians in 1915, with the added horror that it would not have been possible without the aid and silence of Western famine relief."

"Famine relief trucks have been diverted to move people, while grain rots at the ports. The roundups have disrupted harvests and forced abandonment of whole herds of livestock. Grain has been taken from famine areas and sent south to maintain concentration camps. In the meanwhile, government troops have launched their biggest offensives ever in the heart of the famine regions, drawing logistical support from the relief stockpiles while burning the rebels' crops."[11]

Unhappily, the Ethiopian case is not the only one where food aid financed malevolent government persecution of innocent peasants. According to Peter Bauer, "it has been widely and rightly recognized, even by supporters of President Nyerere of Tanzania, that without large-scale external aid he would not have been able to perist for so many years with *forced* collectivization and large-scale removal of people into so-called socialist villages. These policies not only involved brutality and hardship but had devastating effects on food production and distribution, and on economic conditions generally."[12]

The Ethiopian case shows that food aid helps bad governments do bad things to their people. Such "bad things," of course, are not always as extreme as Nazi-like forced deportations. But food aid can—and often does—facilitate classic economic policy errors in recipient countries, which make already poor countries even poorer.

A specific example where food aid facilitated bad general economic policy is India, where the strategy of its second and third

5-year plans focused on import-substituting industry, particularly heavy industry.

It is generally agreed that India could not have pursued its misconceived strategy, which transfers domestic resources from high to low productivity uses, had it not been for generous food aid from abroad, particularly from the United States. Even friends of foreign aid, such as liberal economists Paul Iserman and Hans Singer, point the finger of blame at food aid in this case. They write, "food aid supported and facilitated the import-substitution strategy, primarily by enabling the Indian government to maintain large subsidized distribution programs while, in the eyes of most analysts, not adequately addressing some basic questions of food grain production and distribution."

The point is that import-substitution artificially transfers resources out of agriculture into industry. This reduces agricultural production—which raises the price of food unless food can be imported from abroad. Note that without such food transfers, import substitution would be compelled to cease, particularly in a democratic country like India where government could be expected to be responsive to popular discontent over food shortages and high food prices. This example from India illustrates what may be called the "food aid" trap. The demand for food aid in poor Third World countries indicates severe economic mismanagement. Yet, satisfying that demand only serves to perpetrate the economic mismanagement responsibe for the poverty in the first place.

So far, attention has been focused on the role food aid plays in facilitating bad or foolish policies by bad or foolish government. Next, I would like to turn to the so-called "disincentive effects" of food aid—the direct role that food aid plays in damaging local agriculture in recipient countries.

By increasing the amount of food available for domestic consumption, food aid depresses the price of agricultural products in recipient countries. Such price reductions in turn depress agricultural output, so that what the recipient country gains in food aid it loses to some extent in domestic output. When the offset in domestic output equals the food aid, the marginal effect of the food aid on food availability is zero. In this case the food aid totally fails to increase the recipient's domestic availability of food. The marginal effect is greater than zero but less than unity when the offset of domestic supply is less than the food aid. And it is even theoretically possible for the domestic supply offset to be greater than the food aid, in which case the marginal effect of the food aid is negative.

Whatever, the marginal effect of food aid on domestic food consumption, however, it is clear that it can have a negative effect—and sometimes a devastating negative effect—on domestic food production. For example, a study on food aid to Colombia, by Dudley and Sandilands, showed that, from 1953 to 1971, wheat imported under food aid rose from 50 percent to about 90 percent of total wheat consumption. In that same period, the price for wheat declined by about half, while wheat production declined very sharply to about one-third of its original level.[13] Note the direction of causality. It was not that there was food aid because of low food production, but that there was low food production because of food aid.

Moving down the supply curve is not the only consequence for output of price changes induced by food aid. There are also the income transfer effects of price changes to consider—and these too tend to reduce agricultural production in aid-receiving countries. Income transfer effects relate to the changes in the distribution of income caused by price changes. When, for example, the price of agricultural commodities decline because of food aid, income is redistributed from local producers to local consumers. Whatever one's subjective evaluation of the ethics of such redistribution, it is likely to reduce agricultural production by reducing the means by which investments in agriculture can be made. When agricultural investment suffers, so must agricultural production.

An important consequence of food aid, then, is to reduce agricutural production and make recipient countries more dependent upon foreign nations for their food supply than they otherwise would be. This criticism is not one of agricultural imports, per se—only artificially-induced increases in agricultural imports due to food aid. Such reduction in imports impose an unwarranted dependency of recipient countries on outsiders that can be justified neither by economic nor political considerations.

The analogy between food dependency induced by food aid and

defense dependency induced by military aid is a close one. In both cases, the marginal effect of intervention is less than expected because of offsetting domestic substitutions. And in both, the intervention produces weakness in recipient countries—an inability to defend itself in one case and an inability to feed itself in the other. The only difference between the two is that with military intervention, the offsetting domestic substitutions are the result of free-riding: When the United States does more, its allies do less; in the case of food aid, free-riding is not relevant in that the offsetting domestic substitutions result from the workings of the local marketplace, which cannot absorb the food aid unless food prices are reduced.

The analysis of how food aid creates weakness and dependency in recipient countries can be extended to the case of more general foreign economic assistance. Consider a candidate for foreign aid that is experiencing economic difficulties because of faulty domestic economic policies. If the aid is not given, the difficulties may eventually lead to a policy reversal. The problem can, and often does, correct itself. But rendering economic assistance to the troubled country removes the incentives for domestic policy reform and perpetuates the status quo. In effect, the continuation of the bad economic policies becomes dependent upon the foreign aid: so long as foreign aid is maintained, bad economic policies persist.

TWO EXAMPLES: TAIWAN AND SOUTH KOREA[11]

Taiwan and South Korean are two cases where foreign aid has accommodated poor economic policies. Economic interventionists long have argued that U.S. economic aid was an important springboard for the rapid economic growth these two Pacific Basin countries have achieved during the past two decades. This argument not only is incorrect, but is the reverse of what actually happened. In both Taiwan and South Korea, U.S. economic aid financed and sustained wealth-destroying protectionist and anti–private capital import policies. It was not until the United States threatened to cut off foreign aid in the late 1950s that both countries were constrained to adopt the free-market, pro-foreign capital-import policies that proved responsible for their success. Rather than preparing the Taiwanese and South Korean economies for takeoff, as alleged, foreign aid threatened to ground them permanently.

There were several motives for U.S. aid to Taiwan from 1950 to 1965, of which the least controversial was sustaining a strong Nationalist military posture vis-à-vis Communist China. By 1956, however, U.S. aid objectives gradually shifted from military strength to economic growth. Reflecting the conventional wisdom of the time, Taiwan's development strategy was to use government aid funds to build infrastructure (power, transport, communications), foster agriculture, and develop human resources. Industrial development was to be left in the hands of private enterprise. In other words, U.S. aid was intended to help create a booming private sector by making available increased power, transportation, efficient labor, and low-priced raw materials.

From 1951 to 1965, two-thirds of all U.S. aid went to projects run by public enterprises and agencies. Some 37 percent of the aid in this period went for infrastructure, 26 percent for human resources, 25 percent for agriculture, and 15 percent for industry.

Though designed to benefit private enterprise, the effect of U.S.-financed investment in "social-overhead capital" was to damage private enterprise by diverting scarce resources away from it. This crowding out of the private sector by public projects increased the cost of resources to the private sector as much as an explicit tax on their use would have. Statistics show that private-sector gross investment in fixed capital formation in Taiwan fell from 56 percent in 1954 to 41 percent in 1958. From 1951 to 1963, the public sector accounted for 48 percent of total Taiwanese net domestic investment. U.S. capital assistance accounted for 80 percent of that figure.

Rather than create a model for capitalistic development, as intended, it became obvious by the late 1950s that government-to-government aid was creating a strong socialist state in Taiwan that was suffocating the private sector. This was one of the main reasons Washington wisely chose to discontinue its aid to Taiwan.

The convention wisdom that inspired the practice of letting the public sector crowd out the private sector in Taiwan is what one might call "cart-before-the-horse" economics. Social-overhead capital simply is not the horse to pull private business along with it; indeed, the opposite is true. The lack of infrastructure may well be a bottleneck in economies already experiencing strong private-sector growth, in which case the rate of return from investing in infrastructure will probably be high. But in poor countries, as Taiwan and Korea were at the time, the absence of infrastructure is more a reflection of economic stagnation than a reason for it. The private sector must lead the public one—not the reverse.

An equally important purpose of U.S. aid to Taiwan and Korea during the 1950s was general economic assistance. Grants and concessional loans to finance perpetual balance-of-payments deficits and support the currency in foreign-exchange markets became an important factor in sustaining the protectionist policies of the Nationalists in Taiwan during the 1950s. These policies hurt Taiwanese industry in at least two ways.

First, they artificially restricted Taiwan's exports by drawing resources out of export industries into import-substitute industries. During the protectionist decade of the 1950s, the average annual growth rate of Taiwanese exports was 15.5 percent; during the free-market 1960s, it was 31.5 percent. Second, protectionism helped create stagnation in Taiwanese manufacturing during the 1950s. The annual rates of output growth in the nonfood manufacturing sectors of the Taiwanese economy were (in percentages) 22, 23, 19, 11, 10, and 10, respectively, for the six years from 1953 through 1958. The drop in output growth was particularly severe in textiles, wood products, and basic metals, all of which suffered from severe excess capacity.

In addition to economic stagnation, there were fears in Taiwan that U.S. aid had made the country too dependent on the United States. Independence from foreigners had been a central motif of Nationalist Chinese international economic policy since Sun Yat-sen. The result was that Taiwan, like many Third World countries, opted for protectionist policies in the early post–World War II period. The Nationalists rejected an export-oriented, free capital-import program precisely because they saw it as surrendering Taiwan's future development to private firms and foreign interests, which, they thought, would be preoccupied with profit and unresponsive to the political and historical imperatives that President Chiang Kai-shek had defined for their island-country.

Autarkic economic policies, however, did not bring independence. They brought the opposite. By running the economy into the ground, protectionism forced Taiwan to depend increasingly on the United States for general economic assistance. The Nationalists' fear of dependence on private foreign firms thus led to the reality of "aid dependency" on the United States. In the final analysis, the Nationalist government realized that only the prosperous are truly independent, and that Chiang's earlier fear of foreign capital had been misplaced, if not counterproductive.

Like aid to Taiwan, U.S. aid to South Korea in the early postwar period was linked to containing communism in the Pacific Basin. A food shortage resulted in South Korea from the massive migration southward when the peninsula was split; the United States countered with free food and a half million tons of fertilizer. The fertilizer, in particular, is considered to have been instrumental in restoring agricultural production to its pre–World War II level by the time of the outbreak of the Korean War. Later, however, it was argued that surplus food imports were a prime factor causing stagnation in Korean agriculture because they kept food prices down.

After the Korean War, U.S. economic aid to South Korea was both more substantial and less successful. From 1953 to 1963, U.S. economic aid accounted for 13.4 percent of Korean gross national product, 95.9 percent of Korean gross domestic investment, and 75.6 percent of government expenditure. It is no exaggeration to say that the United States misguidedly financed socialism in South Korea during this period.

Foreign aid on a large scale leads to corruption on a large scale. In the case of the Syngman Rhee regime in South Korea, aid-financed agriculture and industrial projects were used to prop up Rhee's political fortunes rather than the Korean economy. As a result, a fifth of all such projects financed by U.S. aid from 1953 to 1963 proved unsound for reasons of bankruptcy and lack of managerial skills. Korean per capita GNP grew at an annual average rate of 1.9 percent during this period, compared with figures three times that magnitude after both aid and government size in Korea were scaled down in the 1970s.

It is sometimes argued that U.S. aid was vital in stabilizing Taiwan and South Korea because it signaled American willingness to stand firm against Communist aggression. This supposedly gave the Taiwanese and South Korean economies their attractiveness to private investment. In fact, however, foreign and domestic private investment did not take off until the governments of these countries changed their policy orientation from government-led growth and reliance on foreign aid to more emphasis on private-sector growth.

In short, so long as generous U.S. aid was forthcoming, Taiwan and South Korea could forgo private-capital import and export promotion for foreign-exchange purposes. But when the United States discontinued its aid, the generation of foreign exchange by the private sector became critical. It was not mere coincidence that both countries radically altered their domestic economic policies from import substitution to export-led growth in the face of the U.S. aid cutoff. It was a case of cause and effect.

DOES WEALTH MAKE A DIFFERENCE?

The argument that economic aid might be America's strong suit in its contest with the Soviet Union in the Third World because of the success of the Marshall Plan after World War II has been shown to be invalid. A second argument, that America's strong suit may lie in economic aid because this country is richer than the Soviet Union, also is misleading. That the United States is a much richer country than Russia is, of course, beyond dispute. What can be disputed, however, is the value of the greater wealth of the United States in attempting to combat Soviet influence in the Third World.

There would appear to be a natural affinity between aspiring and actual Third World totalitarians and Moscow. The former want power, not wealth, and Moscow can help supply the means to acquire and keep power—at a price. The greater wealth of the United States has proven itself of limited utility in trying to pry Third World totalitarians away from the Kremlin. Economic aid simply does not have the allure many think it does.

Moreover, just because the United States is richer than the Soviet Union does not mean that U.S. leaders have less economic resource constraints on them to give economic aid than do Soviet leaders. The fact that the United States is a real democracy puts it at a substantial disadvantage to the Soviets in the use of economic aid for strategic purposes. In both the United States and the Soviet Union, there is a trade-off between the amount of resources that can be put into economic aid and that available for other uses—

for example, the satisfaction of consumer needs and social services. This is the basic law of economic scarcity which no country—communist or capitalist—can repeal.

In a totalitarian system, the allocation of resources is made by a small group of men, operating in secret. If a consensus exists among these men to put resources into imperialistic adventures, nothing and no one can stop them. The amount of resources the U.S. government can divert to combat Soviet imperialism, however, is limited by public tolerance of the antiimperialistic measures. Historically, public tolerance for economic aid in this country has been rather low. Thus, even though the U.S. economy is more productive than that of the Soviets, U.S. leaders work under more severe economic resource constraints than do Soviet leaders.

American democratic traditions put the United States at a comparative disadvantage to the Soviets in the use of economic aid for strategic reasons in another important respect. When economic aid is given for strategic reasons, its purpose is to create a dependency relationship between the donor and aid recipient such that the aid recipient is made amenable to manipulation by the donor country. Potential for manipulation of aid recipients by the United States, however, is limited by the influence that friends of the aid recipient can have on Congress and in the White House through the democratic process. The relation between Israel and the United States is a case in point. The United States gives more economic aid to Israel than to any other country. There is also a very large, politically active, well-organized Jewish community in the United States that has made economic aid to Israel something of a "sacred cow" in Washington—the politician that dares oppose it faces certain and substantial retribution.

This has not been good for the United States and it has not been good for Israel. From the point of view of the United States, its foreign aid to Israel has not given it the leverage over Israel's foreign policies it would like to have, and should get, given the amount of money the United States has put into Israel. From Israel's point of view, the economic aid has allowed successive Israeli governments to follow ruinous economic policies, which have devastated the country's economic base at a time when a strong economy is badly needed. A country that spends almost 50 percent of its public budget on defense cannot afford the elaborate welfare state Israel has been able to finance because of the economic aid it receives from the United States. Instead of making Israel strong, U.S. open-ended economic aid has made Israel into the "Sweden of the Mediterranean."

Does the Cuban lobby in Moscow (they must have one) possess the same political clout as that of the Israeli lobby in Washington? It is highly unlikely that the Cuban tail wags the Soviet dog, for several reasons. As noted above, in a decentralized political system such as that of the United States, a client state can exert an influence over the most important decision-makers by appeals to public opinion and direct contacts with lawmakers and other influential persons. In a totalitarian system, these avenues of influence do not exist.

Second, Castro's ideological base is so intrinsically anti-American that his bargaining power with the Kremlin is virtually nil. Can anyone seriously imagine Castro trying to hold up the Soviets for more economic aid by threatening to adopt pro-American policies? Yet America's clientele in the Third World consistently threaten the United States that if it does not give—and give generously— they will turn to the other superpower for assistance.

For example, several non-Communist Latin American countries are reported to be warming up to Castro, who, in an interview with a Mexican newspaper in March 1985, said that the Latin American foreign debt of $360 billion simply cannot be paid and must be canceled by U.S. banks. The message the debt-ridden Latin American governments are sending to Washington is obvious enough: Unless you bail us out with economic aid on favorable terms, we will tilt our foreign policies toward Havana and Moscow. Because the ideological orientation of these countries is not intrinsically anti-Soviet, their threat to change political coloration has a credibility in Washington that Castro lacks in Moscow.

PLAYING TO OUR STRENGTH

Those who argue that America's "comparative advantage" in competing with the Soviets in the Third World lies in economic aid are correct in only one respect: that the strength of the United States lies in its economy, and that this country somehow must learn to turn its enormous economic strength to its strategic advantage if it is to impede the spread of communism among the poorer countries. The truth of the matter is that the United States probably has spent too much time and too many resources containing communism, and too little time and resources spreading capitalism. The marketplace is this country's strongest institution, and the United States must learn how to use it to help the poorer countries of the world develop a vested interest in the capitalistic system. Once capitalism spreads, communism will contain itself.

The best way the United States can spread capitalism is through deeds, not words. The poor countries of the world already have had too many lectures from the richer nations about the benefits of free trade, and too few examples of it. Access to the vast American market is what these countries need—and should get—to build their allegiance to a capitalistic system. American protectionism is as subversive to U.S. security interests as Soviet cooperative forces.

That access to the American market is preferred to American aid by at least one of our most important allies recently was made clear by Turkish prime minister Turgut Özal. One look at the map reveals Turkey's strategic importance to the United States. Not only does it guard frontiers with the Soviet Union, Bulgaria, and the straits from the Black Sea into the Mediterranean, but it also shares borders with Iran, Iraq, and Syria. According to a dispatch in *The New York Times*, "Mr. Ozal said Turkey was 'not fairly treated' [by the U.S.] in comparison with the two top beneficiaries of American military aid, Israel and Egypt, the only countries that receive more aid than Turkey." The Turkish prime minister, however, is not seeking additional military aid; instead, he is asking that American protectionism be relaxed. "Mr. Ozal said that on a visit to Washington this year, he stressed an easing of 'American protectionism' rather than more military aid. He said protectionism limited the export of such Turkish products as textiles and steel goods. He also said that Turkey received little help in reducing a trade deficit of $800 million with the United States."

"We are spending a lot for our armed forces," Mr. Ozal is quoted. "This affects our economic development. We have the poorest per capita income in NATO."[15]

The Turkish prime minister's comments make it clear that a link exists between increased American imports on the one hand, and the fight to contain communism on the other. Many U.S. allies would prefer trade to aid, but settle for aid because that is what the U.S. government offers them. When U.S. Secretary of State George Shultz traveled to Turkey in March 1986 to renew American military-base rights there, he offered aid but was told by Sakip Sabanci, chairman of the Turkish Industrialists' and Businessmen's Association, to "assist us not by aid, but by facilitating our export performance." Indeed, Turkey went further than mere rhetoric on this point: it explicitly linked the renewal of the American military-base rights to major trade concessions by the United States.

By increasing the economic resources available to foreign governments, economic aid increases the power that government—and politicians—have over the lives of ordinary citizens in recipient countries. By increasing the exports of the private sector, trade creates ties to, and vested interests in, the capitalistic system. The issue of "trade versus aid," in fact, boils down to whether there should be market or political solutions to economic problems. Unfortunately, the U.S. State Department traditionally has thought more in terms of purchasing the allegiance of public officials in Third World countries with economic aid than in creating an allegiance on the part of the mass of peoples in these countries to an economic system that has the potential to make them "Communist-proof."

The conflict between these two objectives has become a particular problem for the Reagan administration, whose capitalistic ideology has clashed on several occasions with the State Department's business-as-usual policies. The result has been an uncomfortable attempt to square the circle by making U.S. economic aid conditional on the aid recipient undertaking certain reforms designed to make their economies more compatible with capitalism.

This confused policy is not likely to work for the following reasons. So long as the Third World country knows the United States is using economic aid to compete with the Soviet Union, "conditionality" will not be effective. The Third World country simply will take the aid and promise to make the reforms at some future date; then it breaks its promise, claiming severe domestic opposition to the reforms. When the United States counters by threatening an aid cutoff, the aid recipient responds with a threat of its own: "If you cut the aid, we will go for help to the Soviets or to one of its proxy nations." Finally, we decide the aid must be continued for national security reasons. As noted above, several Latin American nations already are using a variant of this scenario to get Washington to bail them out of their enormous foreign debt.

Second, even if U.S. State Department officials can avoid being sandbagged by the "switching allegiance" threat, the policy of giving economic aid in the name of capitalism does not create an allegiance to capitalism in the Third World country—it creates the opposite.

Assume, for example, that the Third World country maintains exchange controls and aid is made contingent upon their removal. In and of itself, the removal of exchange controls makes the private economy more efficient—that is, after the reform, a given amount of economic resources in the private sector can be expected to produce more goods and services than before the reform. But the price of making the private sector more efficient in this instance is to increase the economic resources available to government. Because of this, the new jobs created by the aid-*cum*-reform package will be public sector jobs, not private sector ones. Moreover, politicians will determine who gets how much of the aid. Thus, while the poor country can be presumed to be better off with the reform measure tied to the aid than with the aid alone, conditionality in no way alters the conclusion that economic aid, tied or untied, increases the power and influence of politicians and creates allegiances to government rather than the private marketplace. In wanting to have it both ways, Mr. Reagan's state department gives lip service to the need to create capitalism abroad, but in fact promotes bigger government there.

A U.S.–CARIBBEAN BASIN COMMON MARKET

Instead of playing a game in which the Soviets can compete, and compete effectively—buying foreign leaders with economic aid— we should select a game to play where the Soviet disadvantage is so great as to guarantee a U.S. victory. There is no way, for example, that the U.S.S.R. could possibly match the economic impact of the United States granting unlimited access to its vast market. The United States could use trade against the Soviets as they use aid against the Americans. Let the United States declare war on communism in Central America, for example, not by sending in American troops, but by forming a common market with all countries in Central America who want to participate.

Irving Kristol asks:

> How can the U.S. achieve a reasonable measure of social and political stability in countries such as Grenada, Haiti and the Philippines? The power of example clearly does not work, nor does economic aid, while military occupation goes against the American grain. Is there really nothing the U.S. can do?

Kristol then answers his own question:

> Well, there is something, but at the moment it lies far outside all the possibilities that constitute the political spectrum. There is indeed a way by which the U.S. can offer its client states—many of them, at least—the benefits of economic growth and political liberty while maintaining adequate stability. And that way is economic integration.[16]

The United States should agree to eliminate all obstacles to imports from any Central American country which agrees to reciprocate by removing all obstacles to U.S. exports. A "common market" with the Caribbean Basin countries would help fight communism in four important ways: (1) It would increase the exports and economic well-being of the Central American countries; (2) it would create an allegiance to capitalism in a part of the world where the economic process has been dominated by the political process for too long a period; (3) it would improve the efficiency of the Caribbean Basin economies by imposing more liberal trade policies upon them; and (4) it would place Uncle Sam in a new light. A common market with the Caribbean Basin would help ameliorate resentment against the U.S., by showing the people of that region that the U.S. practices the competitive ethic it preaches. Economic aid, on the other hand, reinforces Uncle Sam's image as a rich bully, all too willing to use its enormous wealth to manipulate others for its own selfish reasons.

Objections to the formation of a U.S.–Central American Common Market can be expected to come from protectionist interests in the United States that fear the increased competition from Central American exports. Countries such as El Salvador, Guatemala, Honduras, and others are rich in labor and thus could be expected to be efficient in the production of such labor-intensive products as textiles, apparel, toys, plastics, and so on. American labor and management in these industries undoubtedly will use their considerable political clout in Washington to try to sabotage the initiative, just as moral isolationists sabotage aid to the Nicaraguan Contras. Under normal circumstances, the protectionists would have a good chance to succeed since the opponents of protectionism usually are not well-organized, and are scattered throughout the population. But the linkage of the Common Market to combating the Communists in Central America gives the plan a much broader base of political support than it otherwise would enjoy. The strategic importance of the proposed U.S.–Caribbean Basin Common Market might be able to defeat American protectionists, just as it might be able to defeat the Central American Communists.

MORE THAN BREAD ALONE

As important as our marketplace can be to help the poorer countries, it will take more than bread alone to combat the spread of communism in the Third World. The United States may be at a disadvantage to the Soviets in the use of substitute forces abroad, but that does not mean the United States should abstain altogether from providing certain types of military assistance to friendly Third World governments under the threat of—or actually experiencing—communist attack. In providing this assistance, however, the United States must restrain itself in one important respect: Except in a narrow set of cases, like Grenada, where U.S. troops can be in, and out, in a short period of time, American ground troops should not be inserted into the area of conflict. This fundamental restraint of behavior must be observed for strategic, not moral, reasons. The indirect approach to containing communism is favored to the direct one, not because it is morally superior but because it works better.

El Salvador is a case in point. If the United States had sent in troops to help the Salvadoran government fight the Communist rebels, the result surely would have been an "Americanized" war: U.S. troops would have done most of the fighting and the Salvadoran army would have politely disappeared. But instead of rushing in to do the Salvadorans' dirty work for them, Washington restrained itself and concentrated its efforts on increasing the efficiency of the Salvadoran fighting forces through advisers, weapons, technical assistance, military aid, and so forth. Since 1980, the U.S. has spent over $1.5 billion to this end, and such efforts are now paying rich dividends. "Progress Is Seen in El Salvador" blares the headline of the May 17, 1985, edition of the *International Herald Tribune*. "For the first time in five years of conflict, many Salvadorans and foreigners are beginning to voice a cautious assessment that El Salvador may have halted its slide into a worsening civil war and that a degree of recovery is now possible."[17]

The media attribute the good news in El Salvador to the fact that human rights violations by the Salvadoran army are presently at a five-year low. "There has been no report of a massacre by government troops for ten months," writes the *International Herald Tribune*.[18] The reason is not that Salvadoran President José Napoleón Duarte put his troops under wraps, as many liberals in the United States argued he should, but that his troops have been made more competent and efficient by American assistance. "The army has significantly improved its performance on the battlefield," according to the newspaper's report. "For the first time in three years, guerrillas have been unable to mount a dry season offensive and have been forced to resort to small-scale ambushes and a new campaign of kidnapping town officials."[19] Thus, as the professionalism of the Salvadoran army increased, two things happened: The human rights violations by government troops decreased and the human rights violations by the Communists increased. The message is clear enough: Human rights violations are not endemic to either side but are a consequence of the relative strength of the combatants. The more competent the armed forces, the less human rights violations they commit.

Just as U.S. moral isolationists argued against military aid to El Salvador because of the human rights violations of government troops, today they argue against military aid to the Nicaraguan Contras on the same basis. If Americans learn their lessons well from El Salvador, however, they will turn a deaf ear to the entreaties of the isolationists and help the Contras help themselves. The human rights violations of the Nicaraguan rebels should lessen with improvements in their competence and professionalism. Thus, rather than being an argument against U.S. military aid to the rebels, the Contras human rights violations actually are an argument that the United States help them improve their competitiveness on the battlefield. The proper interpretation of the human rights violations of the Contras is not that the rebels are bad people unworthy of U.S. support, but that they face a desperate military situation against a better-armed, better-trained, and more numerous opponent.

U.S. isolationists, of course, are the last people to ask advice as to how to combat the growing Nicaraguan menace, since it is they who are responsible for the menace being so close to U.S. borders in the first place. The American people can thank Jimmy Carter for the Sandinista presence in Nicaragua. President Carter was sufficiently concerned with the human rights violations of the Somoza regime that he decided the U.S. government should not be identified with Somoza. When I asked a senior foreign policy adviser in the Carter White House why the administration supported the Sandinista revolution, this official protested: "We didn't support the Sandinistas, we just refused to support Somoza"—a classic distinction without a difference. He added: "The journey from right-wing dictatorships to centrist democracies in the Third World is a hazardous one with the chance for many slips along the way." The Sandinista victory in Nicaragua clearly was one of Jimmy Carter's more costly slips.

CONCLUSION

In countering Moscow's moves in the Third World, Washington must develop tactics and strategies appropriate to America's institutions, values, and strengths—not simply imitate the tactics of our rivals. America's strong suit is its economy, and this country must learn how to use its enormous economic power to improve the material standard not only of its own citizens, but of foreigners as well. Other things being equal, the better off our neighbors, the more secure they—and we—will be.

Harnessing America's economic power for the benefit of the world's poor, however, is a necessary, not sufficient, condition for combating communism. When need be, military aid of all sorts, *except American troops*, should be made available to U.S. allies— weapons, advisers, technical assistance, access to private funds, backup air and sea support, and so forth. Today, some Americans are wary of rendering such support because they view it as a possible prelude to sending in the troops. It is Washington's obligation to convince the skeptics—by deeds as well as words—that, under the widest set of circumstances, U.S. troops will not be sent into the world's trouble spots. The lesson of Vietnam is not that we do not help our friends help themselves, but that we do not "Americanize" their troubles.

12

An Alliance Against
Itself

The conventional wisdom of Western defense strategy is that the United States must be closely linked to the defense of Western Europe because of an inherent imbalance between the military capabilities of Western Europe on the one hand and the Soviet bloc on the other. If the United States did not assume a major role in defending our European allies, the argument goes, the Soviets would dominate them either through Finlandization or outright military invasion.

This book takes a contrary view. While it is true the military balance in Europe presently favors the Soviet bloc, there is nothing inherent in this situation. The sundry states of Western Europe, taken as an aggregate, have four times the population of the Soviet Union, three times its gross national product, and technical superiority. Moreover, Western Europe has no analogue to Moscow's problems with its captive East European states. The Soviets are much concerned lest their East European "allies" not support them if war were to break out in Europe. Poland, East Germany, Hungary, Romania, and other Soviet-bloc countries might decide to "stay home" in case of war, or, what would be more advantageous

233

from the Western point of view, actively work against Soviet interests. This is a negative that must be subtracted from any positives the Soviets might enjoy vis-à-vis Western Europe.

The reason the military imbalance in Europe presently favors the East is not that Western Europe lacks the material resources to compete with the Soviets, but that it lacks the political will to use the ample resources it does have for its own defense. European underinvestment in defense is not an unavoidable consequence of an inherent resource inferiority, but the result of the perverse "incentive effect" of U.S. military guarantees: When the United States pledged itself to the defense of Western Europe, it gave its European allies an irresistible incentive to substitute American military spending for their own. Thus, rather than correct for the military imbalance in Europe, as the conventional wisdom argues, American defense support actually created the imbalance by encouraging Western Europe to do less defense-wise while the Kremlin was doing more.

What makes the West's defense edifice into a particularly insidious arrangement is that instead of blaming "the system" for its faults, the Western allies tend to blame one another. The West Europeans appease the common enemy, not because of inherent weakness or a reduced attachment to Western values, but because the system gives them a powerful incentive to behave this way. Yet, many thoughtful Americans are becoming anti-European precisely because they blame the Europeans rather than the system. If the Europeans will not support us when we are in trouble, they argue, why should we support them?

The United States must abandon NATO, neither because Americans have become anti-European nor that we want to teach our alliance partners a lesson, but because the present system of Western deterrence no longer is working. The distinction between walking out on "the system" and walking out on the Europeans is an extremely important one to make. The United States can leave NATO and still help the Europeans defend their values. There is, for example, a substantial amount of U.S. heavy military equipment, worth billions of dollars, that we can leave in Western Europe. The United States could turn over the keys to the Pershing and cruise missiles to the proper European authorities *gratis*. It could provide technical military assistance to the Europeans, help them develop their own Star Wars system of strategic defense, lend them military equipment, share intelligence information with them, and participate in occasional joint military ventures when mutually advantageous. Indeed, we could even return to Europe if need be.

What this means, in other words, is that the United States could—and should—continue to be a good friend to the Europeans. But the United States can be a good friend by helping them to help themselves, not by substituting its effort for theirs.

The one thing the United States cannot afford to do, however, is to allow the *status quo* of European dependence and appeasement to continue.

> Americans and Europeans [says Senator Malcolm Wallop] have every reason to pray that the future of our alliance will be something, almost anything, other than the logical extension of the trends that have characterized it for over a decade. Those trends are producing precisely the opposite of what Americans and Europeans intended our alliance to produce. Instead of finding in one another the ideas, the moral courage, and the material support necessary to win out in the struggle which Soviet totalitarianism has imposed upon us, one might say of us as Churchill said of the British and French governments a half century ago: "We find in one another the reasons for mistakes that, were we alone, we probably would not commit." Thus, because the allies are there, and for the sake of the alliance, we Americans find ourselves materially and strategically less secure with every passing year, while Europe, for its part, seems to have placed its bets for the future on playing off the Soviet Union against the U.S., and on playing off a Soviet Union against which it no longer prepares seriously to defend itself.[1]

How might the Soviet Union react to a U.S. withdrawal from NATO? No doubt Moscow would hail the withdrawal as a great Soviet victory, and many in this country might well agree with them. Rhetoric aside, however, it is doubtful that the Kremlin would try to take advantage of a phased American withdrawal by Soviet military actions on the so-called fringes of the present NATO structure—in Yugoslavia, Turkey, Greece, or Norway, for instance—for fear of scaring the Western Europeans into the precipitous rearmament and unification the Kremlin hopes to preclude. The guess here is that the Kremlin would be on its best behavior during the process of transition, if only to lull the Europeans into a false sense of security.

The Europeans, for their part, could use this grace period to rigorously pursue rearmament and general remilitarization. If Moscow attempted to short-circuit such rearmament by a direct conventional strike at Europe's heartland, they would have the unknown of an American response to contend with. A pullout of U.S. troops from Europe does not mean they could not return. True, the chances of an American reentry would be unlikely, but just how unlikely is something the Soviet decision-makers would have to calculate for themselves. Deterrence sometimes does not require a certain response, and even if the United States were to withdraw the nuclear umbrella from the Europeans, the possibility that it might be reestablished can be expected to have a certain deterrent value. Moreover, a large-scale conventional attack by the Soviet Union would raise the above-noted issue of the loyalty of Moscow's "slave states" in Eastern Europe. It is a safe bet the Kremlin would like to indefinitely postpone a test of East Europe's behavior during a European war.

But what would happen if instead of using the grace period to rearm and unify, the European states reacted to the American withdrawal by intensifying their practice of détente? The Europeans, after all, have their own perceptions of the Soviet threat, which might lead them to conclude that détente, by itself, is sufficient to ensure the survival of Western values in Europe. This would be the Europeans' choice to make, of course, and there is no way the United States could preclude this possibility. Still, adoption of a "détente only" defense policy by the Europeans appears unlikely.

A "détente as defense" policy makes sense primarily in conjunction with a powerful nuclear threat. The nuclear threat provides the stick, détente the carrot. A détente-only policy would be an "all-carrot" policy. While it is true that European interest in détente has demonstrated a reluctance to pursue an all-stick policy, the Europeans—to this point at least—also have tenaciously resisted the idea of an all-carrot policy up to this point. No European leader—not even Charles de Gaulle—argued that the United States withdraw the nuclear umbrella from Western Europe. Given an American pullout, it is much more in keeping with their own past behavior, and the logic of the present situation, that the Europeans try to establish a stick of their own before giving up on the idea of a stick altogether.

The point is that the optimal mix of policies for the Europeans has been the combination of a (primarily American) nuclear threat with détente. A détente-only policy would be a movement away from that optimal mix.

It is some forty years since World War II ended and the postwar period of adjustment has come to a close. The old enemies—Japan and Germany—have been rehabilitated, developed, and integrated into Western culture and values. The old U.S. ally—the Soviet Union—is now a powerful and determined enemy. Under present conditions, institutions like NATO, which were custom-tailored to postwar realities and needs, not only have lost their rationale but have become counterproductive. NATO, which began as an alliance against the Soviet Union, has degenerated into an alliance against itself.

This book therefore recommends that the United States pursue the following policies toward its allies:

1. Washington should announce a phased withdrawal of U.S. troops over a period of, say, five years. Though the pullout truly would signify a major change in U.S.–European relations, in one sense it merely would be making explicit what has been implicit for many years—namely, a recision of the American nuclear guarantee. The withdrawal must be a phased one, to give the Europeans time to adjust to the new realities. True, the phased nature of the withdrawal gives opponents of the plan additional time to work to undermine it. But if the commitment really is there, they will not succeed. Moreover, forcing the Europeans to go "cold turkey" simply is not acceptable.

In advocating a withdrawal of U.S. troops from Western Europe, a distinction must be made between Europe's flank states and center. Clearly, in terms of resources and the potential to hold together under duress, Europe's center is far stronger than its flanks. Scandinavia is of sufficient concern to the core states of Western Europe that they could be expected to look after the northern flank should the U.S. depart. But what is to become of the flank states, like Turkey, that do not shortchange their defense and have significant strategic value to the United States? Perhaps it would be wise for the U.S. to make a separate bilateral agreement with Turkey after we leave Europe to insure its security. After all, it is not isolationism that motivates the withdrawal proposal but the hope of encouraging those European states that have the material resources for defense to use them.

2. At the same time that the American troop withdrawal from Europe is announced, Washington also should announce a phased withdrawal of American troops from South Korea. Since the European withdrawal would undermine the credibility of a continued U.S. presence in South Korea in any event, it is best to make a withdrawal from South Korea explicit and simultaneous with that from Western Europe.

3. Washington should take no action with respect to Japan at the time of its European and South Korean initiatives. The Japanese will get the message, and undoubtedly respond to the new U.S. policies both by dramatically increasing their national defense expenditures and by taking a more active role in keeping the peace in the Pacific.

The United States should be allied with great nations. The present system of alliances, however, is making our allies weak. To help them become great again—not merely clever in the pursuit of their own national vested interests, but independent, proud, spirited, and generous—will require an act of creative statesmanship on our part, just as creative statesmanship was required at the end of World War II in response to increasing Soviet power and Western Europe's economic ruination. Americans had the wisdom to create NATO when it could do good. We should have the wisdom to dismantle it now that it does harm.

APPENDIX I *Total Population (in millions)*

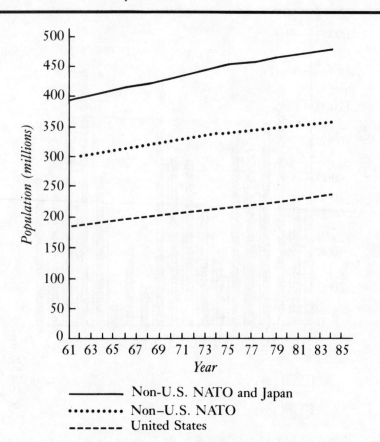

Non-U.S. NATO and Japan
Non–U.S. NATO
United States

Source: "Report on Allied Contributions to the Common Defense," a report to the U.S. Congress, Caspar W. Weinberger, Secretary of Defense, U.S. Department of Defense (March 1985), p. 69.

APPENDIX II *Gross Domestic Product (per capita)*

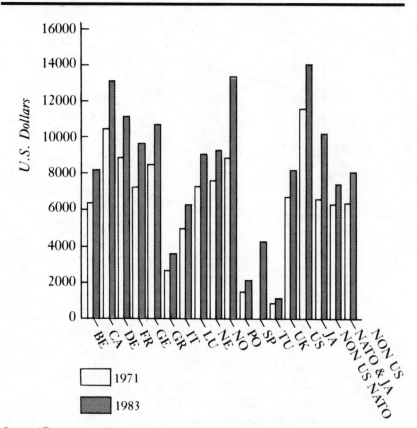

Source: "Report on Allied Contributions to the Common Defense," a report to the U.S. Congress, Caspar W. Weinberger, Secretary of Defense, U.S. Department of Defense (March 1985), p. 70.

APPENDIX III Defense Spending (per capita)

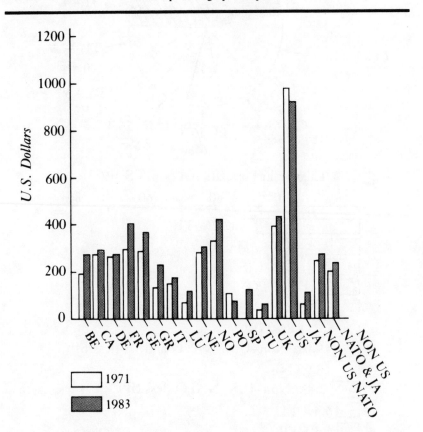

1971

1983

Source: Report on Allied U.S. Contributions to the Common Defense," a report to the U.S. Congress, Caspar W. Weinberger, Secretary of Defense, U.S. Department of Defense (March 1985), p. 72.

APPENDIX IV *Population of NATO and Japan (in millions)*
1983 Total: 747.4

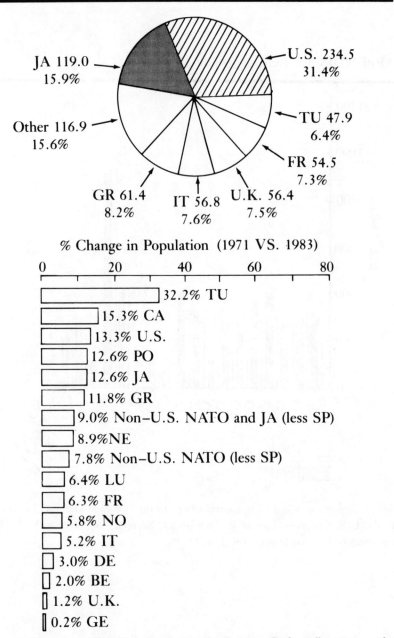

Source: "Report on Allied Contributions to the Common Defense," a report to the U.S. Congress, Caspar W. Weinberger, Secretary of Defense, U.S. Department of Defense (March 1985), p. 70.

NOTES

CHAPTER 1: THE TROUBLE WITH NATO

1. Irving Kristol, "What's Wrong with NATO?", *New York Times Magazine* (September 25, 1983), p. 66.

2. Jay Winik, "Toward a Post-NATO Europe," *The Wall Street Journal* (August 27, 1985), p. 30.

3. Gallois quotation translated from Gerd Schmueckle, "When a Crisis Is Looming, NATO is Hamstrung," in *Rheinischer Merkur/Christ und Welt* (December 3, 1984), p. 18.

4. Henry Kissinger, "The Future of NATO," in Kenneth A. Myers, ed., *NATO: The Next Thirty Years* (Boulder: Westview Press, 1980), pp. 5–8.

5. David Brand, "Europeans Subsidized Soviet Pipeline Work Mainly to Save Jobs," *The Wall Street Journal* (November 2, 1982), p. 1.

6. Keith W. Crane and Daniel F. Kohler, "The Effects of Export Credit Subsidies on Western Exports to the Soviet Bloc," A Rand Note (Santa Monica, Calif.: The Rand Corporation, June 1984), pp. 11, 24.

7. Earl Ravenal, "Europe Without America," pp. 1020–35.

8. Richard Halloran, "Europe Called Main U.S. Arms Cost," *The New York Times* (July 20, 1984), p. A-2.

9. *Congressional Record* (June 18, 1984), p. S-7451.

10. Philip M. Boffey, "Allies Back 'Star Wars' Studies, Not Deployment," *The New York Times* (February 10, 1985), p. 14.

11. Robert V. Daniels, "America's Doubting Allies," *The New Leader* (June 3–17, 1985), p. 7.

12. Henry S. Rowen, "Developing the Supply of Cooperative Forces," paper presented at the Rand Corporation Conference, Cooperative Forces in the Third World, on March 14–15, 1985 (Santa Monica, Calif.: The Rand Corporation, 1985).

13. U.S. Department of State, Report to Congress on Voting Practices in the United Nations. For voting tallies, see pp. 8–9, (Washington, D.C.: U.S. Government Printing Office, 1984). UN Resolution quotes, see Table 9, Appendix, p. 2.

14. Peregrine Worsthorne, "A Tory Critique of Neoconservatives," *The American Spectator* (October 1985), p. 14.

CHAPTER 2: EUROPE ON $134 BILLION A YEAR

1. The figure of 42 percent is derived from Earl C. Ravenal, *Defining Defense: The 1985 Military Budget* (Washington, D.C.: The Cato Institute, 1985), p. 16. The figure of 58 percent is cited in Richard Halloran, "Europe

Called Main U.S. Arms Cost," *The New York Times* (July 20, 1984), p. A-2.

2. Earl C. Ravenal, "The Price and Perils of NATO," in *Beyond the Status Quo: Policy Prospects for America*, eds. David Boaz and Edward H. Crowe (Washington, D.C.: The Cato Institute, 1985), pp. 122–24.

3. Earl C. Ravenal, *Defining Defense*, pp. 15–21.

4. Zbigniew Brzezinski, Robert Jastrow, and Max M. Kampelman, "Defense in Space is Not 'Star Wars,'" *The New York Times Magazine* (January 27, 1985), p. 29.

5. Melvyn Krauss, "It is Time to Change the Atlantic Alliance," *The Wall Street Journal* (March 3, 1983), p. 24.

6. Richard R. Burt, "European Pullout Isn't Deserved or Desired," *The Wall Street Journal* (March 28, 1983), p. 22.

CHAPTER 3: RESTRAINT AND CONTAINMENT

1. George Kennan, *American Diplomacy*, expanded edition (Illinois: University of Chicago Press, 1984), pp. 119–27. Article originally published as "The Sources of Soviet Conduct," *Foreign Affairs* 25:4 (July 1947), pp. 566–82.

2. Eric Severeid, "A Conversation with George Kennan," *Vital History Cassettes*, Encyclopedia Americana/CBS News Radio Resource Library, March 1985.

3. Ibid.

4. Ibid.

5. Charles Krauthammer, "Isolationism, Left and Right," *The New Republic* (March 4, 1985), p. 18.

6. Ibid., p. 21.

7. Ibid., p. 24.

8. Peregrine Worsthorne, "A Tory Critique of Neoconservatives," *The American Spectator* (October 1985), p. 15.

9. Charles Krauthammer, "Isolationism, Left and Right," p. 20.

10. Irving Kristol, "Coping with an 'Evil Empire,'" *The Wall Street Journal* (December 17, 1985), p. 32.

11. Henry S. Rowen, "Developing the Supply of Cooperative Forces," p. 3.

12. Robert W. Poole, Jr., ed., *Defending a Free Society* (Lexington, Mass.: D.C. Heath and Company, 1984), p. xi.

13. Ibid., pp. x–xii.

14. Charles Krauthammer, "Isolationism," p. 19.

15. George F. Kennan, "Morality and Foreign Policy," *Foreign Affairs* (Winter 1985/86), p. 210.

16. Stephen S. Rosenfeld, "'Moral Equivalence': More to It than Dark Subversion," *International Herald Tribune* (May 7, 1985), p. 4.

CHAPTER 4: THE TAIL THAT WAGS THE DOG

1. Konrad Keller, "The New Germans," *The New York Times Magazine* (August 5, 1984), p. 20.
2. Michael Howard, "Reassurance and Deterrence: Western Defense in the 1980s," *Foreign Affairs*, 66:1 (Winter 1982/83), pp. 315–16.
3. Quoted in Robert V. Daniels, "America's Doubting Allies," *The New Leader* (June 3–17, 1985), p. 6.
4. John Vinocur, "Intellectual Europe Changes Sides on U.S. as Hero or Ogre," *The International Herald Tribune* (May 16, 1984), p. 6.
5. James M. Markham, "The Cold War of Letters Raging in Günther Grass," *The New York Times* (February 5, 1986), p. C21.
6. Seth Lipsky, "Polish Move Exposes a Republican 'Soft Underbelly,'" *The Wall Street Journal* (December 17, 1984), p. 34.
7. John M. Starrels, "Talking Trade with the Russians: The Stage Is Set for Better Relations," *The New York Times* (February 10, 1985), p. F-2.
8. Malcolm Wallop, "The Future of the Atlantic Alliance." Address by the senator to a forum at the University of South Carolina (October 5, 1985), p. 1.
9. R. W. Apple, Jr., "Libyan Issues Leaves Many Questioning Role of Allies," *The New York Times* (January 19, 1986), p. 10.
10. Adam B. Ulam, "Western Europe Key Area for Soviet Power Dreams," *Pittsburgh Press* (November 3, 1983).
11. James M. Markham, "Gorbachev Offensive: Splitting Allies," *The New York Times* (October 4, 1985), p. 16.
12. Editorial, *The New York Times* (April 17, 1986), p. 31.
13. Bernard Gwertzman, "U.S. Tries to Clarify Stand on an Israeli Response," *The New York Times* (December 30, 1985), p. A-7.
14. Gwertzman, "Conflicting Currents," *The New York Times* (October 14, 1985), p. A-10.
15. "Craxi Criticizes U.S. on Use of Base in Crisis," *The New York Times* (November 5, 1985), p. A-9.

CHAPTER 5: THE SOVIETS' NIGHTMARE

1. Michel Tatu, "Devolution of Power: A Dream?", *Foreign Affairs*, 53:4 (July 1975), p. 680.
2. G. L. Sulzberger, "Foreign Affairs: Poker as Played in Paris," *New York Times* (February 23, 1966), p. 38.
3. Norman Podhoretz, "Is There a New American Isolationism?", in *The Transatlantic Crisis: A Conference of the Committee for the Free World* (New York: Orwell Press, 1982), p. 62.
4. Quoted in Owen Harries, "Conservative Critics of NATO," *The American Spectator*, 17:6 (June 1984), p. 13.

5. Podhoretz, "Is There a New American Isolationism?", p. 58.

6. Ibid., p. 60.

7. James M. Markham, "Sharp Decline by Communists in West Europe," *The New York Times* (February 3, 1986), p. 1.

8. Flora Lewis, "France's Fading Reds," *The New York Times* (February 4, 1985), p. A-19.

9. James M. Markham, "Sharp Decline by Communists in West Europe," p. 1.

10. Paul Berman, "How a Leading Light of the New Left Learned to Love the Bomb," *Mother Jones* (October 1984), p. 18.

11. Ibid., p. 19.

12. E. J. Dionne, Jr., "Italy's Communists Have Lost Their Grip on City Halls," *The New York Times* (October 6, 1985), p. E-3.

13. James M. Markham, "Green Party Is Fading into the Blues," *The New York Times* (June 27, 1985), p. A-2.

14. Markham, "For West Germany's Young, the Trend Is Conservative," *The New York Times* (February 19, 1986), p. 1.

15. *The Sunday Times*, London (June 20, 1982), p. 3.

16. Michel Tatu, "Devolution of Power," p. 680.

17. Adam Ulam, "Western Europe Key Area for Soviet Power Dreams," *Pittsburgh Press* (November 3, 1983).

18. Ibid.

19. Irving Kristol, "A Transatlantic 'Misunderstanding': The Case of Central America," *Encounter*, 34:3 (March 1985), p. 20.

20. Ibid., pp. 19–21.

21. Peter Norman, "EC to Strengthen Ties with Latin America," *The Wall Street Journal/Europe* (April 18, 1985).

22. Peregrine Worsthorne, "A Tory Critique of Neoconservatives," *The American Spectator* (October 1985), p. 16.

23. Ibid.

24. Ibid., p. 15.

CHAPTER 6: WILL THE REAL GERMANY PLEASE STAND UP

1. Gerhard Herdegen and Elizabeth Noelle-Neumann, "Protest Howls Belied by Opinion Polls," *The German Tribune Political Affairs Review* (June 3, 1984), p. 10.

2. *Die Zeit*, quoted in German Press Review (June 13, 1984), pp. 1–2.

3. Peter Schmidt, "Public Opinion and Security Policy in the Federal Republic of Germany: Elite and Mass Opinion in a Comparative Perspective," Rand Paper (Santa Monica, Calif.: The Rand Corporation, 1984), p. 51.

4. Flora Lewis, "Missiles and Pacifists," *The New York Times* (November 18, 1983), p. A-35.

5. Michel Tatu, "Battle March to a French Tune," *The London Times* (June 20, 1984), p. 10.

6. Stanley Hoffman, "NATO and Nuclear Weapons: Reasons and Unreason," *Foreign Affairs* 60:2 (Winter 1981–82), p. 343.

7. John Vinocur, "Intellectual Europe Changes Sides on U.S. as Hero or Ogre," *International Herald Tribune* (May 16, 1984), p. 6.

8. Cited in Schmidt, "Public Opinion and Security Policy," pp. 38–39.

9. Richard Pipes, *Survival Is Not Enough* (New York: Simon and Schuster, 1984), p. 254.

10. Timothy Garton Ash, "Which Way Will Germany Go?", *New York Review of Books* (January 31, 1985), p. 33.

11. Ibid., p. 34.

12. Meyer, quoted in James M. Markham, "Germany's Trafficking in People," *The New York Times* (July 29, 1984), p. 3.

13. Timothy Garton Ash, "Which Way," p. 33.

14. James M. Markham, "Germany's Trafficking," p. 3.

15. Timothy Garton Ash, "Which Way," p. 34.

16. John Tagliabue, "Warning East Berlin for Slight Lean West," *The New York Times* (August 12, 1984), p. E-3.

17. Quoted in Scott Sullivan, "The Decline of Europe," *Newsweek* (April 9, 1984), p. 44.

18. Hellmut Diwald, quoted in David Gress, *Peace and Survival: West Germany, the Peace Movement and European Security* (Stanford, Calif.: Hoover Institution Press, forthcoming), p. 59.

19. Irving Kristol, "A Transatlantic Misunderstanding," p. 12.

20. Ibid., p. 12.

21. Melvyn Krauss, "Promoting Europe to Better Defend Itself," *The Wall Street Journal* (March 15, 1984), p. 30.

22. Michael Howard, "Reassurance and Deterrence: Western Defense in the 1980s," *Foreign Affairs*, 66:1 (Winter 1982–83), p. 316.

23. Dominique Moisi, "Europe: Frustration in a Land In-Between," *International Herald Tribune* (March 28, 1985), p. 4.

24. Gregory Fossedal, "Western Approaches," *Policy Review* 24 (Spring 1983), p. 178.

25. Gen. Étienne Copel, "Foreign Media," *FBIS* (December 3, 1984), p. 16.

26. Richard Pipes, *Survival Is Not Enough*, p. 253.

27. Raymond Aron, "Anarchical Order of Power," *Daedalus*, 95:2 (Spring 1966), p. 491.

28. Dick Parker, "Giscard: Soviets Won't Allow W. German Nukes," *Atlanta Journal* (December 11, 1984), p. 29.

29. Theo Sommer, "The Objectives of Germany," in Alastair Buchan (ed.), *A World of Nuclear Powers* (Englewood Cliffs, N.J.: Prentice-Hall, 1966), p. 53.

30. Johannes Gross, quoted in H. Joachim Maitre, "Germans Left and Right Chafe Under NATO's Umbrella," *The Wall Street Journal* (May 9, 1985), p. 31.

31. Gen. Étienne Copel, "Foreign Media," p. 16.

32. Bruno Bettleheim, private conversation.

33. H. Joachim Maitre, "Germans Left and Right Chafe Under NATO's Umbrella," *The Wall Street Journal* (May 8, 1985), p. 31.

34. Ibid., p. 31.

35. Helmut Gollwitzer, quoted in Maitre, "Germans Left and Right," p. 31.

36. "D-Day's Absent Actors," editorial, *London Times* (June 4, 1984), p. 17.

37. *Sydney Morning Herald*, editorial, quoted in *International Herald Tribune* (June 7, 1984), p. 4.

38. Quoted in John Vinocur, "Intellectual Europe Changes Sides," *International Herald Tribune* (May 16, 1984), p. 6.

CHAPTER 7: FRANCE AND THE BALANCE OF FEARS

1. Thomas Schwartz, "The Case of German Rearmament: Alliance Crisis in the 'Golden Age,'" *Fletcher Forum*, 8:2 (Summer 1984), p. 307.

2. Daniel Lerner, "Reflections on France in the World Arena," in Daniel Lerner and Raymond Aron (eds.), *France Defeats the EDC* (New York: Frederick A. Praeger, Inc., 1957), p. 216.

3. Dean Acheson, *Present at the Creation: My Years in the State Department* (New York: W. W. Norton and Co., 1969), p. 641.

4. Daniel Lerner, "Reflections on France," pp. 218–19.

5. *Congressional Record* (Washington, D.C.: U.S. Government Printing Office, June 20, 1984), p. S-7782.

6. Ibid. (June 18, 1984), p. S-7451.

7. Ibid., p. S-7458.

8. Ibid., p. S-7736.

9. Ibid., p. S-7743.

10. Ibid., p. S-7458.

11. *The Washington Post*, editorial, "Timely Warning to NATO," quoted in *International Herald Tribune* (June 28, 1984), p. 4.

12. "Die Welt Views Senator's Troop Withdrawal Demand," *This Week in Germany* (July 27, 1984), p. J-3.

13. "Bonn Aide Warns U.S. on Troop Cut Threats," *The New York Times* (July 13, 1984), p. A-5.

14. "Bonn Aide Cautions U.S. on Pressure," *International Herald Tribune* (July 13, 1984), p. 2.

15. Henry Kissinger, "A Plan to Reshape NATO," *Time* (April 5, 1984), p. 24.

16. Ibid., p. 22.

17. Ibid., p. 21.

18. Claude Cheysson, "French Defense Policy and the U.S.," *The Wall Street Journal* (February 25, 1983), p. 26.

19. John Vinocur, "Mitterrand Sees Test for the West's Unity," *The New York Times* (January 24, 1983), p. A-1.

20. "Kohl Interviewed on Positive Ties with France," *FBIS* (June 1, 1984), p. J-2. (Translated excerpt from *La Figaro*, May 28, 1984.)

21. Kurt Becker, "Western European Union: The Sleeping Mummy Comes to Life Again," *The German Tribune* (June 17, 1984), p. 2.

22. "Europe's New Arms Debate," editorial, *The Financial Times*, London (June 13, 1984), p. 16.

23. "Address By President Francois Mitterrand at a Luncheon Offered by the Council of Ministers of the Netherlands, The Hague, February 7, 1984," *French Embassy: Press and Information Service*, 84:6, pp. 7–8.

24. "The French Army: Shield and Sword for Europe?," *The Economist* (June 23, 1984), pp. 37–40.

25. Helmut Schmidt, "Saving the Western Alliance," *The New York Review of Books* (May 31, 1984), p. 25.

26. Ibid., p. 27.

27. Ibid.

28. Ibid.

29. William Drozdick, "Schmidt Proposes Defense Merger by France, W. Germany," *The Washington Post* (June 29, 1984), p. A-21.

30. Dominique Moisi, "Schmidt's Defense Balloon: A Useful Non-Starter," *International Herald Tribune* (July 10, 1984), p. 4.

31. Ibid.

32. See Giovanni Serafini, "Montand Scatena la Guerra in Francia," *La Nazione* (May 20, 1985), p. 9; and also Jacques Richard, "Yves Montand en Premiere Ligne," *L'Actualite* (April 18, 1985), p. 1.

33. Gen. Étienne Copel, *Vaincre LaGuerre: Une autre defense, une autre armee* (Paris: Lien Comun, 1984).

34. Jean-François Revel, *How Democracies Perish* (New York: Doubleday and Co., 1984), pp. 259–60.

35. Zbigniew Brzezinski, "The Future of Yalta," *Foreign Affairs*, 63:2 (Winter 1984/85), p. 299.

36. Quoted in Josef Joffe, "Europe's American Pacifier," *Foreign Policy*, 54 (Spring 1984), p. 81.

37. Ibid.

38. Quoted in Paul Lewis, "European Chiefs Are Deadlocked on Market Issues," *The New York Times* (December 7, 1983), p. A-1.

39. Quoted in Paul Lewis, "Common Market Showdown Today," *The New York Times* (March 19, 1984), p. A-3.

40. Quoted in John Vinocur, "Mitterrand Urges New Common Market Pact," *The New York Times* (May 25, 1984), p. A-9.

41. Quoted in Paul Lewis, "British Diamonds Cause Friction for Europeans," *The New York Times* (March 20, 1984), p. A-1.

42. Ibid.

43. Quoted in Paul Lewis, "Trade Block Fails to End Conflicts," *The New York Times* (March 21, 1984), p. A-11.

44. Ibid.

45. Flora Lewis, "Europe on the Brink," *The New York Times* (March 18, 1984), p. A-21.

46. "Odd Man In," editorial, *The Times*, London (May 25, 1984), p. 13.

CHAPTER 8: ILL FARES THE WELFARE STATE

1. Melvyn Krauss, "Ill Fares the Welfare State," *Policy Review*, 18 (Fall 1981), pp. 133–38.

2. Adam Roberts, *Nations in Arms: The Theory and Practice of Territorial Defense* (New York: Praeger, 1976), p. 105; see also *World Military Expenditures and Arms Transfers, 1971–1980*, U.S. Arms Control and Disarmament Agency (March 1983), p. 68.

3. Roberts, *Nations in Arms*, p. 106; *World Military Expenditures*, p. 68.

4. *Nations in Arms*, p. 106.

5. "Union Institute Says Military Spending Harms Social Welfare," *The Week in Germany* (June 22, 1984), p. 4.

6. Philip M. Boffey, "Allies Back 'Star Wars' Studies, Not Deployment," *The New York Times* (February 10, 1985), p. 14.

7. Gordon Crovitz, *Europe's Siberian Gas Pipeline*, Occasional Paper No. 6, Institute for European Defense and Strategic Studies (1983), p. 16.

8. Ibid., p. 17.

9. Ibid., p. 21.

10. Ibid., pp. 38–43.

11. Ibid., p. 21.

12. "Pipeline Pains," editorial, *The Wall Street Journal* (March 15, 1983), p. 26.

13. Ibid.

14. Crovitz, *Europe's Siberian Gas Pipeline*, pp. 19–20.

15. David Brand, "Europeans Subsidized Soviet Pipeline Work Mainly to Save Jobs," *The Wall Street Journal* (November 2, 1982), p. 2.

16. Keith W. Crane and Daniel F. Kohler, "The Effects of Export Credit Subsidies on Western Exports to the Soviet Bloc," A Rand Note (Santa Monica, Calif.: The Rand Corporation, June 1984), pp. 6, 10–11.

CHAPTER 9: JAPAN: THE KING OF THE FREE-RIDERS

1. Clyde Haberman, "Japan 40 Years After War: A Hamlet on World State," *The New York Times* (August 2, 1985), p. 1.

2. Yomiuri Shimbun (April 6, 1974), quoted in Wythe E. Braden, "Anatomy of Failure: Japan–USSR Negotiations on Siberian Oil Development," *Fletcher Forum*, 5:1 (Winter 1981), p. 92.

3. Gerald L. Curtis, "Japanese Security Policies and the United States," *Foreign Affairs*, 59:35 (Spring 1981), pp. 854–55.

4. Henry S. Rowen, "Japan and the Future Balance in Asia," in F. Weinstein, ed., *U.S.–Japan Relations and the Security of East Asia* (Boulder: Westview Press, 1982), p. 243.

5. Curtis, "Japanese Security Policies," p. 854.

6. "Japan's Northern Territories," brochure (Japan 1982), p. 3.

7. *Sankei Shimbum* (June 20, 1984), p. 1.

8. "Soviet Says Japan Risks Devastation," *The New York Times* (January 20, 1983), p. 5.

9. Daniel I. Okimoto, "The Economics of National Defense," in Daniel Okimoto, ed., *Japan's Economy: Coping with Change in the International Environment* (Boulder: Westview Press, 1982), pp. 247–48.

10. Quoted in Haberman, "Japan 40 Years After War," p. 3.

11. Ibid.

12. Theodore H. White, "The Danger from Japan," *The New York Times Magazine* (July 28, 1985), p. 22.

13. "Japan's Defense: Perceptions and Realities," *JEI Report* (February 10, 1984), p. 11.

14. Clyde Haberman, "Japan Smoothes Over Its Imperial Post" (September 2, 1984), p. E-5.

15. Kei Wakaizumi, "The Problem for Japan," in Alaistair Buchan (ed.), *A World of Nuclear Powers* (Englewood, N.J.: Prentice-Hall, 1966), p. 78.

16. "Japan's Defense," p. 2.

17. William Watts, *The United States and Japan: A Troubled Partnership* (Cambridge, Mass.: Ballinger, 1984), p. 67.

18. William Safire, "Those 'Obscene' Salaries," *The New York Times* (May 7, 1984), p. A-19.

19. William Watts, *The United States and Japan*, p. 19.

20. Theodore H. White, "The Danger from Japan," p. 59.

CHAPTER 10: WITHDRAWING FROM KOREA: THE RIGHT THING FOR THE WRONG REASON

1. Transcript of White House News Conference held by President Jimmy Carter, *The New York Times* (March 10, 1977), p. 26.

2. Richard Halloran, "Carter Sees Pullout From Korea by 1982," *The New York Times* (March 10, 1977), p. 9.

3. Robert E. White, "Cut Loose from Chun," *The New York Times* (March 5, 1985), p. 27.

4. Zbigniew Brzezinski, *Power and Principles: Memoirs of the National Security Advisor, 1977–1981* (New York: Farrar, Straus, and Giroux, Inc., 1983), pp. 124–25.

5. Franklin B. Weinstein and Fuji Kamiya, eds., *The Security of Korea: U.S. and Japanese Perspectives on the 1980s* (Boulder, Colo.: Westview Press, Inc., 1980), p. 2.

6. Ibid., p. 3.

7. *Ethics and Public Policy Center Newsletter* (June 1985), p. 1.

8. *The Security of Korea*, p. 23.

9. Ibid., p. 70.

10. Ibid., p. 73.

11. Ibid., p. 74.

12. Ibid., p. 72.

13. Ibid.

14. Franklin B. Weinstein, "The United States, Japan, and the Security of Korea," *International Security*, 2:2 (Fall 1977), p. 83.

15. James William Morley, "The Dynamics of the Korean Connection," in Gerald L. Curtis and Sung-joo Han, eds., *The U.S.–South Korean Alliance*, (Lexington, Mass.: D.C. Heath and Company, 1983), pp. 12–13.

16. Ibid., pp. 13–14.

17. Ibid., p. 13.

18. *The Security of Korea*, p. 42.

19. Franklin B. Weinstein, "The United States, Japan, and the Security of Korea," p. 73.

20. *The Security of Korea*, pp. 41–42.

21. Ibid., p. 47.

22. Franklin B. Weinstein, "The United States, Japan, and the Security of Korea," p. 47.

23. *The Security of Korea*, p. 44.

24. Ibid., p. 194.

25. *The Wall Street Journal*, Europe (May 8, 1985), p. 26.

26. *The Security of Korea*, p. 47.

27. Gary Saxonhouse, "The United States, Japan, and Korea: Domestic Economic Policies, International Economic Relations, and Global Economic Integration," in Gerald L. Curtis and Sung-joo Jan, eds., *The U.S.–South Korean Alliance* (Lexington, Mass.: D.C. Heath and Company, 1983), p. 179.

28. William Watts, "The United States and Korea: Perception versus Reality," ibid., p. 84.

29. James William Morley, "The Dynamics of the Korean Connection," ibid., p. 23.

30. James William Morley, "The Dynamics of the Korean Connection," pp. 24–25.

31. *The Security of Korea*, p. 41.

CHAPTER 11: FACING THE SOVIET THREAT IN THE THIRD WORLD

1. Charles Wolf, Jr., "Beyond Containment: Redesigning American Policies," *The Washington Quarterly*, 5:1 (Winter 1982), p. 111.

2. Ibid.

3. Charles Wolf, Jr., "Supporting Pluralism in the Third World Through Cooperative Forces: Rationale and Content," paper prepared for Rand

Conference on Cooperative Forces in the Third World, March 14–15, 1985, Santa Monica, Calif., p. 1.

4. Ibid., p. 4.

5. George F. Will, "For the President, A Shattering Defeat," *The Washington Post* (April 21, 1985), p. K-8; and "Reagan in Retreat," *The Washington Post* (April 28, 1985), p. C-7.

6. Suzanne Garment, "Better Not Tangle with Republicans in the House," *The Wall Street Journal* (May 3, 1985), p. 22.

7. Wolf, "Beyond Containment," p. 112.

8. Gottfried Haberler, "Liberal and Illiberal Development Policy: Free Trade Like Honesty is Still the Best Policy," Gerald Meier, ed., *The World Bank Pioneers Series* (Washington, D.C.: The World Bank, 1986), American Enterprise Institute.

9. P. T. Bauer, *Reality and Rhetoric: Studies in the Economics of Development* (Cambridge, Mass.: Harvard University Press, 1984), p. 49.

10. Clifford D. May, "Moving Ethiopians Causes a Dispute," *The New York Times* (January 28, 1986), p. 1.

11. *The Wall Street Journal* (January 27, 1986), p. 26.

12. P.T. Bauer, op.cit., p. 52.

13. L. Dudley and R.J. Sandilands, "The Side Effects of Foreign Aid: The Case of PL 480 in Colombia," Economic Development and Cultural Change 23 (January, 1975): 325–336.

14. This section is based on Melvyn B. Krauss, "Foreign Aid and the 'Gang of Four,'" *The Wall Street Journal* (December 20, 1982), p. 16.

15. Henry Kamm, "Turkey Seeking Changes in U.S. Aid," *The New York Times* (August 4, 1985), p. 3.

16. Irving Kristol, "Now What for U.S. Client States?" *The Wall Street Journal* (March 3, 1986), p. 18.

17. James LeMoyne, "Progress Is Seen in El Salvador," *International Herald Tribune* (May 17, 1985), p. 1.

18. Ibid.

19. Ibid.

CHAPTER 12: AN ALLIANCE AGAINST ITSELF

1. Malcolm Wallop, "The Future of the Atlantic Alliance." Address by the senator to a forum at the University of South Carolina (October 5, 1985), p. 1.

BIBLIOGRAPHY

BOOKS

Acheson, Dean. *Present at the Creation: My Years in the State Department.* New York: W.W. Norton and Co., 1969.

Bauer, P. T. *Reality and Rhetoric: Studies in the Economics of Development.* Cambridge, Mass.: Harvard University Press, 1984.

Boaz, David and Crane, Edward H., eds. *Beyond the Status Quo.* Washington, D.C.: The Cato Institute, 1985.

Brzezinski, Zbigniew. *Power and Principle: Memoirs of the National Security Advisor, 1977–1981.* New York: Farrar, Straus, and Giroux, 1983.

Buchan, Alaistair, ed. *A World of Nuclear Powers.* Englewood Cliffs, N.J.: Prentice-Hall, 1966.

The Committee for the Free World. *The Transatlantic Crisis.* New York: Orwell Press, 1982.

Copel, Étienne. *Vaincre Le Guerre: Une autre defense, une autre armee.* Paris: Lien Comun, 1984.

Crovitz, Gordon. *Europe's Siberian Gas Pipeline.* London: Institute for European Defense and Strategic Occasional Paper No. 6, 1983.

Curtis, Gerald L. and Han, Sung-joo, eds. *The U.S.–South Korean Alliance.* Lexington, Mass.: D. C. Heath and Company, 1983.

Suss, David. *Peace and Survival: West Germany, the Peace Movement and European Security.* Stanford, Calif.: Hoover Institution Press, 1985.

Kennan, George. *American Diplomacy.* Expanded edition. Illinois: University of Chicago Press, 1984.

Lerner, Daniel and Aron, Raymond, eds. *France Defeats the EDC.* New York: Praeger, 1957.

Myers, Kenneth A., ed. *NATO: The Next Thirty Years.* Boulder: Westview Press, 1980.

Okimoto, Daniel I., ed. *Japan's Economy: Coping with Change in the International Environment.* Boulder: Westview Press, 1982.

Pipes, Richard. *Survival Is Not Enough.* New York: Simon and Schuster, 1984.

Poole, Robert W., Jr., ed. *Defending a Free Society.* Lexington, Mass.: D. C. Heath, 1984.

Ravenal, Earl C. *Defining Defense: The 1985 Military Budget*. Washington, D.C.: The Cato Institute, 1985.

Revel, Jean-François. *How Democracies Perish*. New York: Doubleday and Co., 1984.

Roberts, Adam. *Nations in Arms: The Theory and Practice of Territorial Defense*. New York: Praeger, 1976.

Watts, William. *The United States and Japan: A Troubled Partnership*. Cambridge, Mass.: Ballinger, 1984.

Weinstein, Franklin, ed. *U.S.–Japan Relations and the Security of East Asia*. Boulder: Westview Press, 1982.

Weinstein, Franklin B. and Kamiya, Fuji, eds. *The Security of Korea: U.S. and Japanese Perspectives on the 1980s*. Boulder: Westview Press, 1980.

ARTICLES

Apple, R. W., Jr. "Libyan Issue Leaves Many Questioning Role of Allies." *The New York Times*, January 19, 1986.

Aron, Raymond. "Anarchical Order of Power." *Daedalus*, Spring 1966.

Ash, Timothy Garton. "Which Way Will Germany Go?" *New York Review of Books*, January 31, 1985.

"Bashing the Boers." *The Wall Street Journal*, August 2, 1985.

Bauer, P. T. and Yamey, B. S. "Foreign Aid: Rewarding Impoverishment." *Commentary*, September 1985.

Becker, Kurt. "Western European Union: The Sleeping Mummy Comes to Life Again." *The German Tribune*, June 17, 1984.

Berman, Paul. "How a Leading Light of the New Left Learned to Love the Bomb." *Mother Jones*, October 1984.

Boffey, Phillip M. "Allies Back 'Star Wars' Studies, Not Deployment." *The New York Times*, February 10, 1985.

"Bonn Aide Cautions U.S. on Pressure." *International Herald Tribune*, July 13, 1984.

"Bonn Aide Warns U.S. on Troop Cut Threats." *The New York Times*, July 27, 1984.

Braden, Wythe E. "Anatomy of Failure: Japan–USSR Negotiations on Siberian Oil Development." *Fletcher Forum*, Winter 1981.

Brand, David. "Europeans Subsidized Soviet Pipeline Work Mainly to Save Jobs." *The Wall Street Journal*, November 2, 1982.

Brzezinski, Zbigniew. "The Future of Yalta." *Foreign Affairs*, Winter 1984/85.

Brzezinski, Zbigniew, et al. "Defense in Space Is Not 'Star Wars.'" *The New York Times Magazine*, January 27, 1985.

Burt, Richard R. "Europe Pullout Isn't Deserved or Desired." *The Wall Street Journal*, March 29, 1983.

Cheysson, Claude. "French Defense Policy and the U.S." *The Wall Street Journal*, February 25, 1983.

Crane, Keith W. and Kohler, Daniel F. "The Effects of Export Credit Subsidies on Western Exports to the Soviet Bloc." *A Rand Note*, June 1984.

Curtis, Gerald L. "Japanese Security Policies and the United States." *Foreign Affairs*, Spring 1981.

"D-Day's Absent Actors." *London Times*, June 4, 1984.

Daniels, Robert V. "America's Doubting Allies." *The New Leader*, June 3–17, 1985.

"Die Welt Views Senator's Troop Withdrawal Demand." *This Week in Germany*, July 27, 1984.

Drozdick, William. "Schmidt Proposes Defense Merger by France, W. Germany." *The Washington Post*, June 29, 1984.

"Escaping the Marcos Embrace." *The New York Times*, August 8, 1985.

Ethics and Public Policy Center Newsletter, June 1985.

"Europe's New Arms Debate." *The Financial Times*, June 13, 1984.

Fossedal, Gregory. "Western Approaches." *Policy Review*, Spring 1983.

"The French Army: Shield and Sword for Europe?" *The Economist*, June 23, 1984.

Garment, Suzanne. "Better Not Tangle with Republicans in the House." *The Wall Street Journal*, May 3, 1985.

Gwertzman, Bernard. "U.S. Tries to Clarify Stand on an Israeli Response." *The New York Times*, December 30, 1985.

Haberman, Clyde. "Japan 40 Years After War: A Hamlet on World Stage." *The New York Times*, August 2, 1985.

————. "Japan Smooths over Its Imperial Past." *The New York Times*, September 2, 1984.

Halloran, Richard. "Carter Sees Pullout From Korea by 1982." *The New York Times*, March 10, 1977.

_____. "Europe Called Main U.S. Arms Cost." *The New York Times*, July 20, 1984.

Harries, Owen. "Conservative Critics of NATO." *The American Spectator*, June 1984.

Herdegon, Gerhard and Noelle-Neumann, Elizabeth. "Protest Howls Belied by Opinion Polls." *The German Tribune*, June 3, 1984.

Hoffman, Stanley. "NATO and Nuclear Weapons: Reasons and Unreason." *Foreign Affairs*, Winter 1981/82.

Howard, Michael. "Reassurance and Deterrence: Western Defense in the 1980s." *Foreign Affairs*, Winter 1982/83.

"Japan's Defense: Perceptions and Realities." *JEI Report*, February 10, 1984.

Joffe, Josef. "Europe's American Pacifier." *Foreign Policy*, Spring 1984.

Kamm, Henry. "Turkey Seeking Changes in U.S. Aid." *The New York Times*, August 4, 1985.

Keller, Bill. "NATO Chief Finds Conventional Forces Lacking." *The New York Times*, March 2, 1985.

Keller, Konrad. "The New Germans." *The New York Times Magazine*, August 5, 1984.

Kennan, George F. "Morality and Foreign Policy." *Foreign Affairs* (Winter 1985/86).

Kissinger, Henry. "A Plan to Reshape NATO." *Time Magazine*, April 5, 1984.

_____. "The Future of NATO." In Kenneth Myers, ed., *NATO: The Next Thirty Years*. Boulder: Westview Press, 1980.

"Kohl Interviewed on Positive Ties with France." *FBIS*, June 1, 1984.

Krauss, Melvyn B. "Foreign Aid and the 'Gang of Four.'" *The Wall Street Journal*, December 20, 1982.

_____. "Ill Fares the Welfare State." *Policy Review*, Fall 1981.

_____. "It Is Time to Change the Atlantic Alliance." *The Wall Street Journal*, March 3, 1983.

_____. "Prompting Europe to Better Defend Itself." *The Wall Street Journal*, March 15, 1984.

_____. "If the New Zealand Syndrome Spreads." *The New York Times*, February 17, 1985.

_____. "Atlantic Unity Is a Two-Way Street." *The New York Times*, October 30, 1985.

————. "Why Has Reagan Yielded To Europe." *The New York Times*, January 6, 1985.

————. "When the Allies Won't Play Ball, Raise the Ante." *The New York. Times*, April 25, 1986.

Krauss, Melvyn and Fossedal, Gregory A. "Star Wars for the Allies, Usual Terms." *The Wall Street Journal*, May 8, 1986.

Krauthammer, Charles. "Isolationism, Left and Right." *The New Republic*, March 4, 1985.

Kristol, Irving. "A Transatlantic 'Misunderstanding': The Case of Central America." *Encounter*, March 1985.

————. "What's Wrong With NATO?" *The New York Times Magazine*, September 25, 1983.

————. "Coping With an Evil Empire." *The Wall Street Journal*, December 17, 1985.

LeMoyne, James. "Progress Is Seen in El Salvador." *International Herald Tribune*, May 17, 1985.

Lerner, Daniel. "Reflections on France in the World Arena." In Daniel Lerner and Raymond Aron, eds., *France Defeats the EDC*. New York: Praeger, 1957.

Lewis, Anthony. "Theater Nuclear Politics." *The New York Times*, December 27, 1982.

Lewis, Flora. "Europe on the Brink." *The New York Times*, March 18, 1984.

————. "France's Fading Reds." *The New York Times*, February 4, 1985.

————. "Missiles and Pacifists." *The New York Times*, November 18, 1983.

Lewis, Paul. "British Demands Cause Friction for Europeans. *The New York Times*, March 20, 1984.

————. "Common Market Showdown Today." *The New York Times*, March 19, 1984.

————. "European Chiefs Are Deadlocked on Market Issues." *The New York Times*, December 7, 1983.

————. "Trade Block Fails to End Conflicts." *The New York Times*, March 21, 1984.

Lipsky, Seth. "Polish Move Exposes a Republican 'Soft Underbelly.'" *The Wall Street Journal*, December 17, 1984.

Maitre, H. Joachim. "Germans Left and Right Chafe Under NATO's Umbrella." *The Wall Street Journal*, May 8, 1985.

Markham, James M. "For West Germany's Young, The Trend Is Conservative." *The New York Times*, January 19, 1986.

_____. "Germany's Trafficking in People." *The New York Times*, July 29, 1984.

_____. "Green Party Is Fading into the Blues." *The New York Times*, June 27, 1985.

Moisi, Dominique. "Europe: Frustration in a Land In-Between." *International Herald Tribune*, March 28, 1985.

_____. "Schmidt's Defense Balloon: A Useful Non-Starter." *International Herald Tribune*, July 10, 1984.

Morley, James William. "The Dynamics of the Korean Connection." In Gerald L. Curtis and Sung-joo Han, eds., *The U.S.–South Korean Alliance*. Lexington, Mass.: D. C. Heath and Co., 1983.

"Odd Man In." *The Times* (London), May 25, 1984.

Okimoto, Daniel I. "The Economics of National Defense." In Daniel I. Okimoto, ed., *Japan's Economy: Coping with Change in the International Environment*. Boulder: Westview Press, 1982.

Parker, Dick. "Giscard: Soviets Won't Allow W. German Nukes." *Atlantic Journal*, December 11, 1984.

"Pipeline Pains." *The Wall Street Journal*, March 15, 1983.

Podhoretz, Norman. "Is There a New American Isolationism?" In The Committee for the Free World, ed., *The Transatlantic Crisis*. New York: Orwell Press, 1982.

Ravenal, Earl C. "Europe Without America: The Erosion of NATO." *Foreign Affairs*, Summer 1985.

_____. "The Price and Perils of NATO." In David Boaz and Edward H. Crane, eds., *Beyond the Status Quo: Policy Prospects for America*. Washington, D.C.: The Cato Institute, 1985.

Richard, Jacques. "Yves Montand en Premiere ligne." *L'Actualité*, April 18, 1985.

Rosenfeld, Stephen S. "'Moral Equivalence': More to It Than Dark Subversion." *International Herald Tribune*, May 7, 1985.

Rowen, Henry S. "Developing the Supply of Cooperative Forces." Paper delivered at the Rand Corporation Conference on Cooperative Forces in the Third World, Santa Monica, Calif., March 14–15, 1985.

_____. "Japan and the Future Balance in Asia." In Franklin Weinstein, ed., *U.S.–Japan Relations and the Security of East Asia*. Boulder: Westview Press, 1982.

Safire, William. "Those 'Obscene' Salaries." *The New York Times*, May 7, 1984.

Saxonhouse, Gary. "The United States, Japan, and Korea: Domestic Economic Policies, International Economic Relations, and Global Economic Integration." In Gerald L. Curtis and Sung-joo Han, eds., *The U.S.–South Korean Alliance*. Lexington, Mass.: D.C. Heath and Co., 1983.

Schmidt, Helmut. "Saving the Western Alliance." *The New York Review of Books*, May 31, 1984.

Schmidt, Peter. "Public Opinion and Security Policy in the Federal Republic of Germany: Elite and Mass Opinion in a Comparative Perspective." *A Rand Paper*, 1984.

Schmneckle, Gerd. "When a Crisis Is Looming, NATO Is Hamstrung." *Rheinischu Mackuc/Christ und Welt*, December 3, 1984.

Schwartz, Thomas. "The Case of German Rearmament: Alliance Crisis in the 'Golden Age.'" *Fletcher Forum*, Summer 1984.

Serafini, Giovanni. "Montand Scatena la Guerre in Francia." *La Nazione*, May 20, 1985.

Sommer, Theo. "The Objectives of Germany." In Alaistair Buchan, ed., *A World of Nuclear Powers*. Englewood Cliffs, N.J.: Prentice-Hall, 1966.

"Soviet Says Japan Risks Devastation." *The New York Times*, January 20, 1983.

Starrels, John M. "Talking Trade with the Russians: The Stage Is Set for Better Relations." *The New York Times*, February 10, 1985.

Sullivan, Scott. "The Decline of Europe." *Newsweek*, April 9, 1984.

Sulzberger, G. L. "Foreign Affairs: Poker as Played in Paris." *The New York Times*, February 23, 1966.

Tagliaube, John. "Warning East Berlin for Slight From West." *The New York Times*, August 12, 1984.

Tatu, Michel. "Battle March to a French Tune." *The London Times*, June 20, 1984.

————. "Devolution of Power: A Dream?" *Foreign Affairs*, July 1975.

"Time for Action." *The Stanford Daily*, July 30, 1985.

"Timely Warning to NATO." *International Herald Tribune*, June 28, 1984.

"Transcript of White House News Conference Held by President Jimmy Carter." *The New York Times*, March 10, 1977.

Ulam, Adam B. "Western Europe Key Area for Soviet Power Dreams." *Pittsburgh Press*, November 3, 1983.

"Union Institute Says Military Spending Harms Social Welfare." *The Week in Germany*, June 22, 1984.

Vinocur, John. "Intellectual Europe Changes Sides on U.S. as Hero or Ogre." *The International Herald Tribune*, May 16, 1984.

————. "Mitterrand Sees Test for the West's Unity." *The New York Times*, January 24, 1983.

————. "Mitterrand Urges New Common Market Pact." *The New York Times*, May 25, 1984.

————. "West Europe Likes Reagan, Bitburg Aside." *The New York Times*, April 29, 1985.

Wakaizumi, Kei. "The Problem for Japan." In Alaistair Buchan, ed., *A World of Nuclear Powers*. Englewood Cliffs, N.J.: Prentice-Hall, 1966.

Wallop, Malcolm. "The Future of the Atlantic Alliance." Address by the senator to a forum at the University of South Carolina on October 5, 1985.

Watts, William. "The United States and Korea: Perception versus Reality." In Gerald L. Curtis and Sung-joo Han, eds., *The U.S.–South Korean Alliance*. Lexington, Mass.: D.C. Heath and Co., 1983.

Weinstein, Franklin B. "The United States, Japan, and the Security of Korea." *International Security*, Fall 1977.

White, Robert E. "Cut Loose from Chun." *The New York Times*, March 5, 1985.

White, Theodore H. "The Danger from Japan." *The New York Times*, July 28, 1985.

Will, George F. "For the President, a Shattering Defeat." *The Washington Post*, April 21, 1985.

————. "Reagan in Retreat." *The Washington Post*, April 28, 1985.

Winik, Jay. "Toward a Post–NATO Europe." *The Wall Street Journal*, August 27, 1985.

Wolf, Charles, Jr. "Beyond Containment: Redesigning American Policies." *The Washington Quarterly*, Winter 1982.

————. "Supporting Pluralism in the Third World Through Cooperative Forces: Rationale and Content." Paper delivered at the Rand Corporation Conference on Cooperative Forces in the Third World, held in Santa Monica, Calif., March 14–15, 1985.

Worsthorne, Peregrine. "A Tory Critique of Neoconservatives." *The American Spectator*, October 1985.

GOVERNMENT DOCUMENTS

France. *French Embassy: Press and Information Service.* "Address by President Francois Mitterrand at a Luncheon Offered by the Council of Ministers of the Kingdom of the Netherlands, The Hague, February 7, 1984."

Japan. Ministry of Foreign Affairs Brochure. "Japan's Northern Territories." 1982.

OECD. *Public Expenditure Trends.* Paris, 1978.

U.S. Arms Control and Disarmament Agency. *World Military Expenditures and Arms Transfers, 1971–1980.* March 1983.

U.S. Congress. *Congressional Record.* (Washington, D.C.: U.S. Government Printing Office, June 18, 1984).

————. *Congressional Record.* (Washington, D.C.: U.S. Government Printing Office, June 20, 1984).

U.S. Department of Defense. *Report on Allied Contributions to the Common Defense.* A report to the U.S. Congress, March 1985.

U.S. Department of State. *Report to Congress on Voting Practices in the United Nations.* (Washington, D.C.: U.S. Government Printing Office, 1984).

Index

263

General Account Budget of, 167, 168
gross domestic product (GDP) of, 113
gross national product (GNP) of, 158
as influence in Pacific Region, 171–172, 174, 180, 192, 194–202, 204
intelligence operations in, 172
Korean relations with, 182, 191–202
militarism in, 158, 167, 171, 172, 174, 192–93
national security of, 165, 166, 191
neutralism and, 164–65
Northern Territories of, 162–64, 173
nuclear policy of, 157, 159, 162, 164, 173–74, 202
"one-percent rule" of, 170, 172
"peace" constitution of, 165
social security system of, 167–68, 169
Soviet threat to, 161, 163, 166, 180
Soviet trade with, 158–59, 160
U.S. relations with, 157–58, 165, 166–72, 174, 179–80
welfare state of, 167–69, 177–78
West Germany compared to, 157, 237
Japan Economic Institute, 172, 173
Japanese Export-Import Bank, 160
Japanese Olympic Committee, 160
Jaruzelski, Wojciech, 58, 94
Jastrow, Robert, 31
Joffe, Josef, 134, 135
John Paul II, Pope, 74

Kamiya, Fuji, 184, 195, 198
Kampelman, Max, 31
Keller, Konrad, 56
Kennan, George, 39–41, 50–51
Kennedy, Edward M., 49
Kennedy, John F., 44, 184
Khomeini, Ayatollah, 49
Khrushchev, Nikita, 72
Kim Hyung Wook, 189
Kim Il-sung, 184, 196–97, 200
Kirkpatrick, Jeane, 51, 185
Kissinger, Henry, 22, 44, 45, 118–19, 127
Klinghoffer, Leon, 66
Kohl, Helmut, 122, 127, 135
Kohler, Daniel, 154

Korea, South:
authoritarian regime in, 182–86, 202
defense capability of, 183, 185, 186–94, 202
defense spending of, 186–87
détente and, 188–89
economy of, 186–87, 197–99
"free-ride" strategy of, 186, 191–94
gross national product (GNP) of, 186, 187–88, 218
Japanese relations with, 182, 191–202
morale problems in, 189–90
nationalism in, 189–91
as non-Communist nation, 184, 190, 195–99, 201–2
North Korea vs., 183, 184, 188–91, 193, 194, 195–99
nuclear policy for, 192–94
strategic withdrawal from, 185, 186–91, 199–202
U.S. economic aid to, 215–19
U.S. relations with, 181–86, 188, 189, 194, 195, 196, 199–200, 202, 215–19
West Germany compared to, 190–191, 194, 196
withdrawal of U.S. troops from, 54, 181–202, 238
Korean Air Lines flight 007 shootdown, 57, 172
Korean War, 107–8, 197, 203, 218
Kosaka, Masataka, 184
Krauthammer, Charles, 44, 45, 47
Kriegel, Annie, 72
Kristol, Irving, 21, 44, 45, 47, 79, 80, 97, 225
Kurile Islands, 162–63

Laffer wedge, 140, 141
Lebanon, U.S. troops in, 79, 205
Lenin, V. I., 138
Lerner, Daniel, 109–11
Lewis, Flora, 72, 87, 135–36
Liberal Democratic Party (LDP), 168
Libertarians, 48–49
Libya, U.S. bombing of, 61–62, 68
Lippmann, Walter, 47
Lugar, Richard, 112
Luther, Martin, 104

McCloy, John J., 108, 109
Maitre, H. Joachim, 102–3

ABOUT THE AUTHOR

MELVYN KRAUSS is a professor of economics at New York University and senior fellow at the Hoover Institution at Stanford University. He has published in various scholarly journals and is a regular contributor to *The New York Times* and *The Wall Street Journal*. His books include *The New Protectionism*, *Development Without Aid*, and *The Economics of Integration*. He has taught in the United States, Canada, and throughout Western Europe. His hobby is opera, and he has published reviews in leading opera periodicals.